W9-BZK-784

WITHDRAWN

JUN 09

JUL X X 2015

May Interrupt Speaker?	Second Needed?	Debatable?	Amendable?	Vote Needed?
no	yes	no	yes	majority
no	yes	no	no	majority
no	yes	no	yes	majority
yes	no	no	no	none
yes	no	no	no	none
yes	no	no	no	none
yes	no	no	no	none
yes	no	no	no	none
no	yes	no	no	majority
yes	yes	yes	no	majority
no	yes	no	no	two-thirds
yes	yes	yes	no	majority
no	yes	no	no	two-thirds
no	yes	yes	yes	majority
no	yes	yes	yes	majority
no	yes	yes	yes	majority
no	yes	yes	no	majority
no	yes	no	no	majority
yes	no	no	no	two-thirds
no	yes	yes	yes	majority

REFERENCE

Not to be taken from this

WITHDRAWN

Henry A. Davidson, M.Sc., M.D., is a graduate of the Jefferson Medical College. He is Superintendent of the Essex County Overbrook Hospital at Cedar Grove, New Jersey, Editor of *Mental Hygiene,* a lecturer in psychiatry at the Columbia University College of Physicians and Surgeons, and Parliamentarian to the American Psychiatric Association. He is the author of *Forensic Psychiatry,* published by The Ronald Press Company. Dr. Davidson is an Advisory Councilor to the American Institute of Parliamentarians and a Registered Parliamentarian with the National Association of Parliamentarians.

HANDBOOK OF PARLIAMENTARY PROCEDURE

HENRY A. DAVIDSON, M.D.

PARLIAMENTARIAN, AMERICAN PSYCHIATRIC ASSOCIATION;
REGISTERED PARLIAMENTARIAN, NATIONAL ASSOCIATION
OF PARLIAMENTARIANS

SECOND EDITION

CUMBERLAND COUNTY COLLEGE
LIBRARY P.O. BOX 517 VINELAND N.J.

THE RONALD PRESS COMPANY • NEW YORK

Ref.
JF 515.
D32
Ha
1968

68- 5516

Copyright © 1968 by
THE RONALD PRESS COMPANY

Copyright 1955 by
THE RONALD PRESS COMPANY

All Rights Reserved

No part of this book may be reproduced
in any form without permission in writing
from the publisher.

Library of Congress Catalog Card Number: 68–12886
PRINTED IN THE UNITED STATES OF AMERICA

To my long-suffering captive audiences—

THE COUNCIL AND THE MEMBERS OF THE
AMERICAN PSYCHIATRIC ASSOCIATION

Preface

This handbook aims to present in simple step-by-step terms the rules and practices of parliamentary procedure for the small organization—the local business association, professional or scientific society, union, civic group, lodge, and social club. The reader can cover the entire volume in a few hours. He can then keep it on his desk and refer to it swiftly.

I have tried to do more than present the what, how, and why of parliamentary procedure. This volume contains as well a workable manual of organizational tactics and operations: how not to get pushed around, how to handle a heckler, how to construct a constitution, how to organize a budget, and how to make maximum use of committees. Numerous examples of resolutions, reports, and other forms for the chairman, secretary, treasurer, and committee member to follow are provided in a separate section. The key points of parliamentary procedure have been distilled in a chart in the front of the book so that the chairman will have at a glance the rulings for all common troublesome situations. Quick reference is made possible by the glossary of all common parliamentary terms and the comprehensive index citing section rather than page.

What is written here has been largely hammered out on the anvil of experience. I have served as parliamentarian to a number of organizations and as president of many others. At first I followed the procedure laid down in whatever book was the authority of the moment. But it was soon obvious that the standard codes were unsatisfactory for the small and often less formal type of organization. Furthermore, many of the standard works were poorly arranged for quick reference. When a chairman or a parliamentarian needs a citation, he needs it fast. Out of this need, I developed a series of ready reference cards. The rules thereon were, at first, the rigid ones of the formal codes. Later I found that actual experience rubbed the edges off some of the rules, and slowly there developed the simple and practical manual which constitutes the backbone of this book.

In preparing this book I have necessarily examined the standard parliamentary works. In some places here I have followed the general rule and made no original contribution either to the wording of the rule or to its rationale. In other places I have developed new rules which I have found in my experience to be more workable or which I believe are better designed to protect both the minority's right to be heard and the majority's right to rule. For example, I have realistically renamed "previous question." This ancient motion (at least, as traditionally worded) is wretchedly confusing. It is easier and more lucid to move to "close debate."

Unsophisticated persons sometimes assume that parliamentary procedure is distilled out of natural law (such as that the square root of sixteen is four). It is not like that at all. What one parliamentary authority adopted last year can be changed by another next year. For it is the organization itself that is always sovereign. Many members do not realize this. Yet in truth, the organization can say (if it wants to) that a motion to adjourn is always debatable or never debatable or that a motion has to be thirded as well as seconded. Procedure is what the members want, and when the established parliamentary rule seems to be sabotaging the operations of the society, they can change the procedure. To this only two reservations are made: It is not right to change the ground rules in the middle of the game. And there will always be points not covered by the newly adopted rules, and hence the need for a residual authority to fall back on.

Most organizations that have adopted this handbook have found it useful—especially smaller organizations but also larger ones that find a rigid and over-formalized set of rules impractical. The favorable reception and the passing of time have made a second edition desirable. In revising, the author's primary purpose has been to expand on definitions of terms and discussions of procedures that are most confusing and troublesome for the inexperienced chairman.

A writer should express gratitude toward authors whose works he has consulted—works from which he has, perhaps unconsciously, lifted some ideas and maybe even some phrases. While I cannot at this stage separate out the contributions of individual parliamentary authors, I want here to insert a general word of thanks to all my predecessors.

Special words of thanks are also due Dr. Kenneth Appel who, when he was President of the American Psychiatric Association, named me parliamentarian of this 15,000-member body, and to the succeeding presidents who have reappointed me.

HENRY A. DAVIDSON

Cedar Grove, New Jersey
January, 1968

Contents

CONTENTS

2

Precedence of Motions

3

Agenda: The Order of Business

4

Mr. Chairman

5

The Nature of Parliamentary Debate

CONTENTS

6

All in Favor Say "Aye"

7

Points and Motions of Privilege

CONTENTS

8

How To Put Off Until Tomorrow

9

How To Amend a Motion

10

Committees, Councils, and Boards

CONTENTS

11

Second Thoughts: The Motion To Reconsider

12

Adjournment and Recess

CONTENTS

13

Hints on the Construction of a Constitution

Form

Content

14

How Not To Get Pushed Around

CONTENTS

15

How To Handle a Heckler

16

The Society's Budget: Its Form and Its Function

17

Warehouse of Forms and Documents

CONTENTS

HANDBOOK OF
PARLIAMENTARY
PROCEDURE

The art of association is the mother of action. In America as in no other country has the principle of association been more successfully applied to a multitude of different objects. If an obstruction occurs in a road, the neighbors immediately form a deliberative body. Out of this assembly develops an executive power which remedies the inconvenience and removes the obstruction before anybody thought of appealing to civic authority. In America, societies are formed to resist moral enemies, to diminish vice, to promote order, and to advance commerce: for Americans seem to know that there is no end which the human will, seconded by the collective exertions of individuals, need despair of attaining. . . . No one can attack the right of association without impairing the very foundations of democratic society.

—Alexis de Tocqueville, *Democracy in America* (1835).

Parliamentary Traffic Control

101. Mr. Chairman

A chairman really has to know more than how to call "All in favor say 'Aye.'" He needs a skill in leadership which he will never acquire by reading this book—or any other book. However, part of his skill comes from feeling at home with parliamentary procedure—and this he can learn. He has to know whether or not one motion is in order while another is pending. This depends on the relative "rank" or precedence of motions—a matter explored in Chapter 2. He has to have the answer *at once* (or have a fast-talking parliamentarian at his elbow). It is better to be wrong but firm than right but hesitant. An erroneous ruling can be corrected by an appeal (see 408). But, short of getting a new chairman, there is no corrective for weak leadership.

The chair has to know when a rule is not worth enforcing. He has to know how to give members a sense of participation without losing control of the threads that run to all parts of the hall. He has to rule out frivolous, disruptive, or parliamentarily incorrect motions and arguments, but must do so graciously and gracefully. He has to know how to turn off the tap when a garrulous member is boring everyone. He has to maintain the flow of ideas at a brisk tempo without taking over the platform as a debater himself.

So chairmanship is not an assignment to be accepted lightly. However, any one of average intelligence *can* do it with a little help from a handy book like this, plus self-confidence. In the absence of the self-confidence, an air of self-assurance will do almost as well. Most of the apparently well-poised persons on platforms have some inner palpitations, doubts, and qualms. What one uneasy but determined human being can do, another can do.

102. Formal and Informal Sessions

In a large meeting it is helpful to follow standard parliamentary procedure. But it is not necessary to do so if no one objects to a more informal procedure. In this connection, the chairman should remember that the purposes of parliamentary procedure are (1) to expedite business, (2) to assure legality, (3) to protect the rights of minorities to be heard subject to (4) assuring the rule of the majority. Thus, a procedural formality which strangles business or otherwise fails to make sense is a bad procedure.

(a) In a meeting in which all voting members sit around a table, or around a series of adjacent tables, the procedure is generally informal, as described in 104(e) below. This is known as "committee procedure" because it is usually followed in committee meetings. It is perfectly proper, however, for meetings of an entire membership if they are seated in this "around the table" style, and if no one insists on formal procedure.

(b) A meeting at which the presiding officer faces the other members, who sit in rows of chairs, is an "auditorium" arrangement. If the group is large—say more than forty or fifty members—some formal parliamentary procedure will be necessary. If it is smaller—say under forty or fifty members—a committee procedure may be followed if no one objects.

(c) Sometimes the group meets in "parlor style" rather than in auditorium or around-the-table format. In a parlor style meeting, the chairs are arranged casually, in an officer's sitting room, parlor, or hotel bedroom; on a patio or terrace or lawn. Here the committee procedure is the rule.

The degrees of formality, in descending order, are:

1. Flawless and formal parliamentary procedure
2. Flexibly formal parliamentary procedure
3. Informal discussion with formal vote on matters of finance or major importance
4. Informal session
5. Executive session
6. Committee of the whole (For this see 1024 to 1032.)

103. Formal Procedure

(a) In formal procedure no one speaks until he is recognized by the chair. The member rises and calls, "Mr. Chairman," and remains standing until recognized or until someone else gets the floor. No one interrupts a speaker except as provided in 506(b). Nothing is ever discussed until some member has offered it as a motion, and then only after it has been seconded.

(b) The rules of parliamentary procedure may be followed with obsessional care. Such rigidity, however, is rarely necessary. Indeed, it is undesirable because it always slows the tempo of the meeting and bleaches out much of its interest. This kind of obsessional adherence to rules is required only by compulsive chairmen or persistent hecklers. See Chapter 15 for suggestions on how to deal with the heckler who wants to air his knowledge of parliamentary procedure no matter whom he bores.

(c) Under ordinary circumstances, a flexibly formal parliamentary procedure is good enough for even the largest meeting. The chair may conduct the business in a highly informal manner if no one objects (see 104). By "flexibly formal" is meant that kind of procedure which insists on an orderly consideration of business without an absolute demand that every "i" in the rule book be dotted, and every "t" crossed. For example, a member is allowed to make a motion without rising, without even being recognized—if no one objects. The chair might allow a topic to be discussed when no one has yet framed a motion. Indeed, this could be a good thing: the actual wording of the motion might be hammered out of the discussion. If it is obvious that something is the "sense of the meeting," the chair says so. He announces that it will be so recorded if no one objects. The procedure described below (104(e)) is followed, where appropriate unless or until some member insists on a more formal procedure; however, the informal procedure is not suitable for decisions which appropriate money or authorize a public release. These actions should be processed formally.

(d) Informality may be achieved by agreeing to an informal procedure, by going into executive session, or by resolving into committee of the whole (see 104, 105, 1024, and 1025).

104. Informal Procedure

(a) If no one objects, and if the rights of the minority (see 108) are not jeopardized thereby, the chairman—or any member—may suggest that the session (or this part of it) be conducted informally. Or, after a matter has been proposed, a member may make, and the group pass, a motion "that we proceed to an informal consideration of this matter." The actual final disposition, however, is by formal vote. If the agreement is to proceed informally throughout the entire session, then the informal procedure continues until the meeting adjourns or until, by motion, formal procedure is restored.

(b) Possible reasons for considering one specific matter informally are: to permit off-the-record discussion; to take up a matter that has not been clearly formulated, and to think it through aloud; to suggest revisions in a poorly worded proposition; to permit members, including the chairman, to speak more freely; to take a preliminary sounding of the sense of the meeting as a guide to the subsequent drafting of formal resolutions; or to assure that there will be no hasty shutting off of debate by a motion to commit, close debate or table.

(c) Good reasons for conducting the entire meeting informally are a desire to avoid entanglement with parliamentary red tape, a small attendance, a widespread sense of reciprocal cooperation and good will with no fear of interruption by hecklers, or a desire to expedite matters.

(d) An entire meeting cannot be conducted informally if two or more members object. If two members object, one can move to restore formal parliamentary procedure and the other can second it. It is not necessary to vote on such a motion. If two members feel that way, it would be unwise to continue informally lest the legality of the entire meeting be later challenged.

(e) In the informal part of a session, members need not rise to address the chair; there is no restriction on debate; a matter may be discussed even though there is no formal motion before the house; the chair himself may participate fully in discussing the merits of a question; a member may cut in while another is speaking (but should avoid this discourtesy if possible, and should not press it if the speaker resents the interruption); the chair may interpret the sense of the meeting by saying, for example, that "I take it that we are all in favor of (or against) this proposition, and we will so record it, unless there is objection." If any person objects, a formal vote is taken. Otherwise, the matter is considered disposed of by silent assent. During an informal discussion, debate cannot be shut off. A matter is not referred to a committee or laid on the table unless there is unanimous consent. (This is to protect the minority. By consenting to an informal procedure, the minority forfeits some of its traditional safeguards. The members of the minority should not also be deprived of the right to speak on a matter.) In general, the chair may conduct the meeting as freely and informally as he wishes, provided he preserves the majority's authority (see 107) and the minority's rights (see 108).

105. Executive Session

An executive session is an informal meeting from which all nonmembers are excluded. Motion is made and passed that "we go into executive session for the remainder of the meeting," or "that we go into executive session for the consideration

7

of this matter." Or the chair may suggest that, if no one objects, we will go into executive session; will nonmembers
please withdraw? Once in executive (closed) session, the
meeting generally proceeds informally as outlined in 104(e)
above; but it will follow formal parliamentary procedure if
two or more members insist.

106. Committee of the Whole

See 1024 to 1032.

107. Rule by Majority

(a) The touchstone of sound parliamentary practice is not
slavish adherence to rules, but the preservation of majority
rule and the protection of minority rights (see 108 for note on
minority rights). Majority rule is assured by (1) an understanding that the meeting cannot be forced to consider anything if a majority does not want to dispose of it at that time;
(2) by the right to adjourn or recess at any time; and (3) by
the fact that the majority can place any matter on the table
(see 802) and can recall anything from the table (see 806).
The majority must retain the right to amend a proposition
even over the resistance of the maker of the motion, as well as
the right to reconsider or rescind a previous decision.

(b) No matter how informal the session, the chair must see to
it that the majority rights (listed in 107(a) above) are preserved; and that action is not taken, nor money appropriated,
nor commitments made without approval of a majority of
those voting and assurance that a quorum was present (see
111) during that vote. A majority means a majority of those
willing to vote, and not necessarily a majority of those present.

108. Rights of the Minority

The minority must be permitted to retain certain rights unless two thirds of those voting want to withdraw those rights.
This includes the right to debate or discuss a matter (which is

withdrawn if two thirds of those voting vote to close the debate); the right to have a matter considered, which is lost if two thirds of those voting vote against a motion to consider the matter (see 116); the right to insist that matters be considered in the order announced in the agenda—unless two thirds of those voting agree to suspend the rules; the right to expect that the constitution and bylaws will be followed, unless two thirds vote (in accordance with the prescribed procedure), to amend the constitution or bylaws. The members of a minority have a right to assume that a previous action will not be rescinded without notice—though here too, two thirds of the members present can nullify this (see 1112). Furthermore, a minority has the right to suspend immediate action on a major matter just adopted by moving to reconsider it later (see 1109). This is to prevent a temporary but unrepresentative majority from taking irrevocable action contrary to the wishes of the organization's actual majority. In voting for candidates, the minority has the right to insist that its identity be protected. This means a written ballot, and it also means that there can be no motion to make the election unanimous except on the initiative of the defeated candidate. (Otherwise those who voted for him would have to give unwilling consent to unanimity, or show their position by voting against unanimity.)

109. Motions, Questions, and Resolutions

Usually an association can *do* nothing except by passing motions. It can talk, debate, and elect officers. It can applaud, endorse, or file committee reports. But it cannot *do* anything without passing a motion or resolution.

In modern usage there is no substantial difference between a motion and a resolution. A stickler for verbal form would have to agree with the older authorities that until the proposition is stated by the chair it is a motion; after it is stated but before it is passed, it is a *question;* and after it is enacted it is either a *resolution* (if for public consumption) or an *order* (if for operation within the organization). Hence: "I make a motion that . . ."; but "The question before the house is . . ." These nice distinctions are of little practical importance.

9

Generally a proposition that is offered orally is a motion, whereas one submitted in writing is a resolution. A resolution follows the rigid form detailed in 120. A motion is flexible in wording. A matter of major importance or considerable length is usually offered as a resolution. Material is postponed or referred to committees by motion rather than by resolutions. If the maker has a lengthy proposition, he frames a resolution (see 120) and then says, "I move the adoption of this resolution," or words to that effect. See 112 for motions, 120 for resolutions, and Chapter 2 for order (precedence) of motions.

110. Call to Order

As soon after the announced time of meeting as a quorum appears to be present, the chair taps with the gavel (or uses some other appropriate signal) and says: "The meeting will please come to order" or words to that effect. If the chairman is absent at the stated time, it is courteous to wait fifteen or twenty minutes (unless he had previously indicated he *would* be absent) before the vice-president or other second in command calls the meeting to order.

111. Quorum

A quorum is the minimum number of members legally required for the conduct of business (see 1319(10)).

(a) The quorum rule is usually laid down in the constitution or bylaws of the organization. If no quorum rule is stated, general parliamentary practice is that an absolute majority of the members constitutes a quorum. This works out well for a board or for a committee, but for a general membership meeting such a rule may stall all business. A society of more than a hundred members will rarely get 50 per cent or even 30 per cent in attendance. A nationwide body with an annual convention may readily get a majority of the official "delegates" at a meeting, particularly if the society pays their way. But if all members are entitled to vote, it would be an unusual convention that would find as many as 15 per cent of the members sitting down in the hall at one time. Hence for large organizations with general membership voting, the quorum may be as low as 5 or 10 per cent. Some organizations follow this pattern: "Five per cent of the members or one hundred members, whichever number is smaller, shall constitute a quorum." If that society had a thousand members, fifty would constitute a quorum. If it grew to have three thousand members or more, then one hundred would be a quorum, no matter how large it became.

(b) At any time he can get the floor, any member may call for a quorum count. If the membership roll is small—say fewer than thirty or forty members—this takes the form of "I demand a roll call, Mr. Chairman." If it is a larger body, the form is "I see no quorum present, Mr. Chairman, and demand a quorum count." If it is perfectly obvious that this is a simple delaying tactic (if it is manifest that a comfortable quorum is present), the chair says: "A quorum is obviously present, and the demand is rejected." A member can appeal from this ruling (see 408) and, if the appeal prevails, he gets the quorum count or roll call. If the demand seems reasonable, the chair agrees. He counts the attendance himself, has the Secretary do so, appoints tellers, or calls the roll, as appropriate. If there is still dispute (either as to the accuracy of the count or the chair's interpretation of the quorum rule), the chair's ruling is again subject to appeal (see 408).

(c) A member may not interrupt a speaker, a vote, or another member to demand a roll call or quorum count. A simple shout, "Roll call," or "No quorum," is insufficient. Once recognized, he may demand a quorum count regardless of the business pending. In that sense, the demand for a quorum tally is almost always in order—if the caller can get the floor. It need not be seconded.

(d) In the absence of a quorum, resolutions, letters, and statements of policy may be read, offered, and discussed; they may even be amended. But they are nonoperative and no definitive action may be taken on them. The following motions may be made and effectively disposed of in the absence of a quorum: motions to adjourn, to recess, to fix the time for the next meeting, or to do something about rounding up absent members. Under exceptional circumstances, when the welfare or existence of the organization is jeopardized by failure to act, those present may attend to the necessary business, subject to subsequent ratification, but may not make binding commitments.

(e) A majority of those voting (not necessarily a majority of the quorum) is enough to pass a motion. If members present fail to vote, they cannot then complain that the decision was made by a minority. The decision of the quorum is that of the whole body, but this implies a majority of those who took the trouble to vote during a quorum meeting.

112. Form of Motions

A motion is expressed in one of these forms:

1. I move that . . .
2. I make a motion that this organization . . .
3. I here present (offer) the following (attached) resolution (motion) and move its adoption.

113. Motion Should Be Worded Affirmatively

(a) If at all possible, a motion is worded affirmatively rather than negatively. It is better to "move that the invitation (or contract) be accepted" than to "move that the invitation (or contract) be rejected." This is to prevent confusion. If the motion were "move that the contract be rejected" there would be members who would vote *for* the motion in the belief that they were voting *for* the contract. There would be members vigorously opposed to the contract who would delightedly vote *against* the motion, not realizing that they are voting *for* the contract. To prevent this confusion, the rule is: state the motion in the affirmative form. This means that a member who is opposed to something may move that it be done; in this example, if opposed to the contract, he may move that the contract be accepted; and then when the motion is seconded, he opens debate by explaining why he is going to vote against his own motion. So it happens that a member may make a motion with the hope that it will be defeated; and so it happens that sometimes a motion is defeated unanimously even though someone must have made and seconded the motion in the first place. And that is why an appeal from the chair, though originated as a rejection of the chair's ruling, is actually voted on in the form of "Shall the chair be sustained?" and never in the negative form of "Shall the chair be overruled?" (See 408.) And that too is why a motion cannot be amended by inserting the word "not."

(b) It is often possible to express a negative idea in affirmative words, and when this is possible, the motion should be worded that way if the maker wants the negative idea to prevail. For example, suppose he does not want our delegates to be instructed. He should not say "I move that we do *not* instruct our delegates." This is a negative wording and therefore objectionable; it would confuse members who might think that by voting "aye" they were voting to instruct the delegates. The maker of the motion could phrase it this way: "Move that our delegates be uninstructed." This is negative in intent, but positive in form, since it is the same as if he moved "that every delegate be given a blank check so far as instructions are concerned." Such a motion (that our delegates be uninstructed) is perfectly acceptable and causes no confusion. A member does not move "that the report be not accepted." He asks "that the report be filed without further action." Here too a negative idea is clothed in affirmative words.

114. Unconstitutional Motions

A motion that conflicts with the organization's constitution or bylaws is not acceptable and the chair will not receive it. Such a motion cannot be made acceptable by moving to suspend the rules (see 306). It can be made acceptable only when the constitution or bylaws have been formally amended.

115. Repetition of Motions

(a) A society cannot be compelled to listen over and over again to a matter it has already disposed of. Once a primary motion (see 202) has been rejected, referred to a committee, tabled, or postponed, it cannot, at the same meeting, be introduced again—except that a motion to reconsider or rescind might be in order. See Chapter 11 for an explanation of this.

(b) This not only bars the identically worded motion from being renewed; it also means that a motion which is substantially the same cannot be re-introduced simply by making some minor changes in wording.

(c) A secondary, subsidiary, or incidental motion (unlike a primary motion—see 202) may be renewed provided some business has intervened. Under those circumstances (that is, if other business has intervened) the following may be renewed: motions to lay on the table, to take from the table, to reconsider, to refer to a committee, to close debate, or to amend. A motion to suspend the rules, a point of order, or a motion to postpone may be renewed if rejected previously, provided some business has been disposed of since the matter was rejected. This is also true of motions to adjourn or to recess; they may be renewed if previously rejected provided some business has intervened. (Obviously there would be no occasion to renew a successful motion to adjourn.) A passed motion is not renewable, though it may be reconsidered as explained in Chapter 11.

116. Objection to Consideration

One of an organization's precious rights is its privilege to refuse to consider a matter. This may be because the matter is embarrassing, delicate, or beyond the society's area of competence. It may be something which should not be considered in an open meeting. It may be a subject on which members do not wish to be placed on record. No matter what the reason, if two thirds of the members present do not want to consider a matter, it will not be considered, provided this objection is raised before full debate has been launched. It works this way:

(a) As soon as a motion is made, or just before or after it is seconded, or while the first speaker on it is talking, some member rises to say: "I object to consideration of this question." Once the first speaker has concluded his discussion it is too late to make this motion, though a motion to close debate might then be made. Then see (d) below.

(**b**) If the chair considers the matter out of order, irrelevant, or too delicate to discuss, he may seek to suppress it in one of two ways. He can simply rule that it is out of order, giving his reason. This is subject to appeal (see 408). By sustaining the chair a majority could, in effect, prevent a consideration of a matter. Or, if unwilling to appear so arbitrary, the chair could say: "Before proceeding, let us determine whether the meeting wishes to consider this matter at all. It takes a two-thirds vote to remove a matter from consideration. Does the meeting wish to consider this? All in favor say 'aye.' " (Now turn to 116(e).)

(**c**) An "objection to consideration" is not, strictly speaking, a motion. It requires no second. It cannot be discussed, tabled, postponed, amended, or referred to a committee. Though it cannot be debated, it may be explained. The point may be raised while the maker of the original motion is talking—it is one of the few matters that can interrupt a speaker. Only the first speaker on the motion can be interrupted, however. Once someone else starts talking on a matter it is too late to object to consideration.

(**d**) As soon as "objection to consideration" is raised, the chair halts the speaker (if there is one). If the objection has been raised in time, he says: "There is objection to consideration of this. It will be dropped without further discussion if two thirds of you want it that way. I call for a vote. I ask you to vote on whether this matter shall be considered. Shall the question be considered? All in favor of continued consideration say 'aye' . . . all opposed to any further consideration of this, say 'no.' " (The chair could also phrase it this way: "Shall the meeting consider this matter?" or even "Shall we discuss and vote on this matter?")

Note that the objector puts his point in the negative; he objects to consideration. The chair must put it in the affirmative: "Shall the matter be considered?" See 113(a) for explanation.

(e) If twice as many (or more) say "no" than say "aye," the chair says: "The noes have it by a two-thirds vote. The question is withdrawn; there will be no debate on it; the matter will not be reintroduced at this meeting; and the record will not reflect the introduction of this motion." (Actually, the minutes will show what happened; but any published record, transactions, or proceedings, will ignore the entire incident.)

(f) If more vote "no" than "aye" but if the vote is not a two-thirds majority, the chair says: "Though the 'noes' are in the majority, the majority falls short of two thirds; the motion therefore is defeated, and the matter is up for discussion."

(g) If the motion passes, or if the vote is a tie, the chair says, "The 'ayes' have it," and discussion continues just as if no objection has been raised.

(h) If the motion to consider the matter is passed (or if fewer than two thirds vote "no" on it), then the same motion cannot be renewed nor can the action be reconsidered. This is because, by voting to consider the matter, the meeting has made its choice and cannot be harassed by a protesting member, who keeps objecting to consideration.

(j) If the motion to consider is defeated by a two-thirds vote, it *can* be renewed or reconsidered as explained in Chapter 11. If a meeting does not want to consider a subject, subsequent events may change their minds. But once having agreed to consider a topic, and debate having been launched, it then becomes meaningless to refuse to consider it.

117. Withdrawal of a Motion

(a) If a motion has not yet been seconded, the maker may say, "I withdraw the motion," and it is forthwith withdrawn. No record is made of it.

(b) If it has been seconded, but if the chair has not yet said, "It has been moved and seconded that . . . ," the maker can withdraw it. The seconder can if he wishes make the motion himself at this point if the maker withdraws it.

(c) Once the chair has said, "It has been moved and seconded that . . ." (or words to that effect), the organization comes into possession of the motion. It does not belong to the mover. He cannot withdraw it or object to any amendment.

(d) Except under the conditions described below in 117(m) and 117(n), it is the custom to allow a member to withdraw his motion at any time prior to the announcement of the result of the vote, unless the motion has already been referred to a committee (see 117(k)). In theory the member has to ask permission to withdraw his motion once the chair has stated it. In practice the chair says, "If no one objects we will allow Mr. X to withdraw this motion." If someone does object, Mr. X says: "I ask leave to withdraw my motion." This requires no second and is not subject to debate. The chair cuts in and says, "All in favor of allowing Mr. X to withdraw his motion say 'aye.'"

(e) There is not much point to pressing for permission to withdraw when someone objects, because the objector himself would reintroduce the motion if it were withdrawn. Sometimes a member withdraws a motion because, on second thought, he decides he does not want his name attached to it. In that case, his request for permission to withdraw does make sense even if there is objection.

(f) If there is also pending (but not passed) a motion to amend, refer to a committee, postpone, or lay on the table, all these secondary motions collapse when the primary motion is withdrawn.

(g) The minutes do not record a motion that was withdrawn without objection. If a vote was needed to authorize the withdrawal, the minutes do reflect that.

(h) Sometimes another member suggests a happier way of phrasing a motion. This can be handled (1) by withdrawing the original motion and substituting the rephrased one—which requires cooperation of the original maker, since he must agree to withdraw his motion; or (2) by having a formal amendment made, which does not require the consent of the maker, if someone will second the proposed amendment. For example, the original motion is: "That the Society demand that the Governor veto the Zilch Bill, and threaten him with the displeasure of this Society if he signs that bill." This is seconded, but it is pointed out in the course of discussion that it is phrased very awkwardly, and that it would be more effective (not to say more gracious) to replace "demand" with "urge" and to make the second half somewhat more subtle. If the maker and seconder agree, the original motion is withdrawn, and in its place the new resolution is substituted to read: "That the Society urge the Governor to veto the Zilch Bill, calling attention to the fact that this request is respectfully made on behalf of the 350 united and like-minded members of this organization." If the maker refuses to withdraw his motion, the motion is then amended by replacing "demand" with "urge" and having this amendment approved. Then a second amendment is proposed replacing "threaten him with the displeasure . . ." with the phrase "calling attention to the fact that . . ." If this amendment is passed, the main motion (as amended) is then voted on. See Chapter 9.

(j) A matter laid on the table or postponed can be withdrawn if no one objects. If someone objects, a vote is taken on the withdrawal. If the primary motion is withdrawn, nothing is left of it "on the table" so it cannot be revived by "taking from the table."

(k) If a matter has been referred to a committee, the motion to withdraw is out of order. The maker may, however, move to discharge the committee (see 1017(b)).

(m) If there is a deadline to making a motion, then, obviously, it cannot be withdrawn after the deadline has passed. For example, suppose the rules require that a "motion to reconsider" be made within twenty-four hours after the primary motion had passed or failed. A member waits until the last minute, then makes a motion to reconsider. An hour later he wants to withdraw his motion. But it is now too late for anyone else to move to reconsider. It would, therefore, be improper to allow him to withdraw the motion because no one else could propose it and the meeting would be deprived of an opportunity to vote on it. If a deadlined motion could be withdrawn at the whim of the maker, a person hostile to a motion could kill it by first moving it, then (as soon as the deadline had passed) moving to withdraw it.

(n) In many organizations, there is a rule that forbids a matter's being reintroduced until a certain time has passed. For instance, the rule may be that if a proposed amendment to the constitution is defeated, the same amendment cannot be reintroduced until a year has elapsed. In a municipal body, it is a common rule that once a zoning variance is denied, the same request cannot be reintroduced until a year (or some other period) has passed. Such rules are needed so that one individual does not constantly harass a body by reintroducing a matter that is repeatedly rejected.

Where such a rule exists, it is to the interest of the organization that the matter be disposed of rather than that the introducer be permitted to withdraw it. For example: the organization has a rule that the name of a rejected applicant for membership cannot be proposed again until six months have elapsed. Mr. A has proposed that Mr. X be elected to membership. He hears the discussion and realizes that Mr. X has no chance of election to membership. So he seeks to withdraw the motion. Ordinarily this will be allowed as face-saving. But the organization may feel that Mr. A is simply withdrawing the motion today in order to reintroduce it next week when, he knows, only a handful of members will be present. To prevent this, the group has the right to insist that the motion be disposed of now. They can refuse to let Mr. A withdraw his motion, as explained above in 117(d). Accordingly, when the chair says, "Does anyone object to letting Mr. A withdraw his motion?" Mr. B calls out, "I object." Mr. A then asks formal permission to withdraw the motion, and, presumably, the "noes" have it, and the motion is *not* withdrawn. It is voted on then and there unless Mr. A can muster a majority to lay it on the table or to postpone it to a definite future time.

118. Seconding

(a) With the exceptions indicated in 118(c) every motion, nomination, or resolution must be seconded before it can be discussed, considered, or voted on. Any one except the maker of the motion or the chairman may second. This is done simply by the call, "I second it." The member need not rise and the secretary need not record his name. Only a member eligible to vote is eligible to second a motion or nomination. While the maker of a motion has the right to speak first on it, the seconder has no special debating priority. Seconding a motion does not always imply agreement with it. A hostile member may second a motion in order to get it before the house so that it may be defeated.

(b) If no one seconds a matter, the chair has the choice of saying either (1) "There being no second, the matter is not before the house and we will proceed to the next item," or (2) "Do I hear a second?" If no one seconds the motion, resolution, or nomination, then (unless it is one of those listed below), the matter is abandoned and no note is made in the record or minutes of the unseconded proposition.

(c) No second is required to get a ruling on a point of order, information, inquiry, or personal privilege. No second is needed when a maker asks permission to withdraw his motion. An objection to consideration of a question (see 116) is disposed of at once without waiting for any one to second it. The call "Division" (which requires a chairman to count the votes after he has announced the result) does not require a second (see 612). A motion to take from the table *does* require a second (see 807), but to call up a motion to reconsider later (see 1109(f)) does *not* require a second. To get a vote on an appeal from the chair (see 408) *does* require a second, but to get a decision on a point of order does not.

119. Motions To Ratify

Sometimes action is taken by an officer, committee, or a nonquorum meeting, which needs formal ratification later. The motion to ratify is a primary motion, subject to debate, amendment, commitment, and the like. Such a motion is passed if the vote is a tie. When passed, this motion is retroactive: it gives approval to something done previously and the approval dates back to the time of the action.

120. Resolutions

A resolution is a formally written motion. Two forms are in common use: the short form or "resolve," and the long form or "whereas style" resolution.

(a) A short-form resolution is a single paragraph beginning with the word "Resolved." For example:

Resolved that the Bleat and Bragg Company be retained as public relations counsel to this Society at a fee of $25,000 per year.

This is offered by the maker of the resolution in these words: "Here is a resolution (or resolve), and I move that it be adopted." Written copies of the resolution may be distributed or announced as being available; and the maker reads the entire resolution. It is then acted on exactly as if it were an ordinary motion.

(b) A long-form resolution consists of a prologue plus one or more "resolving" clauses. Any language which conveys the idea with exactness is acceptable, but the quaint and decorous language of the traditional form appeals to many persons. For those who are devoted to the ancient form, here is how it is done:

The prologue begins with the word "Whereas." This is followed by a comma. Periods are not used anywhere in the prologue. A comma follows each "whereas"; a semicolon is placed at the end of each of the prologue ideas; and the word "and" without any punctuation mark follows this semicolon. The "resolving" clause begins with the word "resolved" (followed by a comma) or with the phrase "Be it Resolved." Here is the way it looks:

WHEREAS, There is no mental hygiene clinic in this county; and

WHEREAS, There is now in the county treasury a surplus of $300,000 from liquor licenses; and

WHEREAS, No better use for such money can be found than to use it to promote the mental health of our fellow citizens; therefore,

Resolved, That this Society favors the establishment of a mental hygiene clinic in this county; and be it further

Resolved, That this Society favors diversion of liquor tax moneys into the county's welfare fund for this purpose; and be it further

Resolved, That the President of this Society appoint a committee of three members to meet with the County Supervisors and discuss this resolution.

Note that in the prologue the word "Whereas" introduces each idea; it is followed by a comma; the next phrase begins with a capital letter (which is a grammatical solecism but a parliamentary canon); the phrase ends with a semicolon; following the semicolon is the sole word "and" except for the last line of the prologue. The last word of the last line of the prologue is always "therefore," followed by a comma.

In the sample above, the first word in the resolving clause was "Resolved." The phrase "Be it Resolved" would have been equally proper, and is illustrated in the sample below. In either usage, the first letter of the word immediately following is capitalized. The word "Resolved" is followed by a comma, and then by the word "That" with a capital "T."

If there is more than one resolving clause, the drafter has his choice: he may connect them without periods, as in the sample above, or make a separate sentence of each clause as in the sample below. If he uses the first method (sample above), each resolving clause—except the last—ends with a semicolon followed by the phrase "and be it further . . ." There is no punctuation after the word "further"; see sample above.

If he prefers to make a separate sentence out of each resolving clause, then a period terminates each as in the sample below:

WHEREAS, The unspoiled atmosphere of this village has long been its pride and joy; and

WHEREAS, Certain commercial interests are now seeking to erect a bacon rendering plant within a thousand feet of the village green; and

WHEREAS, This would lead to traffic congestion, bad odors, loud noises, and other undesirable effects, therefore

Be it Resolved, That this Society opposes a bacon rendering plant for our village.

Be it Resolved, That this Society urges the Zoning Commission to rezone the Parker tract so that it lies entirely in an AAA Residential Zone.

Be it Resolved, That the Secretary be instructed to attend the next meeting of the Zoning Commission and file the protests of this
Society.

The compulsive or sentimental secretary who wants to keep
the old form unsullied will follow this format rigidly. Of
course it is stilted, ungrammatical, and anachronistic. There
is nothing illegal about the use of more modern language,
provided the resolving clauses are clear.

(c) Each resolving clause is voted on separately. That is because each one is, in effect, a primary motion. Each is debatable, and subject to amendment, commitment, placement on
the table, and postponement. If one or more of the resolving
clauses are passed, then the prologue is put to vote, each paragraph separately. The maker starts the ball rolling by offering
the entire resolution, "I move that this resolution, which I shall
read, be adopted," or words to that effect.

He reads the resolution. Someone seconds it. The chair
says: "It has been moved and seconded that this resolution
be adopted. The first Resolving Clause is: . . ." (The chair
reads it. In the example immediately above it would be "That
this Society opposes a bacon rendering plant for our village."
In the previous example, it would be "That this Society favors
the establishment of a mental hygiene clinic in this county.")

The chair then says "Any discussion?" The matter is then
processed like any other motion, and so on with each resolving
clause, and then with each prologue clause.

121. Debate

(a) After a primary motion has been made and seconded, the
chair asks "Is there any discussion?" This signals the opening
of debate. The rules of debate on motions are detailed in
Chapter 5, and will be summarized here only briefly. Any
primary motion is debatable; so is a motion to amend a matter,
to postpone it, or to refer it to a committee. However, there
is no debate on a motion to close debate, nor on a motion to
lay on the table, to adjourn, or to recess. Debate may be
closed if two thirds of those present want to shut it off. The
motion to close debate is not itself debatable. If twice as

many vote for it as against it, debate stops and the chair calls for a vote on the question. The maker of a motion has a right to be the first to debate on it. The seconder has no particular priority. If a secondary motion is made—(such as a motion to refer something to a committee or to postpone it or to lay it on the table)—the secondary motion puts a stop to debate on the primary motion. If it is a motion to lay the matter on the table, this is not debatable at all and is voted on at once. The other motions (to amend, postpone, or refer to a committee) are debatable but discussion must be focused on the propriety of the secondary motion, not on the merits of the main question.

(b) Ordinarily no one may interrupt a speaker, but there are some exceptions to this. A person may interrupt to raise a point of order, inquiry, or privilege (see Chapter 7), or to appeal from the immediately preceding decision of the chair. He may not interrupt to move adjournment.

(c) The right to debate does not automatically include the right to read long letters, extracts, or documents; and if a member wants to insert such communications as part of his debate he needs permission (see 508).

(d) The debate must be germane to the motion and the chair can rule that a speaker is out of order if his discussion is hopelessly irrelevant to the topic. The chair's decision in this regard is appealable (see 408).

122. Statement of the Motion

When debate has come to an end (or as soon as an undebatable motion is seconded) the chair restates the motion before calling for a vote. As a matter of fact the chair restates the motion *before* calling for discussion if the matter is complex or there is any possibility that some members are not clear about it, as well as before calling for the vote. The statement is simply a common-sense rephrasing of the motion or summary of the resolution, as, for example:

It has been moved and seconded that we create a committee to look for a permanent headquarters building.

It has been moved and seconded that we adopt this resolution which, in essence, protests against the recent decision of the Board of Aldermen on parking meters. If you oppose the action of the Aldermen you vote "yes" on this motion, because this is a protest against the Board's action. Is that clear?

It has been moved and seconded that we lay this matter on the table. This is not a debatable motion so we will have to vote on it at once. If you want to postpone this matter you vote "aye"—that is, you vote to lay it on the table. If you want to keep on discussing it and want to settle it now, you must vote "no" to keep it on the floor. Now, all in favor of laying it on the table say "aye."

These illustrate ways in which the chairman can restate the question to prevent confusion.

123. Voting

(a) Sometimes it is clear from the discussion that almost everyone is either in favor of or against the motion. The chair could then say so. He might say, "It seems to be the sense of the meeting that this motion is acceptable, and I will order it adopted unless there is any objection," if the attitude of the group seemed favorable, or "If no one objects, we will consider the proposition rejected," if a negative attitude prevailed. This is "voting by silent assent." If someone does object, a more formal voting method is used. In order of formality these methods are (1) *viva voce*, that is, by voice vote, (2) show of hands, (3) standing vote, (4) roll call, and (5) written ballot (see Chapter 6 for details). Voice vote (*viva voce*) is the common method. The chair says, "All in favor say 'aye,'" and, after noting the response, says "All opposed say 'no.'" If anyone thinks the chair was in error when he ruled on a voice vote, the skeptical member calls, "Division." Such a demand must be honored, and the chair honors it by calling for a rising vote or, with permission of the group, for a show of hands (for more details on division of the house, see 612). A tie vote passes a motion to sustain the chair, or to ratify action previously taken. In all other cases, a tie vote defeats the motion; but the chair (if he did not vote before) can vote now and break the tie if he wishes. A member may change his unwritten vote any time before the chair announces the result (see 615). A primary motion (see 202) is passed when more

vote for it than vote against it—regardless of how many or
how few vote. That is, a motion has received majority approval when more vote for it than against it even if most of
the members present do not vote at all. A motion which im-
pairs the minority's rights takes a two-thirds vote. So a two-
thirds vote is required for closing debate, closing nominations,
suspending the rules, and refusing to consider a question (see
614). A two-thirds vote means that at least twice as many
vote for the measure as vote against it—and this is so regardless of how few actually vote. If he is a full member of the
group, the chair always has the right to vote.

(b) Unless otherwise specified in the bylaws or in previously
adopted rules of order, a majority means that more voted *for*
than voted *against*. Thus, nonvoters do not count either way,
provided a quorum is present. If one hundred members are
present, and of these two vote "yes" and one votes "no," the
motion is adopted—indeed it is adopted by a two-thirds vote.
The ninety-seven who refused to vote cannot complain, since
they had ample opportunity to vote "no." This rule (that "majority" means a majority of those voting, not a majority of
those present) is the common parliamentary law. It may be
superseded by a previous agreement to the contrary (see
1311). In legislative bodies, it is usual to require either a
majority of the total membership of the house or, at the least,
a majority of those present to enact a law. But this does not
apply to voluntary societies with no law-making powers.
Sometimes a business organization (for instance, the board of
a corporation) has a rule that decisions are made by an absolute majority of the voting stock or by a majority of those
present, rather than by a majority of those who choose to vote.
If the organization is chartered to do business and if it may
encumber funds of members, it is well to have some rule on
this spelled out in the bylaws (see 1311).

124. Contents of the Minutes

(a) If proceedings are recorded verbatim, someone—usually
the secretary—has to edit the proceedings, and bring out a
readable, compact, and correct draft of what took place. Usu-

ally there is no verbatim record. Rough notes are taken by the secretary. A professional stenographer may record verbatim formal motions and the results. Persons who present resolutions or other written documents deliver copies to the secretary, who will work them into the minutes at the proper place. The minutes must include such identifying data as date, place, hour, and type of meeting. At a session of an executive board or other high authority, small-membership unit, the minutes should list every member present. At general membership meetings, it is enough for the minutes to indicate how many were present, or to state that a quorum was present. The presiding officer should be indicated (". . . with the President in the Chair . . ."; or ". . . in the absence of the President, Mr. Jones, the Vice-President, took the Chair"). Every primary motion is noted, including the name of the maker, but not the name of the seconder. Debate is usually not included, but in some organizations it may be desirable to summarize the main pros and cons—this is a matter of local practice. Whether a motion passed or failed is always indicated. The pyramiding of secondary motions is clearly shown in the minutes; for example:

Mr. Jones moved that the Society condemn the water fluoridation ordinance. This was seconded, and during discussion, Mr. Smith moved that it be referred to the Committee on Public Health. This motion was seconded, but before it was voted on, Mr. Brown moved that it be laid on the table, and this motion was passed.

(b) Also included in the minutes are the names of persons appointed as committee members, representatives, observers, delegates, chairmen, and the like. Also included are the names of persons proposed for, considered for, or elected to membership. Committee reports, if readily condensed into short paragraphs, are included; otherwise the report is attached as an "annex" or "exhibit" and the minutes refer to it:

Speaking for the Committee on Zoning and Land Use, Mr. Herbert presented a report urging that Elm Street be retained in zone RA, and giving reasons. (See Exhibit B.) After considerable discussion this was referred to the Executive Committee for further study.

The Committee on Program announced that speakers had been obtained for each regular meeting for the entire year. The report was read by Mrs. Willis. (See Annex 3.) The report was accepted and the Program Committee was discharged with thanks.

(c) When voting is by roll call or by written ballot, the minutes show the number of votes on each side. For a motion requiring a two-thirds vote, the minutes show the number of "aye" votes and the number of "no" votes if they were actually counted. If the vote was by voice (see Chapter 6), and if the chairman's decision that the motion had a two-thirds majority is not appealed, the minutes merely indicate that more than two thirds voted "aye," or that the vote was unanimous if that was true.

125. Form of the Minutes

(a) Minutes are so organized that the *actions* of the meeting stand out clearly and crisply. This may be done in either of two ways. A skeletonized form may be used (see sample in 125(b)) in which the actions are numbered and narrative is omitted; in the second way, debate and narration may be included, but the actions are underlined or are set in bold type or in capital letters, or are set apart from discussion by spacing or margination.

(b) Skeletonized form:

A regular meeting of the XYZ Society was held at the AB building in (city) on Thursday evening, October 20, 19–, with the President in the Chair. Minutes of the previous meeting were read and accepted. There being no old business, the meeting proceeded to new business and took the following action:

—Voted to hold the Annual Social Evening on December 29 at the Club Fatale.

—Voted to admit to membership Messrs. A, B, and C.

—Rejected an invitation from the EFG Society to join with them in a march on the state capital to protest the bill to license fortune tellers.

—Referred to the Committee on Legislation a proposal to protest Senate Bill 1492.

—Heard a paper by M. R. S. Stevenson on "A Sensible Tax Base for Our County."

—Adjourned at 10:15 P.M.

(c) Narrative form with action emphasized by format:

The 187th regular meeting of the XYZ Society was held at the AB building (city) on Thursday evening, October 20, 19—, with the President in the Chair. Minutes of the previous meeting were read and accepted. There being no old business, the Chair called for committee reports. The Committee on the Social Evening, Mr. G. H., Chairman, reported and recommended that the Annual Social Evening be held on December 31. Mr. J pointed out that this would be New Year's Eve, and suggested that the date be December 29 instead. This was acceptable to the Committee, and accordingly the membership

VOTED TO HOLD THE SOCIAL EVENING ON DECEMBER 29 AT THE CLUB FATALE.

The Membership Committee, Mr. J. K., Chairman, reported and recommended that the applications of A, B, and C be accepted. Mr. K also stated that they had one other application which was deferred pending review of his references. The meeting

VOTED TO ELECT MESSRS. A, B, AND C TO MEMBERSHIP.

The Secretary then read a letter from the EFG Society suggesting that our two organizations march on the State House to protest the bill to license fortune tellers. A motion to refer this to the Legislative Committee was defeated and then the Society

VOTED TO DECLINE THE INVITATION OF THE EFG SOCIETY TO MARCH TO THE STATE CAPITAL.

And so on.

(d) The society should adopt a rule indicating whether or not minutes are to be signed by the secretary; if to be signed, whether signed when prepared or when approved; and whether or not the president countersigns or validates the minutes.

(e) Motions which (1) appropriate money, (2) authorize publicity, (3) hire employees, or (4) commit the organization to definite action should be fully and explicitly recorded in the minutes.

126. Disposition of Minutes

(a) At some time during each meeting (usually near the beginning) there is a reading of the minutes of the previous session. If an annual convention consists of several sessions on consecutive days, a society or organization may prefer to consolidate into one narrative the minutes for the entire annual meeting, or it may prefer to read each day the minutes of the previous day's session. A decision should be made on this one way or the other. If there is a long interval between consecutive meetings (longer than four or five months), it would be better to send the minutes out by mail (or to include them in the society's publication, journal, or other printed matter) and invite corrections by correspondence. These minutes could still be accepted at the next meeting, though they would not be read then, the form being:

CHAIR: The minutes were mailed to all of you, and all were invited to submit corrections. Mr. Secretary, were any corrections submitted?

SECRETARY: No.

CHAIR: Then I will entertain a motion that the minutes be approved as distributed.

This could also be done by an executive board or by a special reading committee, or even by silent assent if no mailed corrections were submitted.

If there is not this much time between meetings, the minutes are read, corrected, and then approved at the following session. The word "approved" with the later date and the secretary's signature are then affixed to the last page in the part of the journal covering that earlier meeting, unless the society has adopted a rule against having minutes signed (see 125(d)).

(b) Minutes are usually approved by silent assent (see 603) rather than by formal vote. The chair says: "You have heard the minutes. If there are no corrections, they will be approved as read. Does anyone object?" If anyone does object, the chair entertains a motion to accept the minutes as read, then the objector moves an amendment to permit his correction, and there is a vote on the amendment, then a vote on the primary motion (to accept the minutes as corrected).

If there is no objection, the record states that the minutes of the previous meeting were approved as read. A formal motion to accept the minutes as read (or as distributed) is in order, but is unnecessary, since the chair can present that question for the assembly's decision without a formal motion.

(c) If a motion is passed to expunge a matter from the record, a line is drawn diagonally through the text. In the margin, the secretary writes "expunged by order of the Society," and adds the date. Printed versions completely omit any paragraphs so expunged. See 1113 for more details.

(d) A motion to dispense with the reading of the minutes is in order but requires a two-thirds vote, since it deprives some members of their rights. It is, in effect, a suspension of rules. If such a motion is passed, the minutes become the official journal for that meeting even though not voted on.

(e) If for some reason an error is discovered in old minutes—say those more than four or five months old—those minutes cannot be corrected. However, a resolution may be passed that so-and-so (the correct sentiment) is the sense of the society, and that the different sentiment appearing in the minutes is hereby declared to be in error. The old minutes should then be marginally cross-referenced to this action in the new minutes.

127. Receiving Reports

After a committee report is made, the society, if it likes the report, votes to

1. *Accept* the findings
2. *Adopt* the recommendations

See 1013(c) for further details.

If the meeting does not like the report it may vote to file it, to return it to the committee for further study, to refer it to some other committee, or to lay it on the table. It may vote that the report be divided and certain named items be rejected. See 1014 for action when no motion is made.

2

Precedence of Motions

201. The Parliamentary Keystone

The business end of a business meeting consists of motions. Motions are the vertebrae in the backbone of parliamentary procedure. In a simple meeting, each motion might be made, seconded, and then just passed or rejected. Such a session would present no parliamentary problems; the chairman would need only to know how to call "All in favor say 'aye.'"

(a) In practice, it is not as simple as that. After a motion is made and seconded something else can happen to it. Someone might move to refer it to a committee, or to table it, or to stop debate on it, or to postpone it, or even to refuse to consider it. The chair's mastery of procedure is then tested. If a motion is pending, may someone make a secondary motion to refer it to a committee? And before *that* is disposed of, may another member move to table it? And before *that* is voted on, could someone try to amend the original motion? (The answers are yes, yes, and no in that order.)

(b) The competent chairman has to know about the precedence of motions. There is no substitute for this knowledge. Basically, he has to know how ten secondary motions are ranked. He can keep this in mind in one of three ways. He can learn it by rote; he can learn the reason for precedence, and thus work out the answer logically; or he can keep a list of motions in rank order propped up on his table.

(c) Since there are only ten secondary motions, it is not too difficult to memorize the listing by rote. Learning the rationale of this precedence is a sound idea, but in an emergency there is no time to reason what the rank of motions should be. A memory jogger on the reading desk is also helpful.

(d) To understand this matter once and for all, to understand it so clearly that the "value" of each motion is as familiar to the chairman as the value of each coin in his pocket, it is necessary to review a few fundamentals. This may be ABC for the experienced clubman, but it will be helpful to lay a solid foundation for less sophisticated chairmen.

202. Kinds of Motions

(a) To begin with, there are two kinds of motions. One is the *primary motion,* the main motion, the proposal which, if passed, commits the meeting to doing something or saying something. A primary motion has three characteristics: it is independent of any secondary or incidental motion; it commits the organization to some action or attitude; and it has implications beyond the conduct of this one meeting. Ordinarily, when some one thinks of actions taken at a meeting, he thinks of these primary motions.

Main motions are debatable, amendable, and deferrable; that is, they may be tabled, postponed, or referred to a committee. With only two exceptions (see 614(c)), they are passed by majority vote, and (unless listed in 1105) they may be reconsidered.

(b) All other motions would, therefore, be *secondary* motions. If X moves that we write the Governor and urge him to veto a bill, this is a primary motion: it meets the criteria above. But then, after this motion is made and seconded, B might suggest that it be referred to a committee for study (or that it be "committed," which is parliamentary jargon for the same thing). B's motion is a secondary one, because it is supplementary to, or subsidiary to, X's motion. Perhaps while everyone is debating whether or not to commit the motion, C gets bored and moves that we close debate. This too is a

33

secondary motion. By itself, "close debate" means nothing. It must close debate on something—in this case on B's motion. The motion to close debate is therefore not an independent motion at all; it is subsidiary. And then, perhaps, D moves that we adjourn. This too, is a secondary motion, because the adjournment has no implications beyond this one meeting.

(c) There are various ways of classifying these secondary motions. One is to group together those motions which are supplementary to some other matter and call them all "subsidiary" or "supplementary" motions. Then those secondary motions which are incidental to, rather than dispositive of, primary motions, would be called "incidental" motions: a motion to adjourn, for instance, or a motion to accept a report. It is also possible to classify motions as "privileged" and "unprivileged," the former being matters which require a high priority, such as a motion to adjourn or a point of personal privilege.

Essentially, a *subsidiary* motion is one that amends, commits, or postpones. There are three kinds of postponement: to postpone indefinitely (see 812), to postpone to a time specified (see 811), or to lay on the table (see 802). Motions to close, limit, or extend debate are also usually classed as "subsidiary."

These subclassifications are of little practical importance. It *is* necessary, however, to recognize a secondary motion, realize its purpose, and know its "rank." Knowing the precedence (or rank) of motions is part of the chairman's business. And here is why:

203. Theory of Precedence in Motions

(a) After a motion is seconded, but before it is voted on, various other proposals may be made. Some will be in order and some will not. If Motion X "outranks" Motion Y, then Motion X may be made while Motion Y is on the floor. A motion is "on the floor" after it has been seconded but before it has been disposed of.

Here is the reason for precedence in motions.

(b) No one has a right to keep an assembly in session against its will. Therefore the motion to adjourn has an almost-top priority. It may be made at almost any time, except while someone is speaking. And the reason is obvious: a group has to be able to halt its proceedings whenever most of the members want to.

(c) But the motion to adjourn has to yield, under certain circumstances, to a motion to set the time of the next meeting. If the motion to adjourn has an absolute top priority, the organization might adjourn itself out of existence. So the rule is a logical one: a motion to set the time of the next meeting has Number 1 priority; next under that is a motion to adjourn; then a motion to recess.

That's easy to remember. These three motions concerned with stopping the meeting must rank 1, 2, and 3.

(d) After a society's right to close the session is its right to postpone consideration of a matter for a while. No one can insist that the group must say "yes" or "no" right now, if the majority prefers not to commit itself at this time. So that determines the next priority: a motion "to lay on the table" (see Chapter 8). Unless someone else is speaking, a motion to table may be made while any other motion is on the floor— except, of course, one of the top three. The motion to table has to yield to the top three motions—the ones about adjournment. Except for these "adjournment" and "recess" motions, however, a motion to table has top priority.

(e) After a society has protected its right to adjourn and its right to table a matter, comes its right to shut off debate. No one can compel a group to listen to endless debate if most of the members have heard enough. So the next priority motion is the one that terminates debate. In legislative assemblies this is called "previous question." But "previous question" is not used much in voluntary bodies, since the same purpose is accomplished by a simple motion to close debate.

(f) Here then are the five motions with top priority, and the very sensible reasons why they rank that way:

1. To fix the time of the next meeting
2. To adjourn
3. To recess

4. To lay on the table
5. To stop debate

If no one wants to make any of these five motions, the group will have to listen to a discussion unless they want to postpone it to a more favorable time. Here again, no one has a right to insist on an immediate decision, so next in order is the motion to postpone to a certain time. This differs from the motion to "lay on the table" because there is no specified time to resume discussion when a matter is tabled.

(g) If a matter requires more study than the meeting can give to it now, they can refer it to a committee. So the motion to commit is in order, provided that one of the six higher priority motions is not pending on the floor. The meeting must have the right to adjourn first, to recess next, then to table a matter, then to shut off debate, and then to postpone a subject. If the meeting refuses to dispose of the matter in this summary fashion (after having been given the chance), they must then have the right to send it to a committee. So the motion to commit has a rank lower than the motion to postpone. And the final secondary motion is a motion to amend. This has no priority; it is really a modified primary motion. It has to take priority over its own primary motion (otherwise there would be nothing pending for it to amend), but it is subject to any of these summary methods of disposition.

(h) This, in a nutshell, is the theory of the rank of motions. It is a traffic regulation designed to give the meeting the opportunity of disposing of matters in the way it wants. The rank does not depend on the importance of the motion. Almost the contrary is true, since a primary motion (always the important motion) actually has the lowest rank. But secondary motions must take priority over primary ones; otherwise the primary motion could be disposed of only by passing it or defeating it. There would be no place for amendments, commitments, and so on.

(j) The rank of motions is not whimsical. It was not set up by drawing numbers out of a hat. It was hammered out in the seventeenth and eighteenth centuries in the British Parliament. Secondary motions began to assume their rank in response to very real needs. With respect to its own activities a group has the right, in order to terminate a meeting, to suspend the meeting briefly, to postpone a matter until a more favorable time, to refuse to listen to further talk on it, to schedule a matter for a later but specific time, and to refer it to a committee for further study. The precedence of motions simply freezes this series of rights into a set of compact rules.

204. Roster of Motions Arranged by Rank

In its simplest form, the rank of motions is as follows for reasons above explained:

1. To fix the time for the next meeting
2. To adjourn
3. To recess
4. To lay on the table
5. To stop debate
6. To postpone to a definite time
7. To refer to a committee
8. To amend an amendment
9. To amend a primary motion
10. The primary motion

This is the list which the good chairman knows by heart . . . or which he keeps on a card on the reading desk. It is not complete. A few incidental motions and stray points slip in between Number 3 and Number 4 (these are reviewed in 206 and also in Chapter 7). In all but the most unusual situations, a knowledge of these ten motions will enable the chair to make swift and correct rulings about whether a motion is in order.

205. Precedence in Operation

So much for the theory. To test his skill in handling this "precedence" matter, the aspiring chairman might consider how he would rule in this hypothetical meeting of a dental society planning its annual convention.

Dr. A has moved that "We do not accept liquor displays at

our next convention." There is some discussion. Attendance at this meeting is small, and Dr. B does not think definitive action ought to be taken when so few are present. So Dr. B says, "I move to lay this on the table." The motion to "lay on the table" is seconded, but before it is voted on, Dr. C moves to refer the whole matter to a committee. Are these two motions (lay on the table; refer to a committee) in order?

The answers are "yes" and "no" respectively. Review the table in paragraph 204 and in the end pages. Note that *to lay on the table* is high on the list—Number 4. Unless a motion to adjourn or to recess were pending, this is a top priority motion. So Dr. B's motion was in order. But Dr. C's motion (to refer it to a committee) is down the line at Number 7. Obviously Number 7 has no priority over Number 4. So the *motion to commit* is not in order until the tabling motion (Dr. B's motion) is disposed of. And, of course, it would then be in order only if Dr. B's motion (to table) were defeated. If the motion to table is passed, then there is nothing to refer to a committee. The whole matter of liquor advertising would have been postponed until the meeting moved to "take it from the table."

So far, the moral of the story is this: go back to 204 and note the numbers. A motion is in order when any motion with a higher number is pending; but a motion is *not* in order if one with a lower number is pending.

To proceed with the problem of the liquor displays. The motion to table has been defeated, so Dr. C gets up again and repeats his motion. He wants the whole question studied by a committee. "I move," he says, "that this be referred to the Convention Committee for study and report." This is seconded, and there is some discussion on the wisdom of sending it to a committee. Dr. D is bored with apparently endless debate, so he rises to "move that debate be closed" (or he moves the "previous question," in a legislative or civic assembly).

Is this in order? Yes. A motion to close debate is Number 5, and therefore outranks a motion to commit, which is Number 7.

The motion to close debate passes by the required two-thirds vote. The chair now says, "We will vote on Dr. A's motion to ban liquor displays." Does the chairman know what he is doing?

No, he does not. The pending motion is Dr. C's—the one that wants to refer it all to a committee. What the chair should say here is something like this: "You have voted to terminate debate. There will, therefore, be no further discussion and we will vote on Dr. B's motion, which is to refer to the Convention Committee this question of liquor displays. All in favor of referring it to the Committee say 'aye' . . ."

Before any one can shout "aye," Dr. E jumps up and says, "Mr. Chairman, I move we take a 20-minute recess." Can he get away with that?

If the chair refuses to recognize him, he cannot. But once he was recognized, he would be within his rights to make a motion to recess. This is Number 3 on the list, whereas the pending motion—Number 7—is much lower. The motion to recess, therefore, takes precedence over the motion to commit.

Technically, unless the chair said: "Dr. E," or gave some other sign of recognition, Dr. E's cry would be an empty voice in the meeting. If the chair refused to recognize him and if Dr. E was that kind of fellow, he could rise to a point of personal privilege (see Chapter 7) or demand an appeal from the chair (see 408).

If the chair does recognize Dr. E, then the motion to take a recess is in order—if somebody seconds it. Otherwise it is dismissed. But if seconded, then, without debate, the chair will call for a vote on the motion to recess. If it passes, there will be a twenty-minute break, and then, with every one refreshed, the motion to commit will come to a vote. If the motion to recess is defeated, the vote on the motion to commit is taken at once, since debate was already terminated.

To summarize: While any motion listed in 204 is pending, a member may make a motion with a lower number prefixed to it.

206. Stray Points and Incidental Motions

The list given in 204 is simplified to include only the common secondary motions (all except Number 10 are secondary motions). A few unusual ones must now be considered. These include not only motions, but also "points" which, though not really motions, sometimes have to be allowed to intrude. "Gentlemen, the hall is on fire," for example, would have to be heard regardless of the rank of the pending motion.

The motions and points below outrank the matters to which they refer, but do *not* outrank the motions to adjourn and recess:

> Point of parliamentary inquiry (see 705)
> Point of information (see 704)
> Motion to suspend the rules (see 306(b))
> Objection to considering a matter (see 116)
> Permission to withdraw a motion (see 117)
> Point of order (see 706)
> Appeal from the chair (see 408)

With these motions and points, the rule is that they are in order when a primary motion has the floor, but they can be superseded by a motion to adjourn or recess. In the roster of motions (in 204) they fall between Number 3 and Number 4. Thus, if a motion to lay on the table is pending, a member may rise to a point of order, information, or inquiry, or the maker of the original motion may ask permission to withdraw it, and has to have the chance of having that voted on before the motion to lay on the table is disposed of.

These points and motions are peculiar in some respects, since their precedence is not fixed, but depend on the circumstances. They are considered more definitively in the sections listed above.

3

Agenda: The Order of Business

301. Business and Scientific Programs

A scientific or technical organization that meets frequently (more than three or four times a year) generally has both a scientific and a business program at each session. An organization that meets only once or twice a year usually has, at its convention, separate sessions for scientific and business matters. The present chapter is concerned with the order of items during business meetings only.

302. Order of Business: General Rule

The standard order of business is simply this:

1. Reports
2. Old business
3. New business

This is easy enough to remember, and it is all that any chairman really has to remember. The schedule can be inflated as much as you please by inserting details such as:

1. Call to order
2. Roll call

3. Reading of minutes
4. Report of secretary
5. Report of executive committee
6. Report of treasurer
7. Other reports
8. Communications
9. Old and unfinished business
10. Nominations for office and/or for membership
11. Elections
12. New business
13. Adjournment

This is sheer padding. The "call to order" and "adjournment" are obvious. The "roll call" is rare, and usually only in response to a demand for a quorum count. The basis of the schedule is the three-part program already mentioned, (1) reports, (2) old business, (3) new business.

303. Reports

(a) Many meetings—particularly meetings of executive boards and similar bodies—are devoted largely to acting on reports. Reports are heard early in the meeting to provide the springboard for subsequent action. An organization should hear a *treasurer's report* at every session and an *auditor's report* once a year. The *secretary's report* would include a summary of correspondence handled and statistics about the growth of or changes in membership. When the secretary serves as clerk of the executive board, he reports a summary of the activities of the executive board to the general membership at *its* meetings. Certain committees might report at every meeting (membership committee, for example). Most committees report only once or twice a year. The custom is for the chairman of a committee to indicate in advance when he will report and to have that report listed in the program or on the agenda.

(b) It is good practice to write out all reports in full, well in advance. These reports are filed with the secretary prior to the meeting; they may be reproduced and attached to the program as exhibits or appendixes, filed in the archives and available on request, or they are reproduced and handed out to each member entering the meeting. Sometimes it is impractical for a chairman or other reporting officer to have his report in final form early enough to permit reproduction. In that case a typed copy and a few carbon copies are filed. The secretary, a reading clerk, or the chairman reads the report. If a report is reproduced and given to each member, it is not necessary to read it in full, aloud. But before taking action which might alter part of the report, that part of it is read.

304. Old Business

(a) Old or "unfinished business" is any matter which was pending but not disposed of at a previous meeting.

(b) To renew a matter which *was* settled before is new business, even though the subject is old. For example, at every meeting a member gets up and makes a motion that the society hold a dinner dance. Every month this is rejected. It is thus, in a sense, old stuff when the member brings it up again, but in parliamentary terms it is *new* business, since it was previously disposed of (by rejection) at an earlier meeting.

(c) A matter is old business if at a previous meeting, instead of being defeated or approved, it was laid on the table, postponed, or left pending because of a motion to adjourn or recess.

(d) The report of the tally of an earlier election is old business. Nominations made by a committee come under reports. Applications for membership are also offered under reports. An election (whether to office or to membership) is new business.

305. The Prepared Agenda

The president and secretary jointly prepare an agenda. This includes details under the major headings. It is good practice to include the agenda outline in the announcement of the meeting, so that members will not only know what is coming up, but will also know in what order the subjects will be considered. Of course, no such announcement is possible unless every member who expects to introduce something new will notify the secretary in advance. Even so, it will always be necessary to have a "miscellaneous new business" item for subjects not announced in advance. These get a lower and later chronologic priority than the preannounced topics. In the following dummy agenda, all items specifically mentioned were those which the interested members had announced they would bring up. Other material would have to come under "other" old or new business.

Monthly Meeting of Neighborhood Parents Association

1. Minutes of previous meeting.

2. Treasurer's report.
    a) Decision about selection of banking depositary.

3. Report of Executive Committee.
    a) Matters for information.
    b) Matters for action.
        (1) Special automobile emblem.
        (2) Recommendation about permanent building.

4. Report of Membership Committee.
    a) Action on applicants for membership.

5. Report of Committee to Draft a Community Resources Map.

6. Unfinished business.
    a) Postponed from 1/6 meeting: sponsorship of handbook for parents.
    b) Postponed from 2/8 meeting:
        (1) Participation in "Better Citizenship Conference."
        (2) Selection of official seal for association.
    c) Pending at time of 3/7 meeting adjournment:
        (1) Acting on report of Legislative Committee.

7. Other unfinished or old business or matters previously laid on the table.

8. New Business:
    a) Mr. Arcularius: Proposed membership directory.
    b) Dr. Bensonhurst: Proposed information center in secretary's office.
    c) Mr. Cassandra: Proposal for legislative News Letter.

d) Treasurer: Suggested change in fiscal year dates.

e) Dr. Darius: Proposal for committee on committees to review possible changes in association's committee structure.

f) Other new business.

306. Deviations from the Agenda

(**a**) Usually no one protests if an item is considered out of its scheduled order. The chair says, "If no one objects, we'll take up Number 6 on the agenda now instead of Number 4 and go back to Number 4 as soon as we have disposed of Number 6." Perhaps he gives the reason. If anyone does object, then the person who wants the order changed will either: (1) move to suspend the rules—see 306(b); or (2) move to table the items between now and his subject, as illustrated in paragraph 306(c).

(**b**) A motion to suspend the rules is made to permit something to be taken up out of its scheduled order. The same motion is also used to modify temporarily some procedure which interferes with the majority's wishes. The motion is not used to make fundamental changes of policy. The bylaws and constitution cannot be set aside by a motion to suspend the rules. This can be done only by the formal amendment process. The simple motion to suspend the rules is applicable only to procedures and not to policies. The motion to suspend the rules requires a two-thirds vote (that is, at least twice as many must vote "yes" as "no") of those voting, regardless of how many are present. The following example illustrates use of suspension of the rules to change the scheduled order.

Suppose the appropriate fragment of the agenda is:

3 . . .
4 . . . Selection of city for next convention.
5 . . . Attitude towards proposed Law Number 1779.
6 . . . Purchase of electronic computer for Secretary's office.
7 . . . Proposal to create committee on budget.
8 . . .

Mr. E, who knows all about electronic computing machines, has to leave early. The subject can be disposed of quickly, but it is Number 6 on the agenda. The selection of a convention city (Number 4) may take hours. So Mr. E asks the chair to consider Number 6 ahead of Number 4. Ordinarily no one objects, and it is done. However, if someone does object, a motion is needed to change the order. Mr. E would say: "Mr. Chairman, I move to suspend the rules that interfere with the immediate consideration of Item 6." This motion is in order while any other (or no other) primary motion is pending. If this motion is seconded, it is put to an immediate vote, since it cannot be discussed, amended, committed, or laid on the table. However, it takes a two-thirds vote to pass. (That is, at least twice as many must vote "aye" as voted "no," regardless of the number present.) If the motion is passed, the chair says: "The 'ayes' have it, and by a two-thirds vote; the rules are suspended to permit consideration of Item 6 at this time. Mr. E . . ." (giving the name of the member who wants to present Number 6).

After Item 6 has been disposed of, the effect of the suspension of rules is exhausted. The agenda then automatically reverts to Number 4.

(c) If this method is not practical (or if there is a majority, but not a two-thirds vote to suspend the rules) it may be possible to get a priority for Item 6 in this way:

Mr. E waits until a motion has been made on Number 4. He then moves to lay this matter (selecting a convention city) on the table. The motion to lay on the table is not debatable, but in making the motion, the member can explain why. ("In order to give the right of way to the matter of the computing machine, I'm moving to lay on the table this motion about the convention city.") If a majority (not necessarily two thirds) votes "aye" on this motion (to table), Number 4 is laid on the table. Number 5 (about the proposed new law) comes next and this may be disposed of swiftly either by referring it to the Committee on Legislation or by tabling it. This clears the decks for Number 6, which can now be disposed of. After this has been done, the original objector to the change in order now has a chance to move that we "take from the table" the matter of selecting a convention city. This is now done and every one is happy. As a technique of deviating from the agenda, this method has one advantage over the suspension of rules: it takes only a majority instead of a two-thirds vote. It has the disadvantage, however, of needing a smoothly co-ordinated plan worked out in advance so that the several tabling motions are neatly made just when they are needed.

307. Special Orders

Almost obsolete in American voluntary societies is the parliamentary device of "special orders." This has the effect of setting a certain time in the near future when a specified subject will be considered, and of giving it an absolute priority for that time. It works like this:

(a) A matter is pending, but it seems unwise to dispose of it now. The friends of the matter are afraid that if it is postponed it never will be considered. So the agreement is that we will absolutely give this matter a top priority for next Tuesday's session. Accordingly, as soon as he can get the floor, Mr. F moves that "This matter be postponed and made a special order for 10 A.M. next Tuesday." This motion is not debatable and is amendable only with respect to date and time. It takes a two-thirds vote, however (since it deprives a minority of its right to dispose of the matter now). If passed, the matter is suspended, but is marked down for a top priority for 10 A.M. next Tuesday. See 307(d) for call for the special order.

(b) A member wants to schedule an item for a future date with an absolute priority. However, it is not now pending. In that case he says: "I have a motion (resolution) which I shall offer now to be made a special order for (day) (hour)." This type of special order motion is debatable, and it is passed by a simple majority (because it is not impairing any one's right to discussion, since nothing on it is already pending).

(c) The special order can be for a fixed hour, or for a fraction of a day ("special order for Thursday evening"). It can be expressed as a special time relationship to some other item, such as ". . . that this be made a special order to be taken up as soon as the convention city has been selected," or even for an entire meeting, as ". . . a special order for the Wednesday afternoon meeting." In the latter case, the chair, in stating the motion, will indicate whether the effect is (1) to make that a special meeting at which no other subject can be considered; or (2) to give this subject the top priority for that meeting with the understanding that when it is disposed of, regular business may be taken up.

(d) The chair should announce the special order as soon as the designated time comes. He does not interrupt a speaker to do so, but he does suspend pending business. For instance: last week it had been agreed to make the revision of the code of ethics a special order for 10 A.M. Tuesday. Tuesday is now here. At 10 A.M. a member is talking on a motion to increase the dues. The chair lets him finish and then says: "It is now after 10 A.M. Another item has been made a special order for this time. That is the revision of the code of ethics. Hence we suspend debate on the motion to increase the dues and come at once to a consideration of the code of ethics. As soon as that is disposed of, we will resume discussion of the dues matter" (or words to that effect).

(e) If the members are so fascinated by the discussion of the dues that they do not want to turn to the code of ethics, the members can renege on their arrangement. This takes a motion to "suspend the rules" (see 306(b)), which requires a two-thirds vote. The form is: "I move that we suspend the rules that interfere with our continued discussion of dues; and that the matter of revision of the code of ethics be taken up as soon as the dues matter has been disposed of," or words to that effect.

(f) If the chair suffers from amnesia, or if the secretary fails to jog his memory, it is possible that 10 A.M. will come and go without any consideration of the special order. Then any member can demand that the item scheduled be taken up at once. He does this by simply saying "I call for the special order," or just "orders of the day"—explaining to a perhaps mystified chairman what he means. What he means is that here it is Thursday afternoon and on Monday we voted to make the matter of a new insigne the special order for Thursday afternoon. This call cannot interrupt a speaker, but otherwise it is always in order (except when a motion to adjourn is pending). No second is required. On hearing the call, the chair listens to the explanation. If he does not accept it, he asks the secretary to check with the minutes. If it appears that the time really has come for the consideration of a special order, the chair has the choice of:

1. Suspending the pending matter by reminding the assembly of the special order, and proceeding with the special order as indicated in 307(d) above; or

2. Asking: "Will the assembly proceed to the question of XYZ, which is the special order for this time? Or do you prefer to suspend the rules and continue discussion of ABC now on the floor? I will entertain a motion to either effect."

The motion could be either (1) to suspend the rules which interfere with the continued consideration of ABC, or (2) to proceed to orders of the day—which means to consider ABC now. To pass Motion 1 requires a two-thirds vote; if it gets less than that, the special order must be considered. To pass Motion 2 requires only a one-third vote. If one third of those voting want to continue in orderly fashion the scheduled business, the other two thirds must respect that right.

(g) In actual practice, special orders are rarely used in voluntary societies in the United States. The matter is normally adjusted by informal agreement between the interested member and the chairman. However, the device of making an item a special order and later calling for it remains for the member who wants to take advantage of it, or who has a fascinated fondness for formality.

308. General Orders

The phrases "general orders" and "orders of the day" appear in standard parliamentary manuals. These are seldom used in scientific, civic, technical, and voluntary societies. Ordinarily there is no need for either of them. However, even a society of scientists may have an occasional persistent heckler in its membership; for the benefit of the chairman the following material is offered.

(a) The phrase "orders of the day" refers to the items listed on the agenda (or in a previously prepared program), or assigned to that part of the day by a previous agreement. A call for the "orders of the day" simply means that the member wants items considered in the order announced in advance. Such a call is not really a motion. It requires no second. The chair must call the items in the previously agreed-on order, unless the group, by two-thirds vote, agrees to "suspend the rules." In this connection see 307(e).

(b) The phrase "general order" is used in two somewhat inconsistent meanings. Sometimes it means simply the order in the announced agenda. The order in which items are considered is the "general order," and a call for a general order is a demand that the assembly proceed in orderly fashion to the next item. The phrase, "general order," is also used to indicate an agreement to postpone an item to a future time. It differs from a special order (see 307(d) above) in one essential respect. A general order is considered at the time scheduled, *after* pending business has been disposed of. A special order is taken up even if it requires interruption of pending business. Review the example in 307(d) above. If the revision of the code of ethics had been made a "general order for Tuesday at 10 A.M.," it could not have interrupted the discussion of the reduction in dues then pending. But as soon as the dues matter had been disposed of, the chair would say: "We now have as a general order for 10 A.M. this question of . . ." By this time it might be 11 A.M. or even 3 P. M. Still, the general order item would have right of way over everything else *after* disposition of the pending question; but it would yield to privileged matters, such as a motion to adjourn.

(c) A motion to make something a general order for a specified future hour, date, or priority is a primary motion requiring only a majority vote. The motion can be introduced only when no other business is pending. Therefore, a matter now under discussion cannot be transferred to a later hour (and debate cut off) by a motion to make the matter a general order. (Proper procedure if this is desired is a motion to lay on the table, to postpone, or to stop debate.)

(d) When the designated or scheduled time comes, the chair announces that this item is now the general order for this time and will be taken up at once. He does not interrupt a speaker or pending business to make this announcement, but when pending business is disposed of, he takes up the general order item. If members do not want to take up the general order when it is due, they can vote to postpone it or lay it on the table, or they can take it up prior to its scheduled time by voting to suspend the rules (see 306(b)) or by voting to lay on the table all intervening matters (see 306(c)). If the chair forgets to call for the general order, any member may remind him by announcing, "I call for the orders of the day," or words to that effect. This requires no second. The call may be made even while someone else is speaking. In effect, it is a point of order suggesting that the speaker is out of order because at this time the scheduled subject should have been taken up. The chair notes the call, but waits until the speaker has finished and until the pending topic has been disposed of. He then has the choice of either (1) bringing up the general order item for disposition, or (2) asking the meeting whether they "wish to proceed to the orders of the day." A vote is taken on this, and if more than a third vote "aye," the item scheduled on general order *is* taken up. If two thirds vote "no," the general order item lapses to the next order of business. The meeting is supposed to adhere to the program, unless two thirds want to suspend the rules. Hence if one third vote "to proceed to the orders of the day" that is done.

309. Effect of Recess on Order of Business

A recess is a brief interruption for the purpose of rest, relaxation, comfort, eating, or attendance at some other function. It has no effect on the order of business. Whatever was pending when the recess was called is resumed in the same posture when the group reconvenes.

310. Effect of Adjournment on Order of Business

(a) If the adjournment is for a period of three months or more, it is considered as adjournment *sine die*. This terminates all pending matters. It terminates motions made but not yet voted on. It terminates all unfinished, pending, and undisposed-of matters. Anything not disposed of is dead. To be considered again, such matters must be introduced as new business at the next session (see 1210(b)).

(b) If an adjournment is for a period of less than three months, all pending and unfinished business is carried over. Matters pending at the time of adjournment get a high priority for consideration at the next session. To get this high priority, they must actually have been on the floor at the time of adjournment. For an example, see 1210(a). The high priority given to pending matters means that these subjects are listed as old (unfinished) business at the next session. It does *not* mean that such items take precedence over reading minutes, receiving reports, special orders, or other high priority items.

311. Nominations and Elections

In the agenda, elections are "new business" and are taken up during that part of the program. The slate offered by a nominating committee is a "report," and as such is received early, under the "reports" part of the schedule. However, it is not in order at that time to receive nominations from the floor, since this is new business. The report of the nominating committee is simply filed (it is not accepted, approved, or adopted). Later, under "new business," the chair calls for nominations from the floor, if permitted. Similarly the recommendation of a membership committee is a "report" receivable under that schedule heading, but the actual election of applicants to membership is "new business." There is usually no need for intransigeant adherence to this schedule. If the chairman wants to, and if no one objects, the election of officers and applicants to membership can take place immediately after receiving the reports of the respective committees. If anyone does object, the order can be changed by a vote to suspend the rules or by tabling intervening matters as explained above in 306(b) and 306(c).

4

Mr. Chairman

401. Title and Mode of Address

During any meeting (or during any part of it), the presiding officer is the chairman, moderator, or speaker, according to the titles in the organization's rules. In the first or third person, he is always "The Chair." Referring to himself, he says "The Chair rules that ABC," and never "I rule . . ." Speaking of his own assent and dissent, he says "The Chair agrees" or "The Chair does not agree." In this guide, and in third person usage generally, he is "The Chair."

In second person usage, he is "Mr. Chairman," "Mr. Moderator," "Mr. Speaker," or "Mr. President." A woman is "Madame Chairman," "Madame Moderator," and so forth. The phrase "Mr. Chairman" is always correct, but "Mr. Moderator" or "Mr. Speaker" should be used when the presiding officer actually has that title. The title "Mr. President" is acceptable if, in fact, the chair is president of the organization, though "Mr. Chairman" is the more common usage.

402. Activities of the Chair

When the entire voting membership of a group sits around a table, the chair may conduct all business while seated. In an auditorium arrangement, where the chairman faces the members, he rises to state or restate a motion, call for a vote, announce a vote, or make a ruling. He need not rise to recognize a member. The chair's duties are:

1. He is expected to be familiar with parliamentary procedure. He may appoint a parliamentarian to sit with him or near him and advise him. However, he is not bound by the parliamentarian's advice, and takes responsibility himself for his rulings.

2. He convenes the meeting, and announces each next item of business.

3. He recognizes members who want the floor. The rule is to recognize members in the order in which they have called for the floor. If two members seem to have called out at the same time the chair recognizes the one who has had least to say at the meeting. If he knows the views of members, he tries to recognize members for discussion alternately so that first the "pro" side and then the "anti" side will be given an opportunity to speak.

4. He restates motions, puts them to vote, and announces the results. In this connection, see 122 and 611.

5. He maintains order and decorum. He calls to order a member who is indecorous, out of order, or making personal attacks on the integrity of other members. In this connection, he refuses to recognize patently frivolous demands or tactics that are only harassing or dilatory.

6. He makes rulings on the acceptability, legitimacy, and precedence of motions, on whether a motion is debatable, renewable, referrable to a committee, postponable, or amendable.

7. He certifies the correctness of the minutes, unless the society has adopted a rule against having minutes signed (see 125(d)).

403. Chair's Right To Discuss or To Make Motions

The chair cannot make or second a motion. He may call for a motion, by asking "Does any one care to move that . . ." or ". . . to make a motion to that effect?" . . . or by saying, "The Chair will entertain a motion to . . ." But that is as far as he can go. He cannot make a motion. Similarly, he may ask if anyone has seconded or will second a motion, but may not himself second a motion.

(a) In large or auditorium-type meetings, the Chair does not discuss the merits of a motion. He may explain factually the implications of a motion, clarify a parliamentary point, or furnish simple information. He may explain why he has made a certain ruling. He may make simple announcements ("Luncheon is available at . . ."; "The Committee will meet at . . ."). All this he may do freely; but if he wants to enter into the merits of a proposal, he must vacate the chair (see 406), except in small meetings around a table.

(b) In committee meetings, the chair is usually an articulate and leading participant in the discussion. In small meetings, the chair may debate if no one objects. If any one does object (and, as a general rule, in large assemblies), the presiding officer will temporarily vacate the chair. He does not literally leave his seat. He simply names a temporary chairman, who presides from the latter's seat. In a large auditorium, the temporary chairman will have to go to the stage or the front of the hall (see 405, 406).

404. Chair's Right To Vote

If otherwise eligible, the chair retains his right to vote. In a voice vote (see 604) he does not usually join in either the "ayes" or "noes," though he may do so if he wishes. If the vote is close, and he thinks his vote will be a factor, he calls for a revote, and this time he does join in the chorus. In a standing or show-of-hands vote (see 605 and 606) he does not participate at the first count. If the motion is passed by one vote, he may, if he wishes, then announce that he is voting in the negative, causing a tie and defeating the motion. If, without his vote, there was a tie, he may then cast the deciding vote (though if he were opposed to the motion, there would be no point to doing so, since it would fail on a tie vote anyway). In a roll call (see 607) he announces his vote when his name is called. In a written ballot (see 608) he receives and turns in a ballot like any one else (see 616).

405. Temporary Chairman

In a general membership meeting, there is usually a constitutional provision for a president-elect, vice-president, or past president to preside in the absence of the regular chairman. If there is no such provision, the secretary (or in his absence, the treasurer) calls the meeting to order and a temporary chairman is elected. A presiding officer who knows, in advance, that he will be absent, cannot appoint a temporary chairman. That right is not his to bestow. However, during a meeting, the chair, finding it necessary to vacate that position, may appoint a temporary chairman from among those present, without restriction. A temporary chairman selected in this way presides until the pending matter is disposed of, and he calls the vote to dispose of it. The regular chairman may not, after he has made his speech, immediately resume the chair, if his purpose in vacating it was to make a presumably partisan talk. This is because he may not preside over the vote on a matter on which he had manifested partisan interest. However, once the vote is announced, he may resume the chair. If the chairman is making a formal, noncontroversial address, he may briefly name a member to sit in the chair, and then he himself may immediately resume it. If a meeting starts in the absence of the regular presiding officer, the temporary chairman surrenders the chair as soon as the regular chairman enters. The status of temporary chairman is terminated by adjournment, but not by recess.

406. Vacating the Chair

The chairman vacates the chair whenever:

1. *He wishes to make a motion.* He designates an acting chairman who remains in the chair until the motion is voted upon or otherwise disposed of.

2. *He is the subject, whether favorably or unfavorably, of a motion made by someone else;* for example, a motion to condemn the chair for certain actions, to give him a vote of thanks, and so on. He returns to the chair when the motion is dis-

posed of. During an appeal (see 408) he remains in the chair if he wishes.

3. *He is delivering a formal, noncontroversial oration.* If this talk is not open to discussion, he resumes the chair when it is concluded; otherwise, he resumes the chair when discussion is closed.

4. *In an auditorium-type meeting (or a large meeting) whenever he wishes to discuss the merits of a motion or other proposal.* In a round-table type of meeting, he remains in the chair unless someone objects or unless his discussion is partisan and the matter highly controversial (see 403(b)).

5. *He becomes ill or otherwise indisposed.* If possible, he designates a temporary chairman who presides until either (1) the meeting adjourns, or (2) the regular chairman is able to resume his duties. If the indisposition is so sudden that he cannot name a temporary chairman, the person present next in line of succession assumes the chair; or if there be no clear ranking, the secretary takes the chair and a chairman *pro tem* is then elected for the remainder of the meeting or until the chairman returns.

407. Chairman of the Committee of the Whole

See 1024 to 1030 for explanation of the committee of the whole. When a motion is passed which resolves the meeting into a committee of the whole, the chair calls some other member to serve as chairman of the committee of the whole. The regular chairman may move to another seat on the platform or he may sit down in the auditorium. In most organizations today, the chairman of the committee of the whole takes the seat vacated by the regular chairman. Under the ancient form, the chairman of the committee of the whole sits at the secretary's desk while the presidential chair remains unoccupied as a symbol that the organization, as such, is not in session. This quaint anachronism is followed only in organizations where such symbolism is highly important. In most modern societies, the chairman of the committee of the whole takes the regular chairman's seat. If a motion is made, early after the committee has formed itself, that a chairman be elected, the *pro tem* chairman must put it to a vote; if a majority votes "aye," he calls for nominations for chairman of the committee of the whole, and then for an election, and he abdicates his seat to the person so elected and resumes a seat in the audience. In practice this is extremely rare. Nearly always the presidential designee serves as chairman of the committee of the whole without protest.

408. Appeals

(a) If a member believes that the chair has made an erroneous ruling, he may appeal the decision. If the ruling concerns the count of a vote, the call is usually for "Division" rather than appeal (see 612). On any other ruling, the proper mode of hearing a grievance is an appeal. Appeals are usually made when some member believes that the chair erred in ruling a motion debatable or undebatable, or amendable or nonamendable; or in ruling that an amendment was or was not legitimate; or in ruling on a point of order, in calling a member to order, or in refusing to recognize a member.

(b) Any member may rise to an appeal if he does so promptly after the questionable decision is announced. He may even interrupt a speaking member to do so. This is one of the few actions that may be taken while someone else is speaking. He does not pause to be recognized, but simply says "Mr. Chairman, I am appealing from the decision of the chair just made with respect to XYZ." The chair stops the other speaker (if any), and asks "Does any one second this appeal?" If no one does, the chair says, "Hearing no second, I cannot entertain the appeal," and the other speaker continues. If someone does second it, the appeal becomes the immediate business and the other matter is temporarily suspended.

(c) The chair then explains briefly why he made his ruling, and asks if the member still presses his appeal. If the member does, the chair announces whether the appeal is debatable. It *is* debatable unless it is intrinsically part of an undebatable matter. For example, member makes a motion which is seconded. Another member now moves an amendment. The original maker protests that the amendment is not acceptable. None the less it is seconded. The original maker insists that the amendment cannot be considered because the motion was his and he wants no amendment to it. The chair rules, as he must, that the amendment is legitimate. The original maker appeals. The chair explains that a maker has no control over the motion once it has been stated. This is not subject to discussion or debate; it is simple, readily verified parliamentary fact. However, the original maker might point out that the amendment would negate his motion. He is allowed to explain this, hence there is some debate. The maker of the amendment may wish to show why the amendment would not destroy the motion. These are legitimate subjects for debate because if, in fact, the effect of the amendment would have been to negate the motion, the amendment is not really legitimate. (For instance, to amend by inserting the word "not" would be an illegitimate amendment.) On the other hand, an appeal on a matter of decorum, courtesy, or priority of business is not debatable, though the chair's ruling on these *is* reversible if the meeting so decides.

(d) After discussion (or immediately after seconding if the appeal is not debated), the chair again explains the appeal, and then asks "Shall the decision of the Chair be sustained? All in favor say 'aye.'" If more vote "no" than "aye," the chair's ruling is reversed. Note (1) that the motion itself must be put in the affirmative—"Shall the decision of the Chair be sustained?" and never in the negative form, "Shall the appeal be sustained?" (2) That a tie vote sustains the chair. This is one of the very few cases where a tie vote passes a motion. If the chair is sustained but the member thinks the chairman miscounted, he may call for a division (see 612) but not for a second appeal.

(e) The presiding officer need not vacate the chair while explaining his decision and calling for the vote on the appeal; but he may do so, if he wishes.

(f) If the motion, "Shall the decision of the Chair be sustained?" is defeated by one vote, the chair may then vote "yes," causing a tie vote, and passing the motion. This assumes that he did not vote in the first place, since he cannot have two votes.

(g) If half, or more, of the voting members vote "aye" on the question, the result is announced as "The 'ayes" have it and the ruling of the Chair is sustained"; or, if more than half of those who vote, vote "no," the announcement is, "The 'noes' have it and the ruling of the Chair is reversed."

(h) In the course of disposing of an appeal, no other appeal can be heard.

(j) An appeal is not an amendable motion. It is disposed of in its original form.

(k) An appeal may be laid on the table (see 802 to 810). After it is made and seconded, and before the vote is taken, a member may rise to say, "I move that this appeal be laid on the table." If this is seconded, it is immediately voted on, since the motion to table is undebatable. If passed, the effect is to suspend any consideration of the appeal and to proceed with the regular business. After other business has intervened, any member may move to take the appeal from the table; if this is passed, the question of the appeal is reopened. In practice, an appeal laid on the table is usually dead, since by the time someone revives it, the issue is generally academic.

If the reversal of the chair's decision would remove from consideration the entire issue, then everything goes "on the table" when an appeal is laid on the table. For example, a matter is introduced which Mr. A says is completely beyond the scope of the organization. "Indeed," he says, "our very existence is threatened if we discuss and take action on this matter." The chair overrules him, and calls for debate on the primary matter. Mr. A appeals the decision of the chair, and a motion is made to lay the appeal on the table. If this is carried, the entire issue goes to the table too. The reason is that if the chair were reversed, the matter would be removed from consideration. To allow the primary issue to be settled and then later take from the table the question of the appeal would be an absurdity.

(m) After an appeal is made and seconded, and before a vote

on it is taken, any of the following motions may be made: to adjourn, to recess, to fix the time for the next meeting, or to lay on the table. Also, a point of privilege must be heard if raised during a discussion of an appeal. But another appeal will not be heard until the first appeal is disposed of.

(n) An appeal once disposed of may not be renewed, and it may not be referred to a committee. However, the general problem presented by the appeal, if of sufficient magnitude, may be made a subject for subsequent committee study, though this will not delay or affect the current appeal. If debate on appeal threatens to become prolonged, a motion to close debate is in order, and is effective if passed by two-thirds vote (see 505).

5

The Nature of
Parliamentary Debate

501. Definition

"Debate" is parliamentary jargon for the discussion that takes place at a meeting. Debate is the oral argument for or against a proposal. Debate is what the chair means when he says "Is there any discussion?" As so defined, debate is an essential part of the proceedings of a deliberative body. The right to debate distinguishes an independent organism from a rubber stamp. Through debate decisions are hammered out.

502. General Rule

(a) Technically debate is not in order unless there is a motion on the floor. Usually, however, no one but a very compulsive chairman would squelch a member who, otherwise in order, wants to explain why he is offering a motion or wants to do some free associating about a matter before he frames the motion. Indeed, by allowing debate prior to the offer of a motion, the chair may make it possible for the group to phrase a better worded motion than would be possible if the motion had to come before any discussion. So unless some member insists on meticulous adherence to the rules (which he can do by rising to a point of order) a member is permitted to discuss an idea before a formal motion is offered.

(b) As a general rule, any primary motion (as defined in 202) is open to debate, and all secondary, subsidiary, and incidental motions, except those listed in 503(a) are also open to debate.

(c) No otherwise debatable matter may be rushed through without debate except by a two-thirds vote. That is, it takes a two-thirds vote to suppress an otherwise allowable discussion.

(d) Debate may be cut off by an "objection to consideration" as explained in 116.

(e) A member wishing to discuss (debate) a matter calls "Mr. Chairman," or "Mr. Moderator." In a large meeting, he also rises as he calls out. He begins speaking when recognized— that is, when the chair calls his name or otherwise identifies him as the next speaker.

503. Nondebatable Motions

(a) The following motions are nondebatable: To adjourn, to recess, to close debate, to close nominations, previous question, to go into executive session, to lay on the table, to take from the table, to suspend the rules, to count for a quorum, to object to consideration of a matter, to allow a motion to be withdrawn, a division of the house, to consider a matter, a point of order, information, privilege, or parliamentary inquiry, or (if the primary motion was not debatable) a motion to reconsider.

(b) When a nondebatable motion is seconded, the chair calls for an immediate vote. He may explain, "Since this matter is nondebatable, I call for a vote. All in favor say 'aye.'"

(c) If the chair refuses to allow debate and a member thinks that the chair is in error, he may interrupt the call for a vote (but not the counting) by an appeal from the chair (see 408).

504. Debatable Motions

All motions not listed in 503(a) are debatable. The chair opens the floor to debate by asking (after a motion is seconded), "Is there any discussion?" The maker of the motion has the right to be the first to speak on it, but he need not exercise that right and may speak later if he wishes. However, he cannot insist on this prerogative after a motion to close debate has been passed by a two-thirds vote. The seconder of a motion has no debating priority. The chair will usually not recognize someone who has already spoken on a matter if someone who has not yet spoken asks for the floor. The meeting may limit debate by specifying a certain amount of time for each speaker.

505. Termination of Debate

Debate may be terminated by:

1. Silent assent
2. A motion to close debate (the old "previous question"; see 513)
3. An "objection to consideration" (see 116)
4. A secondary motion disposing of the matter by tabling it, referring it to a committee, or postponing it
5. A privileged motion or point of privilege (see Chapter 7) which cuts into the debate
6. Adjournment

1. *Silent assent.* When discussion quiets down, the chair says, "Any further discussion?" He waits for a brief time. If no one wants to talk he says, "Are you ready for the question?" If there is no answer (or a call of "yes") he puts the question to a vote. This is terminating debate by silent assent.

2. *Motion to close debate.* In most technical and voluntary organizations, this has replaced the old "previous question" (see 513). Any member who can get the floor may move to close debate. If seconded, this is put to an immediate vote. (This motion is not debatable, of course, since its purpose is to stop the talking.) The chair asks, "All in favor of closing

debate, say 'aye.'" If two thirds of those voting register an "aye," the talk immediately stops, and the chair then calls for a vote on the principal motion. The chair may explain this when he is starting the question. For instance, he might say, "It has been moved and seconded that we close debate on this matter of XYZ. If this motion passes, we will terminate the debate and come to a vote on XYZ. I will call for a vote on closing debate. Remember a 'yes' vote now is *not* a vote for XYZ, but simply a vote to close debate. A 'no' vote now is not a vote *against* XYZ, but simply a vote to continue debate. Is that clear? All in favor of closing debate say 'aye.'"

If this passes (and it takes a two-thirds vote) debate stops. However, it would still be in order to vote to lay the matter on the table. This nondebatable motion could be made at this point (see 802 to 806).

If fewer than two thirds vote "aye," the chair says: "Not having received a two-thirds vote, the motion to close debate fails; discussion will continue." If two thirds or more vote "aye," the chair says: "Having received more than a two-thirds vote, the motion to close debate has passed. We will now consider the main question." He then restates the primary question and calls for an immediate vote. If there is disagreement as to whether or not the votes in favor of closing debate were sufficient, a member may appeal from the chair (see 408) or may demand a division of the house (see 612).

3. *Objection to consideration.* Before debate (or while the first discussant is speaking) a member may "object to consideration of the matter" as explained in 116(a) and 116(d). The chair asks, "Shall the question be considered?" and if two thirds vote "no" the subject is dropped without further debate. Review 116 for fuller details.

4. *A suppressive subsidiary motion.* In the course of discussion a member may make a secondary or subsidiary motion. The secondary motions here are these: (1) to lay on the table, (2) to postpone the matter to a specified time, (3) to refer it to a committee, or (4) to amend the motion. The first of these (lay on the table) is nondebatable and must be voted on at once. If passed, all debate on the main question ceases and the next business is taken up. If one of the other three motions is introduced, the secondary motion may be debated in so far as

discussion applies to the wisdom of postponing the matter or referring it to a committee, or the wisdom of the proposed amendment. General debate on the primary motion stops, though limited debate on the secondary motion is in order. If the meeting votes to postpone it or to refer it to a committee, all debate on the subject then comes to a close.

5. *Privileged matters.* If a member introduces a nondebatable privileged or subsidiary motion, all debate stops until that is disposed of. This may be a quorum call, a point of order, information, or inquiry, a motion to adjourn or recess, or a motion to lay the matter on the table. Debate then resumes if the motion to adjourn, recess, or lay on the table is defeated; if the count shows a quorum present; or if the point of order, information, or inquiry is disposed of (see Chapter 7).

6. *Motion to adjourn.* If a motion to adjourn or recess is passed, the chair immediately declares the session adjourned or in recess. All debate then terminates. If it is a recess, the matter is resumed immediately on reconvening, and debate continues as if there had been no interruption. If the adjournment terminated a session but did not terminate the entire meeting (that is, if the next session is scheduled soon, as part of the whole meeting series), the matters pending at the time of adjournment get high priority when the group reconvenes. However, matters definitely scheduled for the adjourned session are considered first. If the adjournment was *sine die,* as defined in 1204, all pending matters are terminated.

They would have to be reintroduced as new business to get back on the floor. See 1210 for details.

506. Interruption of Debate

As a general rule (and as a matter of common courtesy) a member is not interrupted while speaking. However, the following matters may be introduced even while a member is speaking: (1) Points of order, privilege, or parliamentary inquiry as defined in Chapter 7; (2) an appeal from the immediately preceding decision of the chair as explained in 408; (3) an objection to consideration if the member on the floor was the first to speak on the matter, as explained in 116; (4) a call for "division" (see 612) if the vote had been announced just before the current speaker started.

A motion to adjourn may *not* be made while someone is speaking. Indeed, no matters other than those just listed above may be introduced while a member is speaking.

507. Order of Debate

The Chair recognizes persons in the order in which each raised his hand. If each of two or more persons appears to have raised his hand simultaneously (or to have risen simultaneously, if in a large meeting), the chair will give priority (1) to someone who has not discussed the matter before over someone who has; (2) to someone who, the chair believes, will take a view contrary to that expressed by the last speaker over someone who will, presumably, support him; (3) to one who rarely speaks at meetings over one who frequently does; or (4) to one who is known to have had experience with the matter over one who, presumably, has had none. The chair's decision as to priority is not appealable, so long as the one who was not given the floor eventually gets it during that debate. However, termination of debate, by a vote of the meeting, does not entitle a member to the floor even though he has not had the chance to discuss the matter.

508. Reading of Documents

A member's privilege to debate does not automatically include the right to read documents, book extracts, or lengthy communications. If a member wishes to read a communication of considerable length, he either (1) asks permission to do so, or (2) makes a formal motion to that effect. Or silent assent may be given: he asks such permission and no one objects, so the chair tells him to go ahead. If the document is essential to an understanding of the matter, the chair may order it read in full, or may distribute copies to all members. If, without asking consent, a member embarks on reading a long document, the chair may interrupt and ask how long it is and if its full reading is necessary, and any member may object to the reading of it. Such objection is then put to vote in the affirmative form: "All in favor of hearing this document read, say 'aye.'"

509. Irrelevant Discussion

Debate must be germane to the topic, and the chair may interrupt a speaker by saying: "The relevance of this to the matter under discussion does not seem apparent," or words to that effect. The chair may then, at his own discretion (but after explanation), rule that the speaker is out of order. The speaker must then either (1) sit down, (2) return to the main theme of discussion, or (3) appeal the chair's decision (see 408).

510. Indecorum

The right to debate does not include the right to attack the motives of another member, except in a discussion on a matter of discipline or ethics. Allusions to a member's integrity, honesty, or character are out of order except when these are precisely the issues under consideration (as in a motion to expel a member). Abusive, profane, or grossly indecorous language or behavior is also out of order. The chair will maintain decorum and interrupt any member who violates it. A member may, however, appeal from a decision of the chair which thus suppresses his continuing to debate (see 408).

511. Objection to Consideration

If in the opinion of any member a motion is completely irrelevant to the organization's interest or competence, or if it is too delicate to be openly debated, the member may cut into the first speaker's debate, or he may rise as soon as the motion is made or seconded, and say: "I object to consideration of this." This need not be seconded and it is not debatable, except that the protesting member may briefly state his reason for wanting to suppress the item. Objection to consideration must be raised before anyone has completed discussion on it; that is, before the first speaker on it has finished. See 116 for a fuller explanation.

The chair himself may object to having a matter heard, as explained in 116(b).

The objection to consideration is presented in the form, "Shall this matter be considered?" (or words to that effect). A majority of any size or a minority of more than one third is sufficient to pass the motion, "Shall this question be considered?" That means that the matter is now open to debate. This vote cannot be reconsidered. Once someone has completed his discussion of the merits of a primary question, an "objection to consideration" is out of order. After debate has started, the matter can be suppressed only by a motion to close debate or a motion to lay on the table. See 505(2) for a motion to close debate; see 512, and also Chapter 8, for "lay on the table."

512. To Lay on the Table

A motion to lay on the table may be made any time after the first speaker on a motion has concluded his debate. The member making the motion (to lay on the table) must first be recognized, and then the motion (to lay on the table) must be seconded. If this is done, the chair puts it to vote at once, since it is not debatable. "All in favor of laying this matter on the table say 'aye.'" If this motion passes (a majority vote is sufficient) debate stops and the motion (and all motions attached to it) revert to the files of the secretary where the entire matter remains until the meeting votes to take it from the table. See 802 for further discussion of "lay on the table," and 806 for discussion of "take from the table." If a motion to lay on the table is defeated, debate continues as before.

513. Previous Question: Present Status

Though still recognized by many books, "previous question" is falling into disuse in small voluntary organizations. Its effect is better achieved by a motion "to close debate" and such a motion cannot be misunderstood. "Previous question" is readily misunderstood by an unsophisticated member. Even experienced chairmen may garble it in trying to explain it. Furthermore, "previous question" does not have the same meaning in the United States that it has in other parts of the English-speaking world. Thus, in the British Commonwealth, an affirmative vote has no effect, since all it means there is that the assembly wants to continue considering the question. In the United States an affirmative vote immediately shuts off debate. Conversely, in England a negative vote removes the subject from the floor, whereas in the United States a negative vote has no effect. If a chairman feels that he must recognize it, the form is "I move the previous question." The chair, after the motion is seconded, restates it as "Shall the main question now be put?" If two thirds vote "aye," it stops all debate and the primary motion is voted on. Otherwise nothing happens and debate continues as before. It is best for the chair to say when a member "moves previous question," "It has been moved and seconded that we close debate. This requires a two-thirds vote. All in favor of closing debate at once will say 'aye.' Understand, you are not voting on the main matter, but only on whether to terminate debate. All in favor of terminating debate, say 'aye.'"

One of the reasons "previous question" has fallen into disrepute is that there is no universal agreement as to (1) the vote required to pass it, and (2) the effect of defeating it. If the chairman uses as his authority the articles on "Parliamentary Law" in either the *Encyclopaedia Britannica* or the *Encyclopedia Americana,* he will rule that a majority vote is sufficient to pass previous question. If he follows another much quoted authority, he will require a two-thirds vote to pass previous question. Furthermore, the effect of a negative vote depends on what authority the chair cites. One of the older, but still popular, authorities insists that if previous question is rejected, the matter has to be removed from the agenda for the day. But an equally eminent and perhaps more popular authority says that if "previous question" is rejected, discussion continues as before. Under the circumstances, it seems best to abandon "previous question" entirely and use the simple motion "to terminate debate" if that is desired.

6

All in Favor Say "Aye"

601. Methods of Voting

For voting on motions and resolutions, six methods are used:

1. General or silent assent (See 603).
2. Voice vote ("All in favor say 'aye'") (See 604).
3. Standing vote (See 605).
4. Show of hands (See 606).
5. Roll call (See 607).
6. Written ballot (See 608).

602. Selection of Method

(a) After discussion has ground to a halt, the chair asks "Are you ready for the question?" If no one asks for the floor, the chair calls for a vote. Similarly, as soon as an undebatable motion (see 503) is seconded, the chair calls for a vote, explaining if necessary why he is not calling for discussion. If the chair feels that discussion has dragged on to the point where it is no longer fruitful, he may suggest that debate seems to have gone on long enough, and "Are you ready for the question?" He cannot arbitrarily choke off debate, however, and if someone still wants to talk, he must let him debate, or call for a motion to close debate (see paragraph 505(2)). If similarly for some reason it is imperative to come to a vote at once, the chair explains that and calls for a motion

71

to terminate debate (see 505(2)) unless there is general assent to do that.

(b) Ordinarily all motions and resolutions are disposed of by voice vote. However, the chair may at his own discretion call for a vote by show of hands or by standing vote. He cannot, without authorization from the meeting, call for a roll call or for vote by written ballot except on elections to office or matters of discipline.

(c) Any member may, just before or just after the chair calls "All in favor . . . ," formally move that the vote be taken by standing vote, written ballot, or show of hands. Such a motion, if seconded, is voted on at once, and voted on by any method the chair may prescribe. If this motion is passed, the method indicated is used for the vote on the matter under consideration. In general membership meetings of an association, a roll-call vote is not taken; a motion to that effect is not in order.

603. General Assent

If appropriate, the chair may suggest that a certain decision seems to be the sense of the meeting. For example, he may say when the minutes are read: "Are there any corrections?" (*Pause.*) "Hearing none, the minutes will stand approved as read." If at that point no one objects, the minutes will have been approved by "general assent." Perhaps a matter is obviously approved or disapproved by all present; then the chair may say "If no one objects, we will consider this matter approved" (or "rejected"). Before such action is concluded, opportunity must be given for protest. If one member objects, a formal vote, by voice or by other method, must be taken. Motions rejected or passed in this way are recorded as having been disposed of by "general assent" or by "silent assent."

604. Voice Vote

The chair repeats or summarizes the motion and then says, "All in favor say 'aye,'" or words to that effect. This is called "putting the motion." The ancient form, still favored by some authorities is "As many as are in favor of . . ." or even "As many as are of the opinion that . . ." Most authorities today recommend the simpler "Those in favor say 'aye.'" In actual practice, the question is usually slimmed down to "All in favor say 'aye.'" After he hears that response, he says "All opposed say 'no,'" or "those opposed say 'no,'" or "those contrary-minded," or "as many as oppose," or some such form. Even if the response on the "aye" side is overwhelming, even if it is obviously unanimous, the chair still calls for the "no" vote. He judges, by the volume of response, which side had a preponderance. If in doubt, he may call for a revote, also by voice; or for a revote by show of hands (see 606); or for a revote by standing (see 605).

If he is satisfied with the voice vote, he says either (1) "The 'noes' have it and the motion is lost" (or "defeated"); or (2) "The 'ayes' have it and the motion is carried." He may also add a word of explanation, particularly with subsidiary motions, as ". . . and the matter is now laid on the table."

If a member thinks the chair erred, he may either (1) call for a division as explained below in 612; or (2) appeal the decision of the chair as explained in 408.

605. Standing Vote

A standing vote may be ordered by the chair at his discretion on any matter except one which requires written ballot, or he may first call for a voice vote, and then ask for a recount by standing vote; or any member may move for a standing vote, and, if this motion is passed, a standing vote will be taken.

The form is "All in favor please stand" (or "please rise," or "please stand until counted"). The number standing is then counted. Then the chair says "Please be seated. All opposed, please rise" (or "stand"; or "stand until counted"). The number standing is tallied and the result announced. In small meetings the chair and the secretary each count, independently, and confer and agree on the count. In larger meetings, tellers divide the hall into convenient sections. They report their counts to a chief teller or to the secretary. The announced result is not subject to a call for a division of the house (see 612 below) but may be appealed in the manner described in 408.

606. Show of Hands

A show of hands may be ordered by the chair on taking a vote on any matter except where written ballot is required. Also, the chair may first call for a voice vote and then ask for a recount by show of hands. Or any member may move for a show of hands, and, if this motion is passed, the voting will be done by show of hands. Or, after the chair has announced the result of a voice vote, any member may call for a division of the house (see 612) and the chair will (without further request) order a recount by show of hands. The method is simply to call "All of you in favor, please raise your right hands," or words to that effect. After the hands have been counted, the chair says "Thank you. And now, all who are opposed, please raise your right hands." The counting may be done by the chair and secretary independently, with comparison of results, or by tellers appointed for the purpose.

607. Roll Call

(a) This method, known more formally as "voting by yeas and nays," is appropriate only for a body which has a constituency to which it is responsible. This is because the roll-call method puts on record the way each member voted. In a general membership meeting this is improper; no member should be compelled to make his personal vote a matter of open and permanent record. On the other hand, this is an acceptable method in meetings of executive boards, councils, trustees, executive committees, and similar bodies. The constituents of those boards or committees do have a right to know how their representatives voted.

(b) At such board, committee, or council meetings, a roll call is not taken unless the group itself orders it. This may be done in either of two ways:

1. After a motion has been made and seconded, someone moves, as an amendment, that the vote thereon be a matter of record. Such an amendment, though out of order in general membership meetings, would be in order at meetings of a board, council, committee, or constituent body. Thus: motion has been made and seconded that the contract be approved. After some debate, a member hostile to the motion moves the following amendment: "I move that this be amended by adding, '. . . and that the vote to approve the contract be by roll call (or by yeas and nays).'" If seconded, this amendment is voted on at once (by voice) and without debate. If it passes, the motion to approve the contract (when it does come up for action) is voted on by roll call.

2. After a debate closes and before the vote starts, any member may move that the vote be by roll call. He says, "I move that this be a roll-call vote"; (or "a record vote," or "a vote by yeas and nays"). This motion, if seconded and passed (it is not debatable) requires that the roll-call method be used, unless it is a general membership meeting. If it is, the motion calling for a roll call is out of order.

(c) On being required to call a record (roll-call) vote, the chair says "The secretary will now call the roll. Each member will answer 'yea' or 'nay.'" The secretary then calls the roll, pausing briefly after each name. Every member present must give one of four answers: yea, nay, present, or not voting. The last two calls count as "present but not voting." The secretary makes a mark on the roll after each call. If there is no response, the secretary marks the roll "absent" if the member is absent, or "not voting" if the member is present. After the last name is called, the secretary says "According to my record, the following voted 'yea.'" He then calls off the names of those who voted "yea," and asks if there are any corrections. Any member may change to or from a "yea" vote in this way, or make a correction. The chair then asks if any other member desires to change his vote, and if any does, the change is made. The secretary then reports the net corrected tally. The chair announces and interprets it. A member who does not wish to vote may call "present" instead of "not voting." The effect is the same.

608. Written Ballot

Written ballot is used for:

1. Contested elections
2. Disciplinary actions
3. Acceptability of new members

No other matter is voted on by written ballot unless the meeting so orders. This may be accomplished in one of these ways:

(a) The chair says: "We will vote by written ballot if no one objects." If no one does object, ballot slips are distributed. If someone does object, the chair then says, "I will entertain a motion that we vote by written ballot on this matter of . . ."

(b) Any member may move "That the voting on this matter be by written ballot." This motion, if seconded, is put to vote (voice vote, standing, or show of hands) at once, since it is undebatable, nonamendable, and cannot be laid on the table. If this secondary motion carries, written ballot is used. The motion (to use written ballot) may be made as amendment to the motion being voted on, or as a motion by itself.

(c) The chair appoints tellers to distribute the slips of paper, and while they are doing it, he instructs the members, explaining, for example: "Write the word 'yes' or 'no' "; or, "Write the name of the candidate you prefer"; or "After you have written your ballot, fold it once, lengthwise, like this." Tellers may then pass through the hall and collect the ballots, or members may file by a ballot box. Tellers later open, count, and certify the results.

Sometimes a variant of this is used—a sort of symbolic turnstile. The secretary calls the name of each member. The members stand in line, more or less taking their places in the queue, in the order in which they are listed in the roll. The line moves past a ballot box. As each member drops his ballot into the slot, he is identified either by his showing of his membership card or by a teller who recognizes him. This slow and cumbersome method is needed for very large organizations with meetings so open that nonmembers might have infiltrated the hall. Or it may be necessary to meet a legal challenge asserting that nonmembers had voted. See 622(c) and (d).

(d) A contested election for office is always by written ballot, and either of the two methods described under (c) above may be used. A nomination to fill a vacancy or to name a delegate, representative, or observer may be by open ballot if placed in the form of a primary motion, such as "I move that XYZ be named as our representative to ABC." This may be voted on by voice vote, show of hands, or standing vote, unless, on motion, the meeting specifically agrees (by majority) to a written ballot. Written ballot is not used in an uncontested election unless the constitution or bylaws require it.

609. Tellers

Tellers, when needed, are named by the chair, *ad hoc*, unless some other method of selecting tellers is provided. The teller first named is chief teller. He divides the hall into natural sections, one to each teller, to permit distribution and collection of ballots, or to permit standees or hands to be counted in convenient groupings. In unwritten ballots, each teller reports the score for his section to the chief teller or to the secretary, who adds them. If a written ballot is used, the chief teller receives all ballots from the section tellers. Then he has one teller count all ballots while another tallies the call, or he divides the package into groups and has one pair of tellers tally each group, and he himself adds the scores. The chief teller exposes a questioned or questionable ballot to the group of tellers and rules on the acceptability and counting of the disputed ballot. If any teller objects to the chief teller's ruling, the matter is referred to the chair for decision, or if necessary to the entire meeting.

The chief teller certifies the result to the secretary and chair, simultaneously indicating the number of votes for each candidate, the number of blanks, the number of disallowed ballots and reason for their rejection. Tellers, if otherwise eligible, are entitled to vote. In written ballots, each teller includes

77

his own •ballot in the package he delivers to the chief teller. In unwritten voting, each teller adds his own vote to the appropriate side before reporting the score for his section. Persons ineligible to vote may be named as tellers.

610. Doubtful Tallies

If the chair is in doubt after an unwritten vote, he may call for a revote by the same method, or by any other method except roll call or written ballot. Any member who believes the chair erred in announcing a result may call for a division of the house (see 612) or he may appeal (see 408). The meeting may order a written ballot (see 608) either on a seconded and passed motion to that effect, which is in order in lieu of a division call, or after a division call, before the recount has been started.

611. Announcement of Result

When a vote is concluded, the chair announces the result. He says first whether the motion was passed (or carried), usually by saying "The 'ayes' have it and the motion is carried," or words to that effect. If there was a counted vote (that is, any method except voice) he also gives the score: "Four voted 'yes' and seven 'no,' so the motion is lost." A lost motion is announced as having been lost, defeated, or rejected. If a motion is lost even though a majority voted for it, the chair explains: "Although a majority voted to close debate, this motion requires a two-thirds vote, and since the affirmative vote is less than two thirds, the motion is lost"; or "The motion at this time cannot be passed unless a majority of all members favors it; and while more voted 'yes' than 'no,' those who voted 'yes' are less than a majority of the entire membership." If any other than a primary motion was just voted on, the chair explains the implications: "You have just defeated a proposed amendment; we will now vote on the main motion"; or, "The matter will accordingly be tabled"; or, "You have voted to reconsider your previous decision on XYZ. This matter is, accordingly, now open for discussion." The chair will also promptly indicate what is next on the agenda if the vote completely disposed of the matter on hand.

612. Division of the House

A "division" is a request that a voice vote be reviewed by counting; that is, by standing vote, by show of hands, or by roll call.

1. Who may ask for a division? Any person eligible to vote may demand a division of the house.

2. How is a division demanded? By saying, "I call for a division of the house," or simply by calling, "Division!"

3. When is it in order? Any time after the chair has "put the question" and before the next business is taken up. As soon as the chair says, "Are you ready for the question?" or otherwise indicates that he is about to call a vote, a member may call "Division"; he may also call "Division" while a voice vote is being taken, or after it has been taken, either before or after the chair "announces the result" (see 611). It may not be demanded after the next business is taken up, but may be called between the time the chair announces the result and the time someone asks for the floor on the next business.

4. What type of vote is subject to a division call? Any voice vote. Some authorities also permit a division call after a show of hands. The more usual procedure in such cases, however, is an appeal rather than a division call. If a "division call" is recognized after a show of hands, the recount is by rising vote (see 605) unless the meeting assents to a vote by show of hands or orders a written ballot. The chair says: "Division has been called. If no one objects, we will tally by show of hands. All in favor, please raise their right hands." If someone does object, a rising vote is taken. A written ballot, or rising, is not subject to the call for a division. However, such results may be subject to reconsideration (see 1101) or appeal (see 408).

5. A demand for a division, if otherwise in order, is effective even if not seconded. The demand is not subject to debate, amendment, postponement, commitment, or being laid on the table.

6. Procedure. After a division is called, the chair says, "Division having been demanded, we will poll the meeting" (or "We will take the vote again," if division is called after a vote had been concluded). He then says "All in favor please stand" (or "rise,") (or "raise the right hand,"), following the procedure outlined above in 605 or 606. Just before he does so, a member may move for a written ballot or roll call if appropriate, in accordance with the principles and procedure outlined above in 607 and 608.

7. If a member or group of members keeps calling "Division!" even though the sense of the meeting has been repeatedly made clear by voice vote, the chair may, after several such delays, refuse to recognize the division call. This decision (to ignore a division call) is subject to appeal (see 408).

8. Division of the house should not be confused with division of a question (see 618).

613. Tie Votes

Subject to the exceptions spelled out below, the effect of a tie vote is to defeat the motion or resolution.

1. A motion to sustain the chair is carried if it results in a tie vote. This is true, even if the chair voted on the motion.

2. After a tie vote has taken place, the chair—if he did not vote (and if, as in 404, he is eligible to vote) may, at his discretion, cast the deciding vote. However, he cannot vote twice. Thus if he voted for a motion, and if the result was a tie, he cannot break the tie by voting again. That motion is lost.

3. After a tie is announced, as a result of an unwritten vote, any member may rise and change his vote. If he had originally voted in the negative, the effect of this would be to carry the motion. If this happens, the chair will ask whether others wish to change their votes. This procedure is not applicable to written ballot, but is appropriate with all other forms of voting. If a tie vote results from a written ballot, the motion or resolution is lost, but it may be reconsidered. See Chapter 11.

4. A vote to confirm the action already taken by an officer is carried by a tie vote.

5. For the effect of a tie vote in an election, see 622(h).

6. A tie vote means simply that as many voted for as voted against. This is true regardless of the number voting. If a hundred members are present, and two vote "yes" while one votes "no," the chairman (if otherwise eligible) may vote "no," thus causing a tie and defeating the motion even though only two of the hundred voted against it.

614. Majority Vote and Two-Thirds Vote

(a) Unless there is some specific (and previously adopted) rule to the contrary, "majority" means that more voted one way than voted another. In other words, "majority" in the absence of any different rule means more than half of those *voting*. It does not mean more than half of those present. The motion to rescind is the only matter which requires a majority of those *present* to be effective; and even in that case, a vote of two thirds of those voting is sufficient to pass a motion to rescind if they constitute less than a majority of those present. See 1111 for motion to rescind.

(b) Under certain circumstances, the word "majority" is interpreted as meaning a majority of those present rather than a majority of those voting. The common parliamentary rule, and the general practice in voluntary societies, is simply this: a motion passes if more vote for it than vote against it, regardless of the number of nonvoters. If a two-thirds vote is required, it passes if twice as many (at least) vote "aye" as vote "no." However, it is often required in legislative bodies that no law can be enacted unless a majority of the house favors it. Often, this rule extends to an executive board type of body, that is, to a small group with delegated authority representing the entire membership. It may be that the members want no action taken except with the approval of a majority of the executive board. If that is their feeling, the rules or bylaws should so state. In the absence of any statement to the contrary, the common law applies: a majority means a majority of those voting. In business corporations, a decision to spend stockholders' money may be challenged in the courts if the decision was reached by a minority of those present. For example: fifty members constitute a quorum and fifty were present, but only three voted. Two voted for, one against the proposal. By common parliamentary law this is a valid decision. The forty-seven who failed to vote have no grievance. They were there and deliberately disfranchised themselves. Yet a stockholder may institute suit on the theory that money should not be disbursed by decision of only two out of fifty members. Some courts would agree with this as a matter of conscience, or would draw a parallel with the legislative practice of requiring a majority of the house. Others would follow the general parliamentary definition of "majority" and approve the action. The safest course is to have written into the bylaws a specific statement as to the kind of majority required to pass a motion or resolution. Sample rulings will be found in 1311.

A motion to rescind, if not noticed in advance, requires a vote of the majority of the entire membership or of two thirds of those present, as explained in 1114. This is the only motion which, by common parliamentary law, requires that its majority be measured from a base greater than the total voting. In all other matters (unless otherwise specified in previously adopted rules) the majority and two-thirds votes are measured against the total voting, not the total present.

The rule with respect to elections to office is similar. Unless specified in the bylaws or constitution, a plurality is sufficient to elect (see 622 and 1315).

(c) A *two-thirds vote* means that at least twice as many persons voted for the motion as voted against it. Here, too, blanks and nonvoters are ignored. If one hundred are present, and two vote for a motion while one votes against, the motion has a two-thirds vote. Any motion is passed by a majority vote, except the following which require a two-thirds vote:

> To close debate
> Previous question (if in order at all)
> To refuse to consider a question
> To suspend a rule

To close nominations
To expel a member
To amend the constitution

615. Changing One's Vote

A member may change his unwritten vote between the time he votes and the time the chair announces the result (see 611). At the moment when the chair says "the motion is carried" or "the motion is defeated," or other words to that effect, a member loses the chance to change his vote without permission.* For example, a motion requires a two-thirds vote, and the chair says: "Seven have voted for the motion and four against it, therefore—." One of those who voted "no" may, at this point, rise to say "I change my vote from 'no' to 'aye.'" The score now becomes eight to three instead of seven to four; and with eight out of eleven votes, the motion is carried, since eight is more than two thirds of eleven; whereas seven is not. Change of vote is acceptable in voting by show of hands, voice vote, roll call or standing vote. With a written ballot, change of vote is not possible, since there is no way of showing how the member voted the first time. However, a member may in such a situation move to reconsider (see Chapter 11).

Once the chair has announced the result, a member may change his vote only by consent. This is done by the member's rising to say "I ask permission to change my vote from 'aye' to 'no'" (or vice versa). The chair says: "Does any one object?" If no one objects, permission is granted by silent assent (general assent) and the change is made. If someone objects, the chair asks the member to make a motion, asking permission. This is made as "I move that I be permitted to change my vote from X to Y." If seconded, this motion is put to a vote at once. It is not debatable and cannot be disposed of in any way other than by voting on it. If a majority of those voting say "aye," permission is given and the vote is changed. If a majority does not agree, the vote stands. This, too, is inapplicable to written ballot.

---

* Unless it was a tie vote. See 613.

616. The Chair's Right To Vote

If he is otherwise eligible, the chairman retains his right to vote, and can vote no matter what method is used (see 404). He also may, if he wishes, refrain from voting until all votes are in, and then he may announce his own vote, or he may function as a tiebreaker only. The chair may, if he wishes, withhold his vote; then, if the motion is passed by a plurality of one, he may vote against it, thus causing a tie, and defeating the motion. He cannot vote twice; that is, he cannot vote against a motion and then, seeing it pass by a plurality of one, vote against it again to cause a tie; nor can he vote for a motion, see it defeated because of a tie, and then vote for it again to break the tie. Even on an appeal from the chair (in the form of a motion to sustain the chair), the chair is entitled to vote. (This motion is passed by a tie vote.)

617. Unanimous Vote

It is sometimes desirable to record that a motion, resolution, or election was approved by unanimous vote, even though the vote at first was *not* unanimous. This may be done either for the purpose of presenting a front of harmony, or for purely complimentary purposes. This is accomplished, with unwritten votes, in either of these two ways:

(a) Some member says: "Let's make this vote unanimous." The chair says: "Are there any objections to making it unanimous?" If no objections are raised, the chair says, "The action is declared to be unanimous and will be so recorded." If there is any objection, he says, "Since there is objection, unanimity cannot be recorded." (At this point the objector may change his mind, permitting unanimity to be recorded. But he cannot be compelled, and should not be pressured into doing so.)

(b) A member rises to say, "I move that the vote just taken be considered the unanimous sense of the meeting." If seconded, this motion is debatable, though it is not amendable and must be disposed of as soon as debate has been concluded.

(It cannot be laid on the table or referred to a committee.) This motion requires unanimous consent. When the chair says "All opposed say 'no,'" he may hear one or more "noes." If so, the motion is lost. In other words, a vote cannot be recorded as unanimous unless, after deliberation, it is in fact unanimous. The chair should explain this.

(c) The procedures outlined above apply only to decisions reached by unwritten vote. If the vote was by written ballot, a request to make it unanimous is out of order unless (1) it referred to an election; or, (2) the request to make it unanimous is disposed of by written ballot. The purpose of a written ballot is to guarantee the privacy of each voter's opinion. If it were possible to vote openly on making it unanimous, then the minority would have to identify themselves, or assent against their will to a show of unanimity. When a written ballot is used for a contested election, a motion to make it unanimous is in order only under either of these conditions: (1) the motion was made or seconded by *all* defeated candidates, or (2) the motion includes a clause requiring written ballot. Thus, "I move that the result of this election be made unanimous and that the vote on my motion be by written ballot," or words to that effect. However, the chair may receive the motion without that addendum, if he adds, "I will accept the motion with the understanding that this motion to make it unanimous be subject to written ballot." If questioned, he will explain the reason: to protect those who voted on the losing side from being obliged to identify themselves openly by standing or voice vote. If there were two defeated candidates in a contested election, and one of them made the motion to make it unanimous, the chair might look at the other defeated candidate; but he cannot ask if he will second it. If the other defeated candidate seconds it, then the motion is acceptable for vote by unwritten ballot. If there were three or more defeated candidates, they should all openly join in making or seconding the motion before it can be considered for an open vote. It is in poor taste openly to ask a defeated candidate to do this.

(d) An election is considered uncontested when only one candidate was nominated for the position (or when the number of candidates nominated equalled the number of vacancies). Even here, the election would not be uncontested if the organization had a tradition of a large write-in vote. The procedure for making such an election unanimous depends on the way the nominations are presented:

1. If an uncontested election is by mail, there is no way of making it unanimous, unless in fact there were no legally acceptable write-in votes. In that case, it would be unanimous in fact.

2. If a nominating committee brought in a panel with only one name for a vacancy, and if nominations from the floor are not permitted, then there would be no other candidate. In that case, the chair would say: "Since there are no other nominations, the candidate is unanimously elected, and I will order it so entered on the record."

3. If nominations from the floor are permitted, then after one candidate has been named for a vacancy (or as many candidates as there are vacancies, but no more), someone may move to close nominations. If seconded, this motion is put to vote at once, since it is not debatable. It requires a two-thirds vote (see 614(c)) and if it receives a two-thirds vote, the chair says: "The motion to close nominations has received the required two-thirds vote and is passed, and XYZ is unanimously elected to the position of ABC."

(e) The Secretary cannot cast a unanimous or single ballot for the society. The meeting itself does that as indicated above.

618. Division of the Question

(a) Sometimes a single resolution or committee report is so complex or lengthy that it appears best to consider each of its parts separately. If the resolution or report was presented as a unit, a member may ask for a "division of the question." Ordinarily the maker of the motion or presenter of the report agrees to divide it into sections so that each may be discussed and voted on separately.

If he does not consent, the chair rules. Either the maker of the resolution, the presenter of the report, or the maker of the motion to divide may then appeal the chair's ruling (see 408). The general rule is that each part of the question must make sense in itself. A report is usually divided into paragraphs; each may be voted on separately, or the noncontroversial ones may be considered as one section, and each controversial item as a separate section. In any event, each section is separately discussed and separately voted on. If this is done, there is no need to vote on the committee report as a whole. If many changes were made in the course of partitioning the report, however, the chair may order the entire report read as amended, and put that to a vote too, for the sake of clarity.

(b) Any member may call for division of the question, but this is not sufficient to effect the division. The form is: "I call for (or I move) a division of the question." The motion (for that is what it is even if in the form of a "call") may, if practical, indicate the points of division. For example, "I call for a division of the question, with debate and vote first on the findings, and then separately on each numbered recommendation." Or, perhaps, ". . . call for a division of the question: the part referring to the new clinic to be debated on and voted on first, and then the rest of the report."

(c) The call for a division of the question is ignored unless seconded. If seconded, it is debatable with respect to the wisdom of dividing it into parts. It is not debatable on the merits of the main question itself. It is amendable with respect to the points of division but not as to content. Obviously the call for a division may *not* be laid on the table (because it would become meaningless once the undivided question were passed or rejected). A call to divide a question may not be referred to a committee.

(d) If a formal resolution is ordered divided, this is done by discussing separately and then voting on each clause beginning "Be it resolved" or "Be it further resolved." If one or more of these passes, then each clause beginning "Whereas" is discussed and voted on (see 120). If not a single one of the resolving clauses is passed, there is no need to vote on any of the "whereas" clauses; the resolution is obviously defeated.

(e) Division of the question must not be confused with "division of the house," as explained above in 612.

619. Filling Vacancies

Sometimes a council, committee, house, or board must select delegates, observers, or representatives, or fill vacancies. If more persons are named than there are positions to fill, any of these three procedures may be followed:

(a) Nominations from the floor, following the procedures detailed in 621 below. Election would then be by written ballot.

(b) A motion may be made naming a person (or panel of persons) to fill the vacancy or receive the appointment. This is an ordinary motion and must be seconded. It is debatable. If a member objects to this motion, he may move to amend by "striking out XYZ" (names of the persons) and substituting "such persons as are here and now elected by written ballot." If this amendment is passed, then a written ballot is taken in the fashion usual for elections. If this amendment is not passed, then the original motion (naming XYZ to the position) is voted on without debate, and if passed the person is designated; and if the motion does not pass, other names are offered.

It would not be proper to amend by substituting one specific name for another. If the motion includes the name of Mr. E, the friends of Mr. F cannot get a free ride on that motion and substitute F's name for E's. They should vote against the motion, and then make a motion naming Mr. F.

(c) The chair may call for suggestions for each vacancy. As a name is called, the chair repeats it, the secretary notes it. Since these are "suggestions" rather than "nominations," the names need not be seconded. However, this is not an election in the sense that each member votes for the candidate of his choice. In this "filling vacancy" procedure, it works this way. The chair reviews the list and asks, "All in favor of Mr. A." (Mr. A is the first name suggested.) He notes the result. He then asks all opposed to indicate. If more favor than oppose,

Mr. A is elected. Otherwise, Mr. A's name is dropped. The meeting then proceeds to consider the second name on the list: Mr. B. If more favor B than oppose him, Mr. B is elected. If not, the chair calls for a vote on Mr. C, and so on. If a panel of several vacancies is to be filled, the chair uses this method for each name separately.

620. Proxy Voting

While proxy voting is common in stockholders' meetings, it is unusual in technical, scientific, voluntary, professional, or civic organizations. As a general rule, proxy or absentee voting is not permitted. To be sure, a member who expects to be absent may relay his views and ask to have them presented. This is done as follows:

(a) For a general membership meeting, the member sends his communication to the president or secretary. If it is not too long, the secretary will read it during the discussion. If it *is* too long, the secretary or president will announce that he has received the letter, indicate who sent it, and state how the member would have voted if present. He then gives a general idea of the length of the communication (in words or pages) and asks if the meeting wants it read. If there is demand for the reading, a motion is made and seconded. This motion is not debatable, and if passed, the secretary will read the communication.

(b) At meeting of a council, committee, or board, a member who expects to be absent may send a letter to any member of the group. The person receiving the letter will, during discussion of the matter, report that he has this communication, and indicate how the absent member would have voted. If he believes it helpful to do so, he will offer to read it, stating in advance its approximate length. The chair will ask if anyone objects to hearing it. If no one objects, the recipient of the communication will read it. If a member objects, the question of reading it will be put to vote, and the recipient will be guided by that vote.

621. Nominations

See 1316 for sample systems of nominations.

(a) When nominations are from the floor, the chair announces that nominations will now be received. A member raises his hand, is recognized, says "I nominate XYZ for the position of ABC." In most organizations a nomination is not valid unless it is seconded. It is sometimes said that a nomination needs no second. This is contrary to the practice of most organizations. Unless the bylaws otherwise state, or unless a standing rule to that effect has been adopted, a nomination should not be considered as official until it has been seconded. After the nomination has been seconded, the chair calls for additional nominations.

Debate, discussion, and speeches about nominations are not in order unless the society has a rule or tradition to the effect that nominating and seconding speeches are made. The named candidate, if present, may decline the nomination, and if so his name is withdrawn. If he is absent, or if (being present) he is silent, the nomination is presumed to have been accepted. A motion to close nominations is not in order unless and until the chair has allowed a reasonable time for additional nominations. When such a motion is made, the chair says, "Before considering this motion, are there any additional nominations?" or words to that effect, and pauses. If no further nominations are made, he calls for a vote as soon as the motion is seconded. It is an undebatable motion, but requires a two-thirds vote (that is, two thirds of those voting on the motion (see 614(b)) to pass. If passed, the chair calls for the election unless there was only one candidate named; and in that case, he declares him elected (see 617(d)(3)).

(b) The motion to close nominations may *not* be compounded with "and that the secretary cast the unanimous ballot . . ." This affix is unnecessary. If included in the motion to close nominations, the chair will ignore that part of it in stating the question. For explanation see 617(d)(3) and 617(e).

(c) If a recommendation is made by a nominating committee, or if a nomination is made from the floor, the chair will call for other nominations. If he hears none, he may say "If there is no objection, nominations will be closed." A formal motion to close nominations is not necessary, since nominations will have been closed by general and unanimous assent if this procedure is followed.

(**d**) A motion to reopen nominations is in order as follows:

1. If the election was uncontested, a motion to reopen may be made any time before the meeting proceeds to the next business (after election).

2. If the election was contested, a motion to reopen nominations may be made before distribution of ballots has begun but not thereafter. A motion to reopen nominations is undebatable. It requires a majority vote to pass. An amendment is permitted only if that amendment fixes a time to which to postpone the election and allow further nominations.

(**e**) The candidates placed in nomination by the nominating committee do not need to be seconded.

(**f**) A member who has nominated one person may not at the same meeting nominate a different person for the same office, unless the first name has been withdrawn, or that first candidate had declined nomination.

(**g**) All the above instructions (621) apply only when there is no different provision in the constitution or bylaws. If there is, the constitutional or bylaw procedure applies.

622. Elections

Ordinarily, the election procedure is detailed in the constitution, bylaws, or in previously adopted standing rules (see 1315). The general rules are:

(**a**) An election is unnecessary if there is only one legal candidate for each vacancy, or if there are no more candidates than vacancies (see 617(d)). If write-in votes are permitted, however, an election may be necessary even if apparently uncontested.

(b) Contested elections are by written ballot, in accordance with the procedures of 608 and 609 above. But see 1315(b).

(c) Members may execute ballots in their seats, and tellers pick them up as they move through the hall; or, if the situation demands it, members may go to a polling place and deposit ballots in a ballot box. See the "turnstile" procedure in the second paragraph under 608(c) above.

(d) If members go to a polling place, one or more registrars will be appointed who will check each voter's name against a membership list. Registrars need not be members. They are appointed by the president. The polls will be opened and closed at definite and previously announced times. The meeting may, in advance, by majority vote, fix those times; otherwise, the president will do so.

(e) Unless otherwise specified, an elected candidate takes office as soon as the election results are certified. Results are certified by the president on receiving the report of the chief teller, unless some other method of certification is spelled out in the constitution, bylaws, enabling resolution, or standing rules.

(f) A member is expected to serve in office to which he was elected. If he declines to serve, he will resign from office. In that case a vacancy is created, which will be filled in the manner provided in the constitution or bylaws for filling vacancies.

(g) In the absence of constitutional provision to the contrary, a plurality is sufficient to elect; that is, the candidate who receives more votes than any other is elected, even though he received only a minority of the votes cast. If the rules (constitution, bylaws, standing rules, or enabling resolution) require an absolute majority of all votes cast (or any other fraction), then there is no election if the plurality candidate failed to receive a majority. In that case, a second election is held; the candidate who received the smallest number of votes at the first election is disqualified as a candidate at the second election. In like manner, additional elections are held, the low candidate being dropped each time, until one receives an absolute majority. This applies, however, only when an absolute majority is required. Ordinarily a plurality is sufficient. See 1315(b) for details.

(h) If a tie vote occurs, a second election is held; all candidates who received votes at the first election are to be considered candidates at the second, unless one or more withdraw.

(j) If more than one vacancy is being filled, either of these methods may be used:

1. A separate election is held and disposed of for each vacancy, before a ballot is taken on the next vacancy; or
2. A single ballot is distributed and members vote for all vacancies at one time.

If the organization has an established practice with respect to these two methods, that practice will be followed unless the meeting votes otherwise. If no precedent has been established, Method 2 is used. Nominations are made and closed first for one office, then for another, until all nominations are closed. Ballots are then distributed and each member indicates on the same ballot his choice for all offices.

7

Points and Motions
of Privilege

701. Motions of Privilege

(a) A top priority matter that may be introduced no matter what other subject is pending is called a point or motion of "privilege." If it requires a second, it is a privileged *motion*. If it does not require a second it is a *point* of privilege. These are three privileged motions. They are, in priority order:

1. To fix the time of the next meeting
2. To adjourn
3. To recess

These are reviewed in Chapter 12.

(b) A demand that the group take up the matter scheduled for this time is a privileged point, not a motion, since it requires no second. This is explained in 307(f) and 308(a). Eleven other points of privilege are reviewed in 703.

(c) A point of order, point of information, point of privilege, and call for the orders of the day (307(f)) may be raised even while someone else is speaking. The other privileged points and motions cannot be raised until the maker gets the floor, and he may not for this purpose interrupt someone who is speaking.

702. Nature of a Point of Privilege

A member has two kinds of rights: (1) He has certain rights related to his status as a member—the right to vote, to make motions, to debate, to run for office, and so on; and (2) certain physical rights, the denial of which would produce an emergency and choke off his other rights—for example, the right to hear what is being said, hence the right to demand that extraneous noise be suppressed. If this right is denied, the member cannot hear the discussion and thus loses his basic right to participate. But the demand for suppression of noise is an emergency. It does no good to postpone it. Hence the demand that noise be suppressed is a point of privilege. So it is with rights related to physical comfort, light, freedom from abuse, and so on. Also, a member's right to know clearly what is going on is an emergency right. If everyone is talking about a proposal to amend Article VI,3,b of the bylaws, the member has a right to know what this article is, and to insist that the chairman read it. Likewise, his demand that he be informed is based on an emergency right that must be attended to at once. Other examples of emergency rights (points of privilege) are listed in 703.

703. List of Points of Privilege

Here are the eleven "privileged points" which any member may raise, even if someone is talking. In each case, the matter must be disposed of promptly lest the member lose some of his rights to participate:

(a) Point of information; the right to have a simple, basic question answered (see 704).

(b) Parliamentary inquiry; the right to have the parliamentary meaning of something explained, or the parliamentary way of accomplishing something clarified (see 705).

(c) Attention to personal safety or safety of group; calling attention to a hazard such as a falling ceiling, a fire, and so on (see 707).

(d) Attention to personal comfort or comfort of the group; calling attention to the need for better ventilation, heating, lighting (see 707).

(e) Right to hear what is being said; for example, demand that extraneous noise be abated.

(f) Right to have a short basic item read or clarified so that member knows what is being discussed; for example, the right to demand that a motion or resolution be repeated, that the relevant section of the constitution, bylaws, or letter be read, and the like.

(g) Right to be protected against abuse, physical or verbal; right to demand that an insulting statement be retracted or an apology be made; that an abusive speaker be called to order by the chairman (see 706).

(h) Right to insist that the announced schedule or agenda be followed and that the chair promptly take up matters that are supposed to be considered now. This is a "call for general or special orders of the day" (see 307(f) and 308(a)). The group can, by two-thirds vote, suspend the rules and refuse to take up what was scheduled, and the group also can, by majority vote, table it (see 306 and 801).

(j) Right to appeal from the chair if the member thinks the chair ruled erroneously (see 408).

(k) Right to call attention to an error in parliamentary procedure (see 706).

(m) Right to demand that the speaker raise his voice or speak more clearly or more fully, so that member can hear and understand him.

704. Raising a Point of Information

(a) A member who has a bona fide question, permitting a short factual answer, may, at any time, rise to a point of information. He does this by simply calling out "Point of Information." He may interrupt a speaker to do this if the information is essential to understanding the speaker. The chair recognizes him (no second is necessary) and says: "What is your inquiry?" The member states his question and the chair asks the speaker or some other person to answer it, or answers it himself if appropriate. However, the chair will reject a "point of information" that is merely argumentative or intended to challenge the merits of the matter. This privileged point is intended for honest factual questions, answers to which are necessary to understanding the issue.

(**b**) For example, here is a legitimate inquiry. The speaker is saying: ". . . While the proposal is a good one, it seems clear that it would violate the Zilch-Schmutter Law, and therefore . . ."

A member interrupts with: "What is the Zilch-Schmutter Law?" This is a legitimate question; it allows a simple answer; it is not argumentative. And unless the question is answered, the member will not understand the speaker. The chair, if he knows, gives the answer briefly, as: "That's the new law which forbids supermarkets to sell aspirin"; or he calls on the speaker to answer it.

(**c**) Here is an illegitimate inquiry. The speaker is urging that the organization divide itself into five districts and that separate meetings be held monthly in each district. A member says: "Point of information. Does the speaker really believe that we can save money by holding five times as many meetings, or that the allegedly greater participation under this absurd scheme will counterbalance the increased red tape?" The chair here will cut in and say: "I'll have to deny that as a point of information. You are trying to discuss the merits of the motion, and you will have a chance to do that during the debate on it." The member must sit down. If he thinks the chair was unreasonable in banning the query, he may appeal (see 408).

Another example. A member interrupts a speaker with: "Point of information . . . is the speaker now willing to repudiate the malicious and erroneous statement he made last week concerning XYZ?" Although framed as a query, this is obviously an argument, not a legitimate question.

705. Raising a Parliamentary Inquiry

If a member thinks the chair made an erroneous ruling, he raises a point of order (see 706). But if he honestly wants parliamentary information or explanation, he rises and says: "Parliamentary inquiry, Mr. Chairman," or words to that effect. He may interrupt a speaking member, but usually he does not do so, since it seldom happens that this kind of inquiry materially affects the member's understanding of the issue. Here are some examples of parliamentary inquiries:

1. That last motion had an obvious majority. Isn't that enough? [Answer: "It required a two-thirds vote."]
2. If a matter was laid on the table at the last session, may I bring it up again now?
3. Would this be old business or new business?
4. How can we even take this matter up, if the Committee has not reported it?
5. Can he amend my motion, if I object to the amendment?

The chair answers, refers the matter to a parliamentarian for answer, reads from a manual, or says that the point of inquiry is not well taken and refuses to answer it. He would do this when a member uses the form of a "parliamentary inquiry" to get into the record some private opinions; as, for instance, when he says "How can you pass a motion with so few people here and you know perfectly well if more were here it would never pass, and I want to know, Mr. Chairman, why you let them do that." Though in the form of an "inquiry," this is obviously polemical. The chair rules that it is not a bona fide parliamentary inquiry, and does not answer it.

706. Raising a Point of Order

(a) If a member thinks that parliamentary procedure has been violated, or if he is personally insulted by indecorous behavior or abusive remarks, he may rise to a point of order and may interrupt a speaker to do so. Also, the chair may, on his own initiative, "call to order" a speaker who is abusive, insulting, or irrelevant. He may, indeed, order the speaker to change his voice, his language, or the content of his discussion, or to sit down; and may suspend business until he does. The chair may also suspend the discussion if some other member is out of order and causing a diversion.

(b) The member who rises to a point of order says simply: "Point of order, Mr. Chairman," or, more formally: "Mr. Chairman, I rise to a point of order." If someone else is speaking, the latter stops until the point of order is disposed of. The chair asks the member to state his "point," and rules whether it is well taken. A limited amount of debate is permissible; that is, the member is given a chance to explain why he thinks something is out of order, and the chair, if necessary, explains why he disagrees. But since this is not a motion (it is not seconded), it is not appropriate to open it to full debate. If the member is dissatisfied with the chair's ruling, he may appeal (see 408).

(c) Here are some examples:

(1)

MR. JONES:

Point of order. According to parliamentary procedure, you can't move to amend an amendment.

CHAIR:

Not quite, Mr. Jones. One amendment to an amendment is in order. You can't go beyond that. You can't amend an amendment to an amendment.

MR. JONES:

Well, here it is. Page 26. "Only one amendment may be pending at one time."

CHAIR:

That means one separate or different amendment. An amendment to an amendment is part of the first amendment. It is quite in order.
 (*Member could appeal.*)

(2)

MR. BROWN:

Mr. Chairman, I rise to a point of order.

CHAIR:
> (*to interrupted speaker*) Pardon, Mr. Smith. Let's dispose of Mr. Brown's point. Will you please state your point of order, Mr. Brown?

MR. BROWN:
> There is a motion to lay this matter on the table. Mr. Smith is discussing it. As I understand it, a motion to lay on the table is not debatable.

CHAIR:
> The point is well taken. I'm afraid we will have to suspend all debate and vote at once on this matter of laying the motion on the table. All those in favor of laying it on the table, say "aye."

(3)

MR. SNEED:
> . . . and not only that; Mr. Adams' real reason for wanting to locate our headquarters there is not what he has just told you. His real reason is that he owns the tavern next door and he is trying to use his membership in this organization to boost his own business and—

MR. ADAMS:
> Point of privilege. I resent that. It isn't true. Do I have to listen to this, Mr. Chairman?

CHAIR:
> Your point is well taken. Mr. Sneed will please refrain from attacking the motives of members. Confine your discussion to the merits of the proposed site and not the integrity of our fellow-members.

707. Raising a Point of Privilege

When the safety, comfort, convenience, or orderliness of the group or any individual is involved, a person concerned may rise to a point of privilege. He calls out: "Point of privilege, Mr. Chairman," and may interrupt a speaker to do so, if necessary. The chair asks him to state his "point" unless (as in Example 2 below) the point tumbled out in the original demand; for example:

1. Point of privilege, Mr. Chairman—I can't hear the speaker.
2. Mr. Chairman, Mr. Chairman, get that window closed right away; we're freezing and we can't hear what's going on anyway.

As appropriate, the chair may rule that the point of privilege was not bona fide, or that it can be settled just as well after the current business is disposed of. In a sense, all the matters listed in 703 are matters of privilege, but for convenience some are grouped under points of order, information, or inquiry. It is a member's privilege to be safe from abuse. Hence, a member who is being defamed by another could claim a point of privilege or a point of order (see Example 3 in 706). In either event the chair would have to remind the speaker that it is out of order to insult members or attack their motives.

708. Demand that Agenda Be Followed

See 307(f) and 308(a).

709. Appeal from the Chair

See 408.

8

How To Put Off
Until Tomorrow

801. Legitimate Dilatory Motions

No one may compel a meeting to dispose of a matter at once. If the group wants to defer it, they may do so. This is accomplished by passing one of these dilatory motions:

1. To lay on the table
2. To postpone to a specified time
3. To postpone indefinitely
4. To make a special order for a later time

These motions effect the desired delay in different ways:

(a) If a matter is *laid on the table,* it is removed from consideration until the group, by majority vote, agree to take it back "from the table" and dispose of it. Thus, this does not destroy a matter, since at any later time—perhaps with only a bare quorum present—the group can vote to take it from the table. In legislative bodies, and in large organizations with infrequent meetings and heavy programs, a motion to table may effectively kill the matter. If the pace of business is such that the society never back-tracks, then once a motion is tabled it is dead. In the ordinary voluntary organization, however, this is not true. A tabled matter may be revived later at the same meeting or at any subsequent meeting within the limits detailed in 808.

(b) If a matter is "postponed to a specified time," it then gets a priority at the time specified, and must be considered then. Unlike a special order, however, a postponed matter does not get the floor while other business is pending. It operates more like a "general order" than a "special order" (see 308). If a matter is postponed to a specified time, it is certainly going to come to the floor then. Therefore, only those friendly to a proposition are likely to move to postpone it to a specified time. By contrast, those hostile to a motion would vote to table it. See 811 for more details.

(c) To postpone indefinitely is a device to kill rather than to delay a matter. If it is voted to postpone indefinitely, then the matter cannot be brought up again during the current meeting-year (see 812).

(d) To make a special order for a later time means that, when the specified time comes, this matter will be considered, even if it means interrupting pending business (see 307).

802. Form and Purpose of "To Lay on the Table"

(a) The form is: "I move we lay this (matter, proposal, motion) on the table." Colloquially this is acceptably offered by the phrase: "I move we table it." If passed, its effect is to stop debate at once and to remove the matter from the floor. It ceases to be pending. It remains in suspended animation, on the shelf (theoretically on the secretary's "table") until, by majority vote, the group decide to consider it and dispose of it. This is done by voting to "take it from the table" (see 806 to 810).

(b) The purpose of the motion is to remove a matter from consideration at this time, in order (1) to give right of way to something more pressing, or (2) to avoid a temper-trying, embarrassing, or violent continuation of debate, or (3) to suppress a matter (usually temporarily) without being openly recorded as in favor of it or opposed to it.

803. Lay on the Table: When in Order

Except for proposals concerned with recess or adjournment, this has the top priority of all definitive motions. It may *not* be made (1) when someone is talking, or (2) when a motion to recess, adjourn, or fix the time for the next meeting is being considered. Otherwise it is always in order, if the mover can get the floor. The motion requires a second. The chair will not receive the motion to lay on the table if the mover of the primary motion has not yet been afforded a chance to speak on it. The one who made the primary motion must be allowed to have his say first; then the group, if they want to, can vote to lay it on the table (also see 116).

804. Parliamentary Features of Motion To Table

The motion "to lay on the table" is not debatable. As soon as it is seconded, the chair calls for a vote: "All in favor of laying this XYZ matter on the table, will say 'aye.'" (If someone wants to continue discussion, the chair explains that the motion to table is absolutely nondebatable). The motion ("to lay on the table") cannot be amended. In ordinary (nonlegislative) assemblies a motion to reconsider cannot be laid on the table (see 1107(d)), and in no meeting may a motion to lay on the table be reconsidered. (If the motion passes, the primary matter can be put back on the floor by a motion to take from the table; if the motion to table fails, it can be renewed if debate has advanced since it failed; hence there is no need to reconsider a motion to lay on the table.) A motion "to lay on the table" cannot be postponed or referred to a committee. It must be acted on when made. It requires a majority vote only (more voting "aye" than "no") to pass. It is defeated if as many vote "no" as vote "aye."

805. Lay on the Table: Series of Connected Motions

Because of its high rank, the motion to lay on the table may be made when a matter has several secondary motions attached to it. For instance, a motion to do XYZ might have attached a proposed amendment to strike out X, and then a motion to refer it all to a committee. Then, perhaps, someone moves to lay on the table. What does he want to lay on the table? The motion to commit? The amendment to strike out X? Or the motion to do XYZ? The answer is that the entire complex of motions has to be laid on the table. There is no way of disentangling them, except by disposing of certain parts of it now. In the example cited, a motion to lay on the table would put into the deep freeze the motion to do XYZ, the proposed amendment to make it just YZ, and the proposal to refer the whole matter to a committee. If and when a motion is made to take it from the table, the entire matter is reproduced on the floor in the same posture it occupied when it went into the freezer. In this example, the question before the house when taken from the table is whether to refer the XYZ matter to a committee; if this is lost, the question is whether or not to strike out X.

806. To Take from the Table: Purpose

The purpose of this motion is to remove from the secretary's "table" a matter that was previously laid there. It revives and brings on the floor the matter previously tabled.

807. To Take from the Table: Form

The form is: "I move we take from the table the matter of XYZ."

808. To Take from the Table: When in Order

The motion to take from the table is in order at any time after the matter was laid on the table, provided some other business has intervened, and provided:

(a) If the organization meets once in three months, or more frequently, a matter tabled at one meeting may be taken from the table either

1. At that same meeting
2. At the next business meeting

If it is not taken from the table by the close of the next meeting it lapses. This rule is needed to avoid the situation where a tabled matter hangs suspended forever over the heads of the assembly. A matter is tabled with the intent of reviving it soon. If it were to be put forever in limbo, it should have been postponed indefinitely. The rule works no hardship. If the matter is not revived at the next business meeting it dies. But it can be revived easily enough by a new motion under new business.

(b) If an organization holds a meeting only once, twice, or three times a year, then a matter which remains on the table at the time of adjournment is dead. This rule is needed to prevent the unsatisfactory state of unsettled matters forever haunting the agenda. However, a matter laid on the table may be taken from the table at the same meeting—that is, at the meeting which laid it on the table. If a matter dies on the table it can, of course, be later revived by reintroduction as new business.

(c) When a meeting consists of several sessions in close proximity (as, for instance, a three-day annual convention, a two-day session of an executive board, and the like), a matter laid on the table may be taken from the table any time up to the *sine die* adjournment. A matter lying on the table is destroyed by a *sine die* adjournment. It can then be revived only as new business (see 1204).

809. Who May Make Motion To Take from Table

Any voting member may make the motion regardless of how he voted on the subject previously. The motion must be seconded.

810. Parliamentary Features of Motion To Take from Table

The motion may be made only when no other business is actually on the floor. The motion is neither amendable nor debatable. As soon as it is seconded, the chair says: "All in favor of taking from the table the matter of XYZ which was previously laid on the table say 'aye.'" If passed, the matter is restored in the form it had when it was laid on the table. Debate is reopened and any matters affixed to the primary motion (such as amendments) are also in the same status. If defeated, the motion to take from the table may be renewed after other business has intervened. (There is, therefore, no need to move reconsideration.) The motion to take from the table may not be referred to a committee, postponed, or laid on the table.

811. Postpone to Specified Time

(a) This motion may be made while a primary motion, or an amendment to it, is being discussed, or after a motion to commit (refer to a committee) has been made, but before it has been acted on. It replaces a motion to postpone indefinitely (see 812). If a motion to postpone indefinitely has been made and seconded, the friends of the primary matter can rescue it from a silent grave by moving to postpone to a specified time. This, if passed, nullifies the motion to postpone indefinitely.

(b) The motion is worded: "I move that this matter be postponed to–." The time could be specified, as "to 10 A.M. tomorrow"; or simply the day, as "to Friday"; or "to our next meeting"; or "until after the XYZ matter has been disposed of." In any event the maximum period of postponement is one year, plus a few days or weeks if this brings it to an annual convention.

(c) The motion to postpone must be seconded before it can be voted on.

(d) The motion may be amended with respect to the time of postponement. It is not subject to any other kind of amendment.

(e) The motion is open to debate on the wisdom of postponing action, but not to debate on the merits of the primary matter.

(f) The motion cannot be self-stultifying: that is, it cannot be so worded that, if passed, the original matter could never, within reason, come up. For example, the motion cannot be worded (or amended) to read "that the matter be postponed for twenty-one years." Again, a suggestion that we invite Dr. A to speak at the February meeting cannot be postponed for decision at the March meeting. In these two examples, the purpose of the motion was to destroy the matter, not postpone it. The maker should move to postpone indefinitely, not to postpone to a certain time (see 812).

(g) The motion to postpone cannot be referred to a committee nor can it be tabled. However, a motion "to lay on the table," made while a motion to postpone is being considered, will be construed as a motion to lay the primary matter on the table; and this is in order.

(h) A matter having been postponed to a specified time becomes a "general order" for that time (see 308).

(j) The time to which a matter can be postponed by this motion must be within one year. If the matter comes up at an annual convention, it may be postponed to as late as the last day of the next annual convention even if this is a few weeks in excess of an exact one-year period.

812. To Postpone Indefinitely

(a) The intent of this motion is to kill the matter without officially being recorded as voting against it. The effect of passing this motion is to push the item completely off the agenda for the remainder of the program-year. A matter having been postponed indefinitely may not be brought up again during that year, except by a motion to rescind or reconsider postponement (see 1111 et seq.).

(b) The motion to postpone may be made if the maker can get the floor while the primary motion is under debate. It may not be made if there is pending a motion to amend, to refer to a committee, to lay on the table, to recess, to adjourn, or to postpone to a definite time. The motion to postpone indefinitely has the lowest priority of all secondary motions.

(c) If a motion to postpone indefinitely is made and seconded, any member may immediately move to postpone to a definite time (see 811). This is voted on first, and if passed the matter is postponed to the time specified. (The motion to postpone indefinitely is then automatically vacated.) If the motion (to postpone to a definite time) fails, then the motion to postpone indefinitely is voted on.

(d) The motion to postpone indefinitely is not amendable. It is, however, debatable. If the motion passes it may be reconsidered as explained in Chapter 11.

(e) If the motion fails it may neither be renewed nor reconsidered. While a motion to postpone indefinitely is pending (or under discussion), the matter may, by vote, be referred to a committee. This has the effect of killing the motion to postpone. If the motion (to postpone indefinitely) fails, debate continues on the primary matter. If the motion (to postpone indefinitely) passes, debate stops and the primary matter is suspended unless revived by a motion to reconsider. Furthermore, the same primary matter cannot be brought up again until an adjournment has intervened (see 1210).

813. To Make a Special Order

See 307.

814. The Tactics of Delay

See 1414 to 1419, and also 1509.

9

How To Amend
a Motion

901. Amendments in General

Any primary motion (as defined in 202) may be amended. An amendment may be proposed without the permission of—indeed, even against the resistance of—the maker of the primary motion. An amendment is acted upon before the primary motion is disposed of. After one amendment is disposed of, another amendment may be proposed. It is not in order to propose one amendment while another is pending, unless the former is an amendment to the amendment. As explained in 909, the privilege of amending an amendment does not descend down that chain any further. You cannot propose an amendment to an amendment to an amendment.

902. Methods of Amendment

A resolution, motion, or report may be amended in any of these ways:

1. By striking out certain words or phrases without replacing them
2. By inserting certain words or phrases without removing anything

3. By deleting certain words and replacing them with others

4. By adding something

Every proposed amendment takes one or more of these forms:

1. Deletion
2. Insertion
3. Substitution
4. Addition

903. Wording of Proposal

The technical form for proposing an amendment is: "Mr. Chairman, I move that this motion be amended by striking out the words ABC and inserting in their places the words XYZ" (or equivalent terms for deletion, addition, or insertion). In practice, the chair will accept any wording so long as it is clear. For example, the primary motion is: "That applicants be subject to examination before acceptance." A member says: "I move to insert the word 'rigorous' before the word 'examination.'" It is clear that he is proposing an amendment by insertion, so there is no need that he follow the exact form and say "I move that this motion be amended by inserting the word 'rigorous' before the word 'examination.'" Of course, the proposal must be so worded that it *is* clear.

Sometimes, however, the implication is obscure. Most listeners find it hard to follow a proposal that "the number three be stricken out and replaced with four, while the semicolon be deleted and a period be substituted therefor." It is therefore good form for the proponent of the amendment or for the chair to explain the implication of the proposed amendment and to reread the motion the way it would sound if amended.

904. Voting on Amendments

A proposed amendment is debatable if the primary motion is debatable. After debate has concluded, the chair puts the amendment to a vote. The meeting always votes on the amendment first, and then on the main motion. If the amendment is defeated, the primary motion, as originally drawn (or as previously and acceptably revised) is then voted on. If the amendment passes, then the primary motion is rephrased to incorporate the amendment, and it is then voted on. Any of the standard voting methods may be used in voting on amendments. See Chapter 6.

905. Nonamendable Motions

No amendment may be offered to a motion to:

lay on the table
sustain the chair
reconsider
take from the table
adjourn
amend an amendment
go into Committee of the Whole
close debate
close nominations
suspend the rules

The raising of a point of order and a call for a division of the house likewise cannot be amended.

906. Amendable Motions

Any primary motion may be amended. An amendment may be amended once, but only once at a time. It is also in order to propose an amendment to a motion fixing the time for adjournment or recess, or fixing the time for the next meeting, or a motion to rescind, to postpone to a certain time, or to refer to a committee. These are all amendable motions; the other secondary motions (905) are not.

907. Amendments to Previously Adopted Matters

If a motion, bylaw, resolution, report, rule, or provision of the constitution had been previously adopted and is in effect, then a motion to amend it is a primary motion in itself, and is so treated.

908. Status of Mover

It is not necessary to seek or obtain the permission of the mover of the primary motion in order to introduce an amendment. If the mover likes the proposed amendment, he may withdraw his original motion and incorporate the proposed amendment; that is, he may *substitute* the revised version for his original. If no one objects, permission for a substitution is granted, and the revised motion simply takes the place of the original motion. If, on the other hand, the mover does not like the proposed amendment, he can do nothing except speak against it during debate. If the proposed amendment is legitimate (see 911), and if it is seconded, it comes before the meeting and will be voted on. One who has seconded an original motion could refuse to second a revised substitute form, and in that case the chair will call for another seconder. An amendment needs to be seconded before it is before the meeting.

909. Amendment to an Amendment

An amendment to an amendment is in order; but a second amendment is *not* in order while a first amendment is pending.

(a) An amendment to an amendment limits itself sharply to the amendment. For example:

1. Primary motion is: "Students be admitted to the exhibit for a $1 fee." It is now proposed to amend by adding "and apprentices" after "students." If this were adopted, the motion would read: "Students and apprentices be admitted for a $1 fee." The phrase "and apprentices" is an amendment.

2. Now it is suggested that to the phrase "and apprentices" there be added "in the printing trades," so that this would read: "Students and apprentices in the printing trades be admitted . . ." The phrase "in the printing trades" is an amendment to the amendment. It is, therefore, in order.

3. However, suppose that after the "and apprentices" had been suggested (but before it was voted on), a member had suggested: "Let's add that first-year journeymen be admitted

for a $2 fee." This is a different amendment; a second amendment. It is *not* an amendment to the "and apprentices" amendment. Since it is a different (a second) amendment, it cannot be considered until the first amendment ("and apprentices") is disposed of.

(b) Only one amendment may be considered at one time. But one amendment to that amendment (a subamendment) may be considered then too. See example in 909(a).

910. Multiple Amendments

Multiple amendments are considered separately, one at a time. The amendment first proposed is first disposed of, together with a single subamendment if one is offered. Then the second proposed amendment together with its subamendment (if any) is disposed of. See 909(a) for example.

911. Illegitimate Amendments

(a) An amendment is not legitimate unless it is relevant to the subject of the primary motion. For example, the motion is, "That this Society go on record as favoring the rezoning of the Hendry tract." A member now rises and says, "I move to amend by striking out everything after the word 'favoring' and inserting in its stead the phrase 'a higher protective tariff for original works of art brought into this country.'" This is so hopelessly irrelevant to the primary motion that the chair must refuse to receive it as an amendment. He rules it out of order, telling the mover to bring it up later as an item by itself.

(b) An amendment is not legitimate if its effect would be to reverse the intent of the original motion. If the intent of a motion is to praise the chairman for his work during the year, it would not be legitimate to amend it by replacing "praise" with "censure." This is general practice and general opinion. There are, however, a few parliamentarians who take the opposite position and who say that so long as the amendment is germane to the subject, it *may* be stultifying in effect; that it may, for example, replace "accept an offer" with "reject" it, or replace "discontinue the contract" with "renew the contract."

Common sense would seem to rule out an amendment that reverses the primary motion. For example, the motion is "that this Society accept the invitation from the XYZ Association." Another member now moves to "amend by striking out the word 'accept' and replacing it with the word 'reject.'" This is not a legitimate amendment. Persons opposed to the invitation from the XYZ Association should speak and vote against the original motion. Introducing a negative amendment causes confusion (which is sometimes the reason it is introduced) so that members are not sure how they are voting. There is no reason why the opponents of a proposition should ride into the program on the horse furnished by the friends of the proposition.

An amendment that inserts the word "not" is illegitimate; so is an amendment which replaces a verb with its own antonym, as for instance "reject" with "accept," or "censure" with "endorse," or "extend" with "dissolve," and the like.

(c) An amendment, therefore, must be relevant in topic, and reasonably consonant in spirit with the original motion. How far the chair will go in recognizing this spiritual accord is a matter of the chair's discretion.

For example, a member moves that $300 be appropriated to purchase a computing machine for the statistical office. Another member moves to amend by striking out "the sum of $300" and replacing with "whatever sum may be necessary, but not to exceed $400." This amendment is in consonance with the general spirit of the primary motion, and it is obviously germane to it. However, the chair would probably exclude a motion to "strike out purchase of a statistical machine" and insert "purchase of an air conditioning unit." Here the friend of air conditioning is smuggling in his motion under cloak of the statistical machine. To accept the proposed amendment here could destroy the original motion. If most members wanted both the air conditioning and the computing machine they would approve the amendment; but this would wipe out the motion about the computing machine. Thus it would seem best to consider these as two separate primary motions.

(d) A member says: "I move that we present the retiring President with an ivory desk set, purchased from funds in the Society's treasury." Could another member say: "I move to amend by striking out 'ivory desk set' and replacing with 'one pound of spinach' "? No! Apart from the suspicion that the amendment is frivolous and therefore out of order is the fact that it is completely out of accord with the intent of the original motion.

(e) The rule then is this: the maker of a motion is entitled to have the meeting vote on that motion or on a substantially similar version of it. He cannot be compelled to forego this by an amendment which destroys or negates the obvious intent of his original motion.

912. Substitute Motions

The complete replacement of one motion by another is a substitution, not an amendment. Thus, a resolution begins with "Resolved that ABC." After this is before the house, a member can hardly move an amendment by asking that "The resolution be amended by striking out all words after 'resolved that' and replacing with XYZ." This is clearly a complete substitution and the member who wants that should get the floor when appropriate and bring his proposal in by itself. On the other hand, a substitute motion *is* in order if acceptable to the original mover, and to the original (or some other) seconder.

A dissenting, minority member of a committee sometimes tries to replace the majority report with his (or the minority's) views. It would be technically proper to do this by offering a substitute motion, but, for reasons indicated in 1015(c), this would seem to be bad practice.

913. Parliamentary Rank of the Motion To Amend

The motion to amend is practically on the same footing as the primary motion to which it applies. Except that it cannot be postponed indefinitely, the motion to amend is subject to any other secondary motion; it can be debated, referred to a committee, renewed, reconsidered, or laid on the table. In other words, while a motion to amend is being debated, it (the amending motion) can be disposed of by one of these subsidiary actions (lay on table, refer to committee, and the like) if the members so desire; and if done, this leaves the primary motion untouched. The motion to fix the time for the next session and the motion to recess are amendable but not debatable. Otherwise any proposed amendment is debatable.

10

Committees, Councils, and Boards

1001. High Authority Bodies

A large organization usually finds it necessary to establish subordinate bodies to assist in the society's conduct of business. These smaller bodies are of two classes:

1. Committees to study, deliberate, investigate, and/or work with other agencies; committees then submit reports to the parent body
2. Executive bodies having considerable autonomy, usually elected or representative assemblies, known variously as councils, commissions, boards, trustees, managers, executive committees, and the like

Bodies of the first type (pure committees) are hereinafter referred to as "committees." Bodies of the second type are here called "executive boards and similar high authority bodies."

The essential differences are: A committee is generally appointed; an executive board is generally elected. A committee has no authority to act in the name of the parent association; an executive board does. A committee is usually an annual body, terminating either at the end of the fiscal year or at the completion of its mission; an executive board is generally a continuous or overlapping body. A committee has a budget granted by the parent organization. An executive board usually has authority to make appropriations for itself from the organization's treasury, whereas a committee is not empowered to encumber or commit the funds of the parent organization. See 1318 for further details.

COMMITTEES

1002. Types of Committees

Committees may be classified in two ways:

1. In terms of their duration and survival
2. In terms of the source of their authority

(a) A committee appointed for a specific occasion only is a "select" or *ad hoc* committee. Its life comes to an end when it brings in the report required of it, or when it otherwise accomplishes its mission. An *ad hoc* committee appointed by an executive board or other high authority body expires when the term of the executive board or other authority comes to an end. The new executive board might want different personnel on its *ad hoc* or select committees.

A committee which has a term longer than that of the president is called a "standing committee" in some organizations, a "permanent" or "continuing" committee in others. Thus, the president may have a one-year term, whereas committeemen may be appointed to two-, three-, or four-year terms. This arrangement is common and its purpose is to give the committee stability and opportunity to accomplish long range objectives. Unfortunately the phrase "standing committee" is also used to describe a short-term committee—one appointed for only a year or for the duration of an annual meeting. In most American voluntary organizations, such committees are known as "annual committees." A committee that has a long range function should remain "standing" through changes in administration and thus should be a continuing (or "standing") committee with considerable overlap between terms of members. On the other hand, a committee with a function specifically related to the year's program should be created, or at least appointed, anew each year. For example, a committee on program, a committee on nominations, a committee on the annual convention, are bodies which should be annual (one-year) committees.

A committee appointed for a specific task is a special, *ad hoc*, or select committee.

(b) Some committees draw their authority specifically from the constitution or bylaws of the organization. They are "constitutional" committees. Their functions, term of office, and method of selection are usually laid down in the bylaws or constitution. They are not creatures of the executive board but have quasi-independent constitutional status. Most committees, however, are not listed in the constitution or bylaws. They were created by resolution or motion—either made on the floor at a general meeting or by decision of the executive board or corresponding high authority body. Such committees are "derivative" rather than "constitutional" committees; that is, they derive their existence and their power from some other body, not from the constitution. A derivative committee is a creature of the body which established it, and its function, personnel, term of office, and authority can be curtailed by that body.

1003. Creation of Committees

Unless established by the constitution or bylaws, a committee is created by resolution or motion on the floor, at a general membership meeting, or at a session of an executive board or similar agency. Often this is done indirectly: a matter comes up, and a motion is made to refer it to a committee. It then appears that no existing committee is appropriate, so the motion is amended (or reworded) to the effect that "this matter be referred to a special (select, *ad hoc*, standing) committee of four (or five or eight), to be named by the president, with instructions to study (or investigate, or draft resolutions) and report at the next meeting (or at the annual meeting)."

Sometimes, a narrow matter is referred to a special committee in the manner just described; then, during debate on it, it appears that this is part of a larger issue and that there ought to be a committee to make a more general study. In this case, the original motion is withdrawn, and a new primary motion is prepared creating this new committee; and then the matter is referred to it.

In any event, a motion creating a committee should include (1) size of committee, (2) method of appointment, (3) mission of committee, (4) whether any special authority to act is being granted, (5) whether any special funds are being allocated, and (6) first reporting date.

1004. Committee Personnel

(a) In most organizations, the president names all committee personnel. There is usually specific authority for this in the organization's bylaws or constitution. However, even if the constitution is silent on this, the president has an inherent right to name committee personnel unless the organization (either as a general rule or for the occasion) makes other provision. The president is the policy-executing officer of the association and committees are simply his advisers and assistants in that program. Executive boards and committees which partake of the nature of boards, commissions, councils, and so forth are usually elected rather than appointed.

(b) Every organization has a right to select committee personnel by election on the floor of a meeting. (In rare instances, the constitution might specifically limit committee-appointing authority to the president; and then the organization could only nominate members for the president to appoint to the committee.) However, it is usually considered wasteful to name committee personnel by this unwieldy process, since it would require nominations from the floor (or by petition), written ballot, or motions to fill vacancies by naming specific members.

(c) In some organizations, the president's nominees for certain committees must be approved by the general membership or by the executive board or similar high authority body.

Under these conditions, the president announces his panel and then entertains a motion that these nominations be confirmed. This is a primary motion, and is debatable and voted on like any other primary motion, except that this time a tie vote passes the motion. (This is true even if it takes the president's vote to make it a tie.)

(d) There is a long parliamentary tradition to the effect that whoever makes a motion to create a committee is "entitled" to be named chairman of it. In many cases this works out well because the motion is made by a member with special interest in and knowledge of the subject. However, the president is well within his rights in ignoring this tradition if it is apparent that the maker of the motion would be an unwise choice for committee chairman.

(e) The authority naming the committee personnel also designates who will be chairman. If this is not done, the first one named is temporary chairman and the committee selects a chairman at its first meeting.

(f) Occasionally a president names only the chairman of a committee and asks him to select the people he wants to work with. This is a proper procedure, but the chairman should be careful to clear all names with the president before they are announced and should make the appointments on behalf of, and as the surrogate of, the president.

(g) Unless the constitution or bylaws say so, the president is not an automatic or ex officio member of all committees.

(h) An ex officio member of a committee loses that status when he ceases to hold the office that entitled him to the ex officio seat.

(j) If he is otherwise eligible, an ex officio member of a committee has the same voting and other rights as any other committee member. But if he is not a member of the parent organization (or is otherwise ineligible) his ex officio seat cannot confer any new rights on him. For instance, the state health officer might be an ex officio member of a medical society's committee on public health. If this health officer were not a member of the medical society, then he cannot be a voting member of any of its committees. So he would be an ex officio nonvoting member of this committee. But if he were a member of the parent medical society, then he would be a full voting member of this committee by reason of his ex officio seat even though he was not personally named as a member of that committee.

(k) A committee may have advisers, legal counsel, consultants, and other staff personnel. It is better to use this status rather than an ex officio seat when it is desired to place someone on a committee by reason of technical knowledge connected with his official activities. For example, a committee on zoning in a civic association might want one or more real estate experts as advisers or consultants; but there is no need to make them ex officio members. Again, a medicolegal committee to a bar association would want physicians as consultants to the committee but not as ex officio members.

(m) The extent to which a committee is authorized to hire and pay staff personnel, such as clerks, typists, and the like, should be formulated in advance. In many organizations, this kind of staff work is done through the office of the executive secretary or corresponding salaried official in the society's headquarters. But thought should be given to this in blueprinting the operating plan for a committee.

1005. Motions To Commit

A matter is referred to a committee by a motion such as: ". . . that this be referred to the XYZ Committee," or "to the appropriate committee for study and report," or words to that effect. The motion to commit must take precedence over the primary motion to which it applies, and of course to any amendments thereto. But while the motion to commit is pending, the matter (including the proposed commitment) can be disposed of by tabling, closing debate, postponement, recess, or adjournment. This precedence of motions is illustrated by the following example:

A makes a motion to purchase an electronic computing machine for the office. This is seconded. It is the primary motion.

B moves that this be referred to the Committee on Building and Grounds, and this is seconded. This is the motion to commit, and it is in order.

Before it can be voted on, *C* moves to amend the primary motion by adding to it the phrase: "to cost not more than $500." This motion is out of order, because a motion to commit takes precedence over a motion to amend; therefore the lower-ranking motion (to amend) cannot be received while the motion to commit is pending. So the chair says that the motion to amend will have to wait until the motion to commit is disposed of. If the group wants to add a price limit, they can do it by instructions to the committee if the motion to commit passes: or by an amendment to the primary motion if the motion to commit fails.

Before the motion to commit can be voted on, *D* moves to lay it on the table. Now a motion to commit, as such, cannot be laid on the table, though of course the primary motion can be tabled. So *D*'s motion means that he wants to lay on the table the entire question of buying the computing machine. This is in order since a motion to lay on the table has the right of way over any motion except one related to adjournment or recess. And the motion to table is not debatable.

The chair therefore calls for an immediate vote on the motion to table the question. If it passes, the motion to commit is automatically vacated. The whole matter of buying a computing machine is tabled, and remains in limbo until someone recalls it. If the motion to table fails, then discussion is resumed on the motion to commit. If this passes, the question is committed for study by the Committee on Building and Grounds, and, for this meeting, that ends it. *C* could, as a new primary motion, move that we send to the committee an instruction to the effect that no more than $500 be spent for the machine. However, this is really unnecessary, since the committee would not usually have the authority to buy the machine but only to recommend; and the matter of cost could be discussed then.

1006. Parliamentary Features of the Motion To Commit

The motion to commit (that is, to refer to a committee) is debatable, subject to limited amendment, and may not be laid on the table:

(a) Debatable. In theory, debate is on the wisdom of referring the matter to a committee rather than on the merits of the question. In practice, it may be impossible to isolate one subject from the other, so that in most voluntary assemblies the motion to commit is fully debatable.

(b) Amendable with respect to the committee to which the question is to be referred or with respect to instructions to such committee. This practically reopens the question on its merits, however, so that to all intents and purposes the motion to commit is fully amendable.

(c) Subject to having all debate halted by a motion to close debate (previous question). Unless otherwise specified, this would shut off debate only on the motion to commit, not on the main motion (see 505).

(d) Not subject to being laid on the table, except when the entire question is laid on the table. However, a motion to table a primary matter *is* in order while a motion to commit is pending. So the motion "to table it" made under those circumstances is presumed to mean a motion to table the entire question (see 805).

(e) Reconsiderable. If the motion fails, a vote to reconsider is unnecessary since the same effect could be achieved by simply renewing the motion to commit after some additional debate or additional business has intervened. If the motion passes, it may be reconsidered, provided the motion to reconsider is made at the same meeting as the motion to commit. If it is desired at a later date to rescind the commitment, this is done by discharging the committee (see 1017).

1007. Implementation of Motion To Commit

If a motion to commit is passed in its simplest form, without specifying the committee, its authority, or its reporting date, the chair may issue instructions on those points. He announces, "This will be referred to the Committee on Gadgets and Gimmicks with instructions to report their recommendations within sixty days"; or, "I will appoint a special committee to investigate this matter. I'll announce the personnel of that committee before the end of this meeting." If no one objects to the chair's assumption of this authority, it is considered ratified by silent (general) assent. If someone does object, the chair invites motions to implement the action: motions specifying the name of the committee, for instance, or its instructions, its reporting date, its general authority. Or, all this may be done *before* the motion to commit is passed, by calling for amendments or substitute motions spelling out these details.

1008. Committee Procedure

Committees generally follow the procedure described in 104(e). Sessions rarely conform to rigid parliamentary procedure. The chairman calls the first meeting of a new committee. If he fails to do so, any committeeman may ask the president to remind the chairman of the need for an early meeting.

(a) Committees hold two types of meetings: hearings and deliberations. A *hearing* is an inquiry into facts. Every member of the parent association has a right to attend, except when the chairman (or committee majority) has declared an executive session. The committee is under no obligation to notify every member of the parent association of the time and place of a hearing. Any member may be asked to give information. A *deliberative* session is a forum where the resolutions, recommendations, and reports are hammered out. These are generally closed meetings.

(b) In committee meetings it is customary to allow members to talk with about the same informality as would be observed in a social gathering in a living room. A chairman could, of course, insist that no one speaks unless he has risen and been recognized, but this is unusual for a committee. It is not the practice to limit or close debate in a committee meeting, though the committee by two-thirds vote may decide to do so. A committee chairman (unlike the presiding officer in an auditorium-type assembly) is an active discussant on the merits of matters before the committee. If committee attendance is very uneven, it may happen that actions taken at one session are reversed by those present at the next meeting and then this is re-reversed by the original group who come to the third meeting. This is prevented by firm leadership, by taking a mail poll of all members, and/or by having one final session at which every committee member is expected to be present, or bound in advance (beyond right of complaint) by the decision of those who *are* present.

(c) In scientific and voluntary societies, committees may meet by mail or by telephone conference. Thus, the chairman could propound a series of questions and circulate them among committee members, coordinating the answers. He could then shape a report which integrates as many of the views as possible and circulate that among the members for their signatures. While this is not a good substitute for the personal meeting it may be the only practical way to hold a committee meeting if the committeemen are scattered in the four corners of the continent.

(d) A majority of the members constitutes a quorum. If much of the work is done by mail, however, the quorum may be waived. And if repeated calls fail to get a quorum, the members who do attend may prepare a report and have it later ratified by the absent members.

1009. Subcommittees

A committee may by vote create a subcommittee consisting entirely of members of the parent committee. It would be proper to ask persons with special skills to advise the subcommittee or act as liaison personnel for it, though of course (unless they happened to be members of the parent committee) they could not actually be "members" of the subcommittee. The subcommittee is subordinate to, and functions on behalf of, the parent committee. A subcommittee's report is directed to, and is then consolidated with, the report of the parent committee. A subcommittee is a highly informal body in most organizations, and is usually not given any official recognition (as a subcommittee) by the organization itself. Occasionally, for historical reasons, a subcommittee may, over the years, develop considerable autonomy.

COMMITTEE REPORTS

1010. Committee Reports in General

The consummation of a committee's work is, usually, its report. It is this, rather than action, which is the measure of a committee. (There are certain exceptions, such as arrangements committees, program committees, publication committees, and the like where the committee's work is visible in deeds rather than in words. For most committees, however, the report is the climax of the year's activities.) Reports represent views of the *majority* of the committee. Strictly speaking, therefore, there can be no minority reports (see 1015) though there may be memoranda of minority views entered into the record. The report is approved by the committee and then presented to the parent association, usually by the committee chairman. The association then takes some action on the report—adopts it, approves it, changes it, rejects it, recommits it, files it, agrees with it, or votes to implement it (see 1013).

1011. Form of Report

The report is prepared in writing, and signed by the chairman, with the names of other committeemen typed in. If one or more minority members refuse to be associated with the report, their names are not affixed to the body of the report; instead an additional paragraph headed "dissenting members" is used, and their names are listed there. These minority members may then prepare a memorandum of views and submit it through the same channels as the report, or they could present the minority views by asking for the floor during discussion of the committee report. The report may be written in either the first person plural or the third person: "We recommend that . . . in our opinion . . . ," and the like, or "Your Committee finds that . . . recommends that . . . in the opinion of the Committee," and so on. For these purposes the word "committee" is considered a singular noun. Some sticklers insist that the report must always be written in the third person, but this is unnecessarily rigid. The report may be written with stiff formality, divided into numbered paragraphs, and it may bristle with official-sounding words, or it may be written in a breezy and informal style. The most usable report is one in which the conclusions and recommendations are given first, and the background material and comment are grouped in a subsequent section. This permits the reader to get the sense of the report at once and makes it easier to vote on it. The standard conventional phrases may be used, such as, "Your ABC Committee herewith respectfully submits . . ." or "The Committee on XYZ begs leave to report that . . . ," and so forth. But these stereotypes are entirely unnecessary and most voluntary organizations today dispense with them. The complimentary close ("Respectfully submitted"), however, is still in general use.

A lengthy report is divided into logical sections, such as "Recommendations," "Background," "Findings," and the like. Recommendations always appear at or near the beginning of the report. They should be separately numbered, and—if logical to do so—grouped in some functional way. This permits the organization to debate and vote on each operating part of the report as a separate item.

1012. Presenting the Report

(a) In the standard "order of business" and in the typical agenda, committee reports are scheduled immediately after reading of minutes and before old (unfinished) business is taken up. If this is the rule, the chair will call for committee reports at that time. If there is no provision for reports in the society's "order of business" (or if the chair forgets to call for them), the committee representative (usually the chairman) will notify the meeting (usually under the "new business" schedule) that his committee is ready to report.

(b) Ordinarily, the chair will simply tell him to proceed and make his report. If anyone objects, the chair will ask, "Shall this report be received now?" and this becomes an undebatable motion. (It need not be seconded, since the member who is ready to give the report has seconded it by implication.) If the presiding officer is in doubt as to the wisdom of receiving the report, he could say to the committee chairman, "I don't think we should receive this now, but, if you wish, you may make a motion to that effect." A persistent committee chairman will then move "that the report be received now." This requires a second and is debatable as to the propriety of reporting at this time (not debatable on the merits of the main question). If passed by majority vote, the report is read. If defeated, it is not read until a more appropriate time. Dilatory motions (such as "lay on the table") are not applied to a motion to receive a report, since the same effect is accomplished by voting "no" on the motion to receive at this time.

(c) All this is unusual in a community or technical society. Nearly always the report is received by general assent. A *motion* to receive the report is unnecessary. Indeed, if it is made after the report has been read, the motion is an absurdity. The group has already received the report.

1013. Acting on the Report

When a report is presented, what action can the parent association take? The motions that are made to dispose of a report include the following (some of which are unnecessary or improper):

(a) APPROVING ACTIONS:

	received
	accepted
I move that the report be:	adopted
	approved
	implemented by (or put into action)
	spread upon the records

(b) DISAPPROVING, EMENDATORY, OR DILATORY ACTIONS:

	rejected
	returned to the committee for further study
	committed to the XYZ Committee for further study
I move that the report be:	
	laid on the table without action
	divided, and that items 1, 2, 3 be accepted, while items 4 and 5 be . . . filed

(c) The best general rule is to *adopt* recommendations or resolutions and to *accept* findings or summaries of background data. Here is what these words actually mean:

1. *To Receive:* This means to listen to the report. It has no implication of accepting. If in fact the report has already been read, it is useless to make a motion to receive it. The motion is in order only when some question has been raised as to whether the report should or should not be read at this time (see 1012(c)).

2. *To Accept:* To accept a report means that the committee has satisfactorily completed its mission and that the report is acceptable in form. To accept a report does *not* mean that all the recommendations are endorsed. It *does* mean that the organization is taking responsibility for the statements of *findings* and *facts*. The motion "to accept" is the proper one for a report which (or that part of a report which) recites facts, findings, and background data only. It is *not* appropriate for disposing of recommendations.

3. *To Adopt:* This is to agree with the *recommendations*. The parent organization adopts as its own the recommendations of the committee. If a report requires no affirmative action by the association, there is no need to adopt it; it will be sufficient to accept it. (For example, the report of the auditors that the treasurer's books are in good shape. This

report is accepted, not adopted.) When a committee makes specific recommendations, a separate adopting motion should be made for each separately numbered recommendation. Then when the motion to adopt is passed, the effect is to make the recommendation an official action of the organization.

If the recommendation involves the expenditure of money, a motion to adopt the recommendation is ordinarily sufficient to authorize the treasurer to disburse that money. Sometimes in the charter or in the practice of an organization, a specific motion is needed to authorize appropriation of a specific number of dollars (or not to exceed a certain number of dollars) for a specific purpose. If this is so, the motion "to adopt" should be followed by, or amended by, a motion to authorize the appropriation.

4. *To File:* The effect of this is merely to make the report a matter of record without expressing opinion on it. It is appropriate for reports which simply recite facts or findings on which no action is needed. It is also used to express mild disapproval or disappointment with the report if circumstances do not warrant a more vigorous dissent.

5. *To Approve:* In modern usage, reports are seldom "approved." The verb "accept" or "adopt" (as explained above) is less ambiguous and should be used. To approve a report is to accept the findings and to adopt the recommendations. It puts the organization on record as endorsing the report in all its aspects.

Since "to approve" does bind the organization to adopting the recommendations, the word "approve" should not be used unless this is clear. Some members may vote for this motion without realizing that they are implementing the recommendations. Either the phrase "to approve" should be avoided or, before he calls for a vote, the chair should make it clear that an affirmative vote specifically binds the organization to certain actions, positions, or expenditures.

6. *To Implement:* Actual wording depends on the recommendation. Suppose the Hillside Hotel has offered a contract for the next convention and the committee endorses this. The motion then is: "Move that the President and Treasurer be authorized to sign the contract with the Hillside Hotel as recommended by the Committee on Arrangements."

Or, to take another example, suppose the committee had studied a legislative bill, S-1313, and recommended a resolution condemning it. However, by this time the bill has passed both houses and is on the Governor's desk. Here the implementing resolution would be "Move that the Governor be urged to veto S-1313 for the reasons stated in the report of the Legislative Committee."

7. *To Spread upon the Records:* This is usually attached to one of the other motions (though it could be made later and independently). The wording is: "Move that this report be accepted and spread upon the records." It means that the entire verbatim text of the report is entered into the minutes of the meeting. (Ordinarily the minutes will show that the committee reported and the report was disposed of in a certain way, but will not spell out the entire text of the report unless very short.)

The motion "to spread upon the records" is, in modern meetings, used largely as a kind of courtesy. Thus, in adopting a resolution of sorrow at the death of a member, or a resolution of praise for a member who has done an outstanding job, or an accolade for a member, officer, or employee who has reached an anniversary—on occasions like these, the complimentary phrases or the condolences may be "spread upon the records."

1014. If No Motion Is Made

Sometimes, after a report has been read, there is dead silence. The reader of the report (or some other member of the committee) should have sense and alertness enough to make the appropriate implementing motion (see list in 1013(a)). If no one makes the motion the chair has these alternatives:

1. "If there is no objection," he could say, "I shall order this report filed." (See 1013(c)(4) for effect of this.) If there is still no motion, then the filing is approved by silent assent and becomes official.

2. Or he could say, "The Chair will now entertain a motion to accept the findings of this committee" (or "to adopt the recommendations," if more appropriate). By this time it is

probable that some member will oblige with the motion. If not, all the chair can say is, "Hearing no motion for any other disposition, I order the report filed."

1015. Minority Views

One or more members of a committee may dissent from the report as a whole or from certain parts of it. The report, as approved by a majority of the committee, is *the* report. The minority may not submit an official competing report though they may make their dissent known. This can be done in either of the following ways:

(a) They can prepare and sign a memorandum of dissent. Here they point up the reasons for their disagreement, and their alternative recommendations. After the committee (majority) report has been heard, the chairman (or whoever is reading the report) could say: "I have here a memorandum of minority views, and if there is no objection, I shall read it." (If anyone does object, the chair calls for a vote on a motion "to receive the views of the committee minority.")

(b) The committee minority could wait until the motion has been made to accept, adopt, or approve the report. Then, in the debate thereon, spokesmen for the minority could present their views, urging that the motion to accept (adopt) the report be defeated. If the motion to accept, adopt, or approve the report is defeated, then the minority spokesman could make a motion embodying his group's recommendation, which then becomes a primary motion. He might have to wait until the "new business" part of the agenda; but the chair would be justified in hearing this motion in connection with the "reports" part of the schedule. If a motion "to file" the committee report was passed, the minority could still move some contrary action, since the motion "to file" was not a blanket approval of the committee report.

(c) Some parliamentary authorities allow the organization to vote on the minority views before they have a chance to vote on the majority report. This is done by a motion to substitute the minority view for the committee report. One author even says that if this "motion to substitute" is passed, the "minority report becomes the report of the committee." This would seem to be absurd on the face of it. The report of the majority is the report of the committee, and no parliamentary gimmick can subsequently change that fact. Furthermore, the motion to substitute is, in effect, a motion to amend. But it is a matter of parliamentary common sense, as well as common practice, to forbid a motion to amend if it has the effect of simply negativing the primary motion. Generally that is what a minority view does: it would substitute the negative of the proposition for the affirmative. For example:

A seven-man committee considers whether our club should affiliate with The County League of Citizens Associations. Four think we should and three say "no." The committee report concludes with a recommendation that we affiliate. The minority view is, "We should retain our complete independence and therefore should reject the invitation to affiliate."

The committee report (favoring affiliation) is read and it is now moved that we "adopt this recommendation." (In other words: the motion, in effect, is that we affiliate.)

The only honest and clear-cut way of disposing of this is to hear all points of view and then vote yes or no on adopting the recommendation. Source authorities suggest that a member could, during discussion, move to substitute the minority view (rejecting affiliation) for the main motion to affiliate. This is objectionable on three counts:

1. If it is construed as an amendment, it comes under the ban on amendments which negative the primary motion.

2. If it is a straight substitution, one motion for another, it is not in order unless the original mover agreed to the substitution—most unlikely contingency if the majority spokesman made the motion.

3. In any event it is highly confusing. In the case cited, the chair, hearing the substitute motion, would have to say, "All in favor of the substitute motion say 'aye.'" And half of those who call "aye" would assume that they are voting to affiliate instead of the opposite!

Accordingly, it would seem to be bad practice to allow the minority view to replace the majority report by way of a substitute motion. The procedure above (1015(b)) would seem to be the simplest, least confusing, and most clear-cut way of offering the views of the minority.

1016. Changing a Report

The organization is sovereign and can dispose of a report any way it wants. It cannot, however, make a substantive change and call it (as amended) the committee report. It would be, at best, an *amended* committee report. *The* report of the committee is as it was officially read, and, if it is significantly changed, it is no longer *the* report of the committee. This is subject to two contingencies:

1. A committee might change its mind after it filed a report—assuming that the committee was not dissolved at the time of the report. If this happens, the records should show that on such a date the committee filed a report and that at a later and specified date it filed an amended report.

2. Some large organizations submit reports of standing committees to reference committees as explained in 1038 below. The assembly (i.e., the total organization) then votes on the reference committee's report, not on the report of the standing committee. The parent body should have a specific rule on the reference committees' right to amend a report of a standing committee. In some societies, the reference committee can recommend only acceptance or rejection of the report of the standing committee; in other organizations, it may change the form or wording but not the substance of the primary report. In still other bodies, the reference committee may make significant changes in the report. If the bylaws or procedural codes are silent on this point, it is assumed that the reference committee has a free hand to modify the primary committee's report.

If the society has no reference committees, how then can it change all or part of a report? It can reject certain parts and take action thereon contrary to the recommendation, and it can accept and implement the other parts. For example:

The committee has recommended a program for improving the health of automobile drivers. They suggest (1) biennial physical examination of all drivers, (2) automatic disqualification of any driver who has ever had a heart attack, (3) a $5 fee for the routine examination of the driver, the fee to be paid by the state, but the cost of the license renewal to be increased by $5 to provide the funds, and (4) drivers with color-blindness to be forbidden to drive at night.

The parent organization likes recommendation (1); they want to amend (2) by adding "if an electrocardiogram shows unmistakable evidence of myocardial damage"; they are opposed to (3) but they favor (4).

The organization cannot amend the report to conform to this. The report is as it was offered. The organization can do either of these things:

1. The slower but less confusing method would be to adopt a motion "to recommit this matter to the committee with instructions to delete any reference to fees for examinations or charges for licenses, and with further instructions to limit the disqualification for heart disease to those drivers who have had electrocardiographic evidence of myocardial damage."

2. A quicker, but sometimes confusing method, is to have each of the four recommendations voted on separately. Recommendations (1) and (4) would then be adopted, recommendations (2) and (3) would be rejected, and a new resolution touching on the disqualifying of cardiac patients would be offered and adopted as the sense of the society on this point. Net effect of this would be to place the organization on record as it wanted to be recorded, but the report of the committee would not be amended. If the proceedings are published verbatim, the committee report as originally presented would be included.

1017. Dissolution of and Discharging of Committees

(a) A *derivative* committee is a creature of the organization or body which created it, and the committee can be abolished by the same body. It will be recalled that a committee which derives its authority from a resolution or motion is a "derivative" committee, by contrast with one that is mentioned in the constitution or bylaws. A constitutional committee cannot be abolished except by amending the constitution, but any committee not mentioned in the constitution or bylaws is a derivative committee and, as such, can be abolished by the authority which created it. This is true even though there may be on the committee some members with long terms yet to run. They have no vested right to such terms of service.

(b) Any committee may be relieved of a specific assignment by a motion to discharge. This does not abolish the committee. The wording follows this pattern: "I move that the Committee on Buildings and Grounds be discharged from any further consideration of plans for remodeling the second floor." A majority vote is sufficient to discharge a committee of its responsibility for a specific project. (One popular parliamentary authority says that this requires a two-thirds vote since it rescinds previous action. The analogy strikes me as faulty; and I know of no other authority which insists on a two-thirds vote before relieving a committee of a project. Such a motion does not impair anybody's "rights" and therefore there seems to be no logic in the two-thirds rule proposed by this parliamentarian.)

A motion to discharge the committee may, if the sponsors wish, include a plan for considering the question elsewhere. For example: "I move that the responsibility for drafting a resolution on health insurance be transferred from the Committee on Resolutions to the Committee on Economic Problems of Practice." Or: "I move that we here and now consider the plans for a permanent home for the Association and relieve the Committee on Headquarters of that assignment."

There is no need for using the exact form, "the committee be discharged from any further consideration of . . ." This is the conventional wording, but it is perfectly proper to ask that the "committee be relieved of this or that assignment," or "the responsibility for considering XYZ be transferred from the AB Committee to the CD Committee."

(c) A constitutional committee cannot be relieved of a specific constitutional function, except by amending the constitution. However, the committee could be relieved of certain aspects of its function. Suppose the constitution provides that: "All applications for membership are referred to a Membership Committee, which will report its recommendations on such applications at the next annual meeting." There is no way of relieving the committee of this responsibility by any simple motion. However, if the committee has forfeited the confidence of the association, or if it has delayed so long as to have impeded the growth of the society, then it can be by-passed by some such resolution as, "If the Committee on Membership holds an application more than 30 days without report thereon, it will be assumed that the application is approved." Then a special credentials committee could be created to study the credentials of applications for membership. In practice, such parliamentary maneuvering is unnecessary. If the parent body indicates that it has lost confidence in the committee, most of the committeemen will get the message and resign.

(d) An *ad hoc,* special, or select committee terminates when its mission is accomplished. No special resolution is needed. If a committee is appointed for a specific purpose, then the acceptance (approval, adoption, or filing) of its final report is its last activity and its life automatically terminates at that time. If the matter is recommitted, then the life of the committee is extended. The parent body can vote to extend the life of any temporary committee or vote to make it a permanent committee.

(e) As a general rule, a committee created by an executive board or other high authority body does not survive any substantial change in the membership of that body. If following an election (or end of a year) more than two thirds of the membership of the board has changed, then its subordinate *ad hoc* and special committees should resign to permit this substantially new board to have its own immediate committee personnel. This does not apply to constitutional committees or to committees appointed for long term projects with the advance understanding that they will survive changes in administration.

(f) A derivative (that is, not constitutionally created) committee can be stripped of all duties but still left alive by a motion, or series of motions, relieving the committee of all specific assignments, and/or transferring its assignments to other committees, or discharging it from further consideration of any matter currently before it.

(g) Between the time a matter is referred to a committee and the time it starts to study it, the assignment can be taken from

139

the committee by a motion to reconsider the motion to commit. It could also be accomplished by rescinding the motion to commit. The same effect is also achieved by a motion to transfer the project from this committee to another.

(h) A committee terminates individual meetings and sessions by adjournment. But its last meeting is terminated by a motion "to rise." When a committee votes to rise, it votes to abolish itself, or to recognize that its service is coming to an end.

BOARDS AND COMMISSIONS

1018. Boards and Commissions: Functions

In professional and technical societies, it is customary to establish a board or commission rather than a committee to perform such functions as:

1. Operate a long-term or permanent program or project, for example, a board of examiners to qualify scientists or specialists, an editorial or publications board to publish a periodical, or an accrediting body
2. Supervise an award or prize-giving program, for example, an annual cash or medal award, the selection of a prize-winning paper, or the appointment of a commemorative lectureship
3. Take control of or jurisdiction over the organization's major assets, for example, its investment program, its journal, its headquarters building
4. Coordinate with an outside organization in a common long-term project which requires joint meetings of representatives (delegates, commissioners, or the like) from both organizations

1019. Boards and Commissions: Designating Personnel

The enabling resolution usually indicates how personnel are selected. Four methods are available: (1) nominated by president, subject to approval of executive board or general membership; (2) appointed by president; (3) elected by general membership or by executive board; or (4) self-perpetuating; that is, when a vacancy occurs, the surviving members of the commission or board select a person to fill the vacancy. Sometimes certain named staff personnel or officers of the parent association might also be designated as ex officio members of the board or commission.

If the board has authority to raise funds, or if its expenditures are not accountable to the parent body, then the membership of the commission (or board) should never be self-perpetuating. For example, a board or commission which publishes a journal might retain control over income from advertising; one which inspects institutions or agencies might be authorized to retain the fees it charges, and so on. If under these circumstances the membership were self-perpetuating, the board or commission would soon become completely independent of and beyond the control of the parent organization.

1020. Boards and Commissions: Term of Office

Since stability is a major reason for establishing a board rather than a committee, the terms of office are generally long: three to five years, as a rule. To avoid abrupt changes, it is common to provide for overlapping terms; for example, a six-member commission, each member serving three years, two seats becoming vacant each year.

1021. Boards and Commissions: Operations

In general, the procedures applicable to committees (detailed above) are also appropriate for commissions and boards. However, the latter generally have a greater degree of autonomy. They may have fund-raising powers and thus could conceivably be independent of the parent organization in terms of budget. More often, though devoid of fund-raising authority, they do have a moral or legal entitlement to certain funds allocated from the organization's treasury, and a fairly free hand in disbursing such funds. A board is sometimes permitted to issue newspaper releases and other public statements on its own authority. The parent organization, however, would have the right to curtail this. A board or commission usually has a freer hand in hiring staff personnel than does a committee. In spite of all this, it must be made clear to all concerned that in the last analysis the board or commission draws all its authority and status from the parent organization.

1022. Executive Board or Comparable Body

Under modern conditions, few organizations can hold general membership meetings more than eight to ten times a year —and usually less frequently. It accordingly becomes necessary to have some body which can administer the affairs of the organization in the long intervals between meetings. Such a body is known as a board of trustees (or "managers"), a council, an executive committee, an executive board, a comitia majora, comitia minora, house of delegates, an executive council, an assembly, or some other descriptive title. Frequently, even this body cannot meet as often as the business of the association requires, and out of it is distilled a smaller (and more frequently assembled) body. Thus, there might be a board of trustees which could have its own executive committee. The constitution generally sets up this type of executive board, indicating its composition, term of office, and powers. As a matter of parliamentary common sense, this executive board (by whatever title designated) must be considered the heir of all the association's powers in the intervals between meetings. The executive board is accountable for its actions at the next general membership meeting. However, as the agency entrusted with top leadership responsibility, the board must do anything (not expressly forbidden by the society's constitution) which is essential to the organization's welfare. Financial and other commitments, made in good faith by an executive board, cannot be repudiated by the general membership unless there was some provision in the society's constitution which the board violated in making the commitment. On the other hand, the general membership could adopt a policy with respect to future commitments which would bind the board thereafter. See 1318 for more details.

1023. Personal Representatives of the President

The president of an organization has no right to create a committee where none existed. He may—and usually does—have authority to name the members of a committee, provided the committee was already in existence or is being established by a resolution or motion. It may happen that the president wants a study made, a collaboration undertaken, or a project initiated; and perhaps no appropriate committee exists. If it is not convenient to ask the executive board to create such a committee, the president may appoint a personal representative to perform a task, make an inquiry, or bring in a report. For example, he could designate one or more persons to represent the organization at a meeting sponsored by some other group. Such a personal representative could not encumber the funds of the parent association, nor could he create new policy or issue press releases in the name of the organization, but he *could* convey *pro forma* greetings, participate in purely deliberative or ceremonial activities, and act as a reporting observer. Similarly, the president could ask two or three members to make an inquiry or investigation and to report to him. These personal representatives are not committees, but they perform some committee functions. Their report, indeed their entire activity, is validated only as approved by the president whose surrogate these members were.

COMMITTEE OF THE WHOLE

1024. Committee of the Whole: Composition

The committee of the whole consists of the entire membership, or, more exactly, of all the members who happen to be present at the meeting which "resolves into" the committee of the whole.

1025. Committee of the Whole: Function

A meeting translates itself into a "committee of the whole" to discuss a subject with more informality and freedom than would be possible in an assembly which has to follow formal rules of order. The give and take of informal committee discussion does not adapt itself well to a system of asking for the floor, being recognized, being restricted to one discussion of a motion, having statements spread on the record, and the like. Here are situations in which an organization might well resolve into a committee of the whole:

1. In discussing informally, intimately, and confidentially matters of considerable delicacy. Nonmembers are more readily excluded from a meeting of the committee of the whole than from a general membership meeting. And the spirit of free committee discussion is more appropriate for intimate conferring.

2. In discussing matters where it is felt unwise to have any detailed record of the debate. Only the conclusions (recommendations) of a committee of the whole are recorded, not the discussion.

3. In taking a preliminary sounding of the sense of the meeting a as guide to the subsequent drafting of resolutions. This is valuable, for example, in estimating in advance whether a proposed constitutional amendment is likely to obtain a two-thirds vote. It is helpful to those charged with the duty of wording an important resolution and who want some idea of the sense of the meeting before putting the words together.

4. In organizing a debate in which it is desired to avoid any dilatory motions, such as motions to postpone, to shut off debate, or to lay on the table. A committee of the whole assures full discussion without the matter being choked off by any dilatory or postponing motion.

1026. Committee of the Whole: When in Order

(a) A general membership meeting may resolve itself into committee of the whole at any time after a main motion or an amendment has been presented, and before it is voted on; except that if a motion to lay the matter on the table is pending, that motion must be disposed of before voting on whether to go into committee of the whole.

(b) In a meeting of an executive board or similar body, or at a meeting of any other committee, a motion to go into committee of the whole is unnecessary. The same result can be accomplished by going into executive session or by agreeing to consider the matter informally (see 104 and 105).

1027. Motion To Go into Committee of the Whole

The wording is "That this meeting now resolve itself into a Committee of the Whole for the purpose of considering XYZ"; or, more simply, "That we go into Committee of the Whole to consider XYZ." If desired, a time limit may be included, as "And that the Committee report at 3 P.M. today"; or "And that the Committee be in session not more than one hour."

A motion to go into Committee of the Whole is *not* in order if there is pending a motion to (1) adjourn, (2) lay on the table, or (3) postpone. Otherwise, it is always in order if a primary motion is pending. Technically, the motion should not be made until the primary matter (the one to be considered) has been formally moved and seconded. However, this step may be omitted if no one objects. That would work as follows:

The chair says that the next item on the agenda is deciding on a city for the next convention. A member, knowing that informal, off-the-record discussion is desirable, rises to say: "Mr. Chairman, I move that we resolve ourselves into a Committee of the Whole to consider the selection of our next convention city." Strictly speaking, he should first have made a motion that our next convention be held in Kenosha (or some other named city), had this seconded, and then moved to refer this to the committee of the whole. In practice, it is unnecessary to go through this formality unless someone insists on it. The member is allowed to make his motion (that we go into committee of the whole), and then the group can, by vote, decide whether they want to do that.

The motion ("that we resolve into Committee of the Whole") is debatable with respect to the wisdom of presenting the question to the committee of the whole. The chair does not allow extended debate on the merits of the main question because that would stultify the very purpose of having the committee of the whole. After the motion ("to go into Committee of the Whole") is made and seconded, but before it is voted on, it may be amended with respect to the scope of the subject to be considered in the committee. The motion to lay on the table is not in order with respect to the motion to commit; but a motion to lay on the table would have to be received if it applied to the primary question itself; and then this motion (to lay the whole matter on the table) would have to be voted on at once without debate. If carried, the whole primary question would be laid on the table. The motion to go into committee of the whole would simply atrophy from disuse. If it (motion to lay primary matter on table) was defeated, the motion to go into committee of the whole would then come up for vote.

1028. Process of Resolving into Committee of the Whole

(a) When the motion passes, the chair declares the meeting in recess to permit a sitting of the committee of the whole, the recess to terminate when that committee reports.

(b) He designates some member of the society to serve as chairman of the committee of the whole. The presiding officer of the main body (usually the president) vacates his seat as chairman. He may remain seated on the platform or may take a seat in the auditorium. (This is the more gracious way.)

(c) The new chairman (that is, chairman of the committee of the whole) takes the seat vacated by the president or chairman of the general meeting. In assemblies which like to follow the ancient forms, the chairman of the committee of the whole sits at the secretary's desk. The president's chair remains vacant as a symbol of the fact that the organization, as such, is not in session.

(d) The new chairman calls the committee of the whole to order. He invites nonmembers to leave the room (unless there is good reason to the contrary). He asks if the committee desires to elect its own chairman. (Usually there is dead silence, or cries of "no.") If so, nominations and election take place, and the chair changes again.

(e) The chair now restates the primary question and says the matter is open for debate.

1029. Procedure in Committee of the Whole

(a) The committee of the whole is a purely deliberative forum. It may take an informal vote to gauge the sense of the group. But it cannot pass any motions except:

1. To adopt its own report
2. To amend its report
3. To rise—that is, to adjourn and report

So, in a meeting of the committee of the whole, no matters may be laid on the table or postponed; motions to refer items to committees or subcommittees are out of order; new primary motions (except to amend or to report) are also out of order. Except as indicated below in 1032(c) it is improper to introduce a motion to shut off debate. If a member takes advantage of this by trying to filibuster, the chair interrupts to remind him that he has held the floor for a disproportionate time. The chair says he will receive a motion that the Committee rise unless the garrulous member stops talking. If a motion to rise is passed, this dissolves the committee. It may be the only way to silence a nonstop talker. Usually, though, such drastic action is not needed.

(b) The committee of the whole cannot discuss any matter unless it is germane to the topic for which the committee was convened. The chair rules on this, and his ruling is subject to appeal in the usual manner of an appeal from the chair (see 408).

(c) The chairman may participate freely and fully in the deliberations of the committee.

(d) The chair is justified in trying to appraise the "sense of the committee" by asking for a show of hands or a voice vote. This may be a necessary preliminary to preparing the committee's report. Indeed, if the report has many subdivisions, paragraphs, or sections it may be necessary to have repeated showing of hands or calls of "aye" or "no" in order to take soundings of the opinion of the members. This does not contravene the general rule that no matters (other than the report) are voted on at a session of the committee of the whole. These informal measurements of opinion are not recorded as votes, but are needed to guide the leadership of the committee in framing the report.

1030. Rising of the Committee of the Whole

The committee may recess briefly to permit the drafting of a report, and then reassemble to approve of it. Except for this occasion, a committee of the whole can neither adjourn nor recess. When it finishes its work, or when it tires of it, it votes "to rise." This motion when passed adjourns the meeting and dissolves the committee. If no report is being submitted, the form is simply: "I move that this Committee rise." If a report is prepared, the motion is: "I move that this Committee rise and report." This motion must be seconded, and is not debatable. As soon as it is passed, the original presiding officer takes the chair; the chairman of the committee of the whole resumes his seat in the auditorium.

The presiding officer says: "Is the Committee of the Whole ready to report?" and the chairman or other designated spokesman of the committee of the whole then rises to report.

1031. Resumption of Interrupted Meetings

By its very nature a committee of the whole is an *ad hoc* body, which loses all its momentum when it rises. Its session cannot be interrupted by any other than a momentary recess, or a recess long enough to permit framing a report. When it rises, the committee of the whole vanishes into history. If revived, it is a new body, not a continuation of the previous one. So, a new motion may be made "that we resolve ourselves into committee of the whole to consider again the matter of ABC." If this is done, it is a new committee of the whole.

1032. Reports and Records of the Committee of the Whole

(a) In practice, the person who was serving as secretary for the meeting will continue to perform a like function for the committee of the whole. In theory this is not the case because (1) the committee of the whole should have different officers from the general meeting to emphasize the fact that, in a parliamentary sense, they are different bodies; and (2) the transactions of the committee of the whole are not recorded, but only their report. If the same person was secretary to both bodies he might, as a matter of habit or momentum, continue to record the transactions of the committee of the whole. So the chairman of the committee of the whole may ask any other member to serve as "clerk" of the committee, or he may entertain nominations from the floor and have the committee elect a clerk. Usually this is absurdly dilatory, and either the regular secretary serves or the chairman appoints a clerk. In any event, minutes of the discussion are not recorded. Tentative motions, or motions short of their final form, are not recorded either.

One reason for a committee of the whole is to hear material off the record. When the sense of the meeting is being gauged, the clerk—or the chairman—must keep some record, usually informal, so that this appraisal can be used in preparing the report.

(b) When discussion comes to an end, the committee must prepare its report. If the sense of the meeting has been made clear, the chair or clerk can now assemble this and suggest the form and general content of the report, or the committee can recess briefly while the chairman and clerk, assisted by other members as designated, draft the report.

(c) The clerk then reads to the committee the text of the proposed report. This is debatable and amendable. At this point, a motion to close debate would be in order, and would be effective if passed by two-thirds vote. (The committee is now moving to the formal part of the mission, and the informal and free discussion of the prior phase is no longer appropriate.) This part of the committee's agenda follows standard parliamentary practice, so that eventually the committee adopts a report, and then a motion to rise and report.

(d) When the committee rises, the membership meeting instantly resumes. The first order of business is the report of the committee of the whole. Any person may be designated (by the committee's chairman) as spokesman. Usually the committee's chairman performs that function and it will be assumed that he will give the report unless the president is otherwise notified.

(e) The presiding officer asks: "Is the Committee of the Whole ready to report?" The chairman of (or other spokesman for) the committee of the whole then gives the recommendations agreed on by the committee. The minutes note this, and note what happens to the recommendation. The minutes indicate that the society did resolve into committee of the whole and who the chairman was.

The minutes do *not* reflect the debate or discussion during the committee phase of the meeting, nor do the minutes include any tentative forms of the report.

Usually, the report is then adopted immediately. The group now sitting as the organization had only a few moments ago, as a committee of the whole, adopted some recommendations. Presumably they will now ratify what they just agreed on. Theoretically, the meeting could fail to ratify under two conditions: (1) if the basic matter required a two-thirds vote and received only a majority vote in the committee of the whole; or (2) if many members left the hall after the committee of the whole had risen but before the general meeting had reassembled. To prevent the latter, the motion to accept the findings and/or to adopt the recommendation is undebatable and unamendable. A member says, "I move that the report of the Committee of the Whole be approved, that its findings be accepted, and its recommendations adopted," or words to that effect. And the presiding officer calls for an immediate vote. The report of the committee of the whole can be laid on the table only if another meeting is scheduled within the same fiscal year. If this is the last meeting of an annual convention, for instance, the motion to lay on the table would be the same as a motion to reject the report. If this is desired, it is accomplished by voting "no" on accepting the report. A decision to accept or reject the report is subject to reconsideration under the normal rules for reconsideration (see Chapter 11). Members who want to add amendments to the report can do so by proposing them as primary motions later.

UTILIZATION OF COMMITTEES

1033. Committee Check List

This check list will be useful to officers or society officials in making maximum utilization of committees. From time to time, the committees should be reviewed to determine if any can be abolished or consolidated. Certain activities now of uncertain assignment may, perhaps, be allocated to new committees. The list given in 1035 is probably unique. I have nowhere else seen an actual listing of the nontechnical (universal) committees which an organization might want. A scrutiny of the list (at the end of 1035) may disclose operational areas now neglected by the society. Conceivably the creation of an appropriate committee could enormously increase the usefulness of the organization to its members.

1034. Types of Committees

Committees are classed by mission, by term, by constitutional status, and by authority (see 1001, 1002, and 1003 for a review of these classifications). There is also another plane of classification:

1. Universal committees—those which might be found useful in any type of organization (for instance, a budget committee)
2. Idiomatic committees—those which are peculiar to one kind of organization, as, for example, a committee on mouth washes in a dental society

The list of idiomatic committees is practically infinite, since every kind of organization has its own special focus of interest. The maximum number of universal committees, however, is finite. The major ones are listed at the end of 1035.

1035. Universal Committees

No one society could have or should have all the committees listed below. Some would be useless in a particular association. This check list is intended as a stimulus to thinking and as a source of specific data about those committees. This is not an instruction to a constitution-writer. An organization should not have unnecessary committees.

Here is the list of committees:

1. Ad Hoc (see 1037)	24. Insurance
2. Arrangements	25. Legislation
3. Auditing	26. Library
4. Awards	27. Membership
5. Budget	28. Nominations
6. Building and Grounds	29. Personnel
7. On Committees	30. Policy
8. Constitution and Bylaws	31. Printing
9. Convention (or Annual Meeting)	32. Prizes (Awards)
10. Defense	33. Program
11. Editorial Board	34. Publication
12. Educational	35. Publicity
13. Entertainment	36. Public Relations
14. Ethics	37. Reading
15. Executive	38. Reference (see 1038)
16. Exhibits	39. Research
17. Finance	40. Resolutions
18. Grants	41. Standards
19. Grievances	42. Steering
20. History	43. Training
21. Honorary Membership	44. Ways and Means
22. Hospitality	45. Welfare
23. House	46. Of the Whole

1036. Functional Grouping of Committees

It is impossible for an organization, an officer, or an executive body to follow and act intelligently on the reports and recommendations of two dozen committees. Beyond this number, the committee structure is topheavy. No one can keep track of what is going on. Committee reports eat up too much time at meetings. After the first five or six have reported, the other chairmen simply drone on to a sleepy audience. If a review of the list above shows the need for more committees than can be conveniently handled, it may be advisable to group the committees so that reporting may be consolidated. For example, all committees concerned with funds, fund-raising, and fund-auditing could constitute one group; all committees concerned with physical arrangements for and at meetings could constitute another group, and so on. A single person could be designated chairman of the group of committees and report for that group. In fact, this departmental system could also be applied to committee budgeting, as indicated in 1609. For further examples of this grouping see 1039 below.

1037. Ad Hoc Committees

An *ad hoc* committee is one appointed for a specific task. Thus, a committee to study ways of raising funds (that is, a ways and means committee) would probably be a standing committee, because there would always be need for fund-raising. But a committee appointed to arrange a fund-raising dance or picnic next month would probably be an *ad hoc* committee, since it would have completed its mission by the end of the month. The organization might, of course, convert the same personnel from an *ad hoc* picnic or dance committee to a permanent ways and means committee.

Ad hoc committees could be used more often. Many societies are unfamiliar with the concept and as a result they overburden standing committees with short term projects, or they create standing committees when only temporary *ad hoc* committees are needed. Here are examples:

The clubhouse needs painting. The permanent (standing) house committee might look into this, or an *ad hoc* committee could be named for the sole purpose of determining whether a new paint job is needed, what the color should be, and what contractor can best handle it. The *ad hoc* committee could draw up specifications, receive bids, recommend a certain contractor. Once the job is over, the committee is discharged.

It is pointed out that, over the years, the society has developed many educational and training programs—some under the jurisdiction of a committee on training, some under the jurisdiction of individual officers. It is decided that it might be worthwhile looking into the possibility of consolidating all training and education activities into a sort of "department." An *ad hoc* committee is appointed to determine if this is practical, and if so, how the consolidation can be effected.

An *ad hoc* committee may be created by a resolution passed by the general membership; or by action of a board of trustees (executive committee or other high authority body).

1038. Reference Committees

A reference committee is a temporary body to which is referred the report of an officer, official, employee, or committee. In the usual month-by-month work of an organization, there is no need for a reference committee. The committee assigned to study or develop a project spends the necessary time on it, reports it to the assembly, the report is adopted or rejected, and that is that. However, at an annual meeting, convention, or similar body, a great many undigested recommendations are presented. It is impossible for the general assembly to absorb them all. Under these circumstances, each matter is referred to a reference committee which, typically, (1) holds hearings on the matter, (2) deliberates, usually in executive session, (3) frames a report agreeing with the recommendation, or disagreeing, or suggesting changes, (4) presents *its* report to the general body. Not all reference committees follow all these steps. In some organizations the hearings are open to anybody and in some they are very restricted. Sometimes a reference committee has no choice but to accept or reject the original report, and sometimes it is permitted to amend the report. Here are some examples of a reference committee in operation:

1. In his annual report, the treasurer has recommended that the fiscal year be changed so that it corresponds to the calendar year. This is a rather complicated matter, and the presi-

dent says: "The report of the Treasurer is referred to Reference Committee 2. All interested in being heard may appear before Reference Committee 2 at 8 P.M. today in the Elbow Room."

Reference Committee 2 has been assigned the reports of officers. When it meets, it examines all these reports, hears witnesses, and finally comes up with recommendations like this:

Reference Committee 2 reviewed the reports of officers. The President's report is an excellent but modest recital of the accomplishments of his administration. We commend the retiring President on his devotion to duty and congratulate him on his successful term of office.

The Secretary's report reflects the growth of the society in a very creditable way. The report was reviewed carefully and is commended as an example of excellent documentation.

The Treasurer's report with its attached statement from the auditors was reviewed. The auditors report that the books are in good condition. The Treasurer has suggested changing the fiscal year so that it coincides with the calendar year. Three members appeared at the hearing, one in favor of and two opposed to the proposed change. The change has the advantage of making the fiscal year correspond to the year for which dues are paid. But it has two serious disadvantages. It would mean a change of treasurers in the middle of the fiscal year and it would put the fiscal year out of cycle with the program year. Accordingly, your Reference Committee cannot endorse this proposal.

(The assembly, by voting to adopt this recommendation of the reference committee, in effect rejects the recommendation of the treasurer; or *vice versa*.)

2. The committee on membership has brought to the convention a recommendation that a new class of membership, junior membership, be created. This convention has several lettered reference committees, one of which, Reference Committee E, is assigned the reports of the Committees on Publication, Membership, and Personal Practices. The report of Reference Committee E might read:

Reference Committee E has examined the reports of three committees: those on Publication, on Membership, and on Personal Practices. The work of the Publication Committee speaks for itself in our excellent monthly News-Letter, and the committee has made no recommendations. The Committee on Membership urged that a new classification—

that of Junior Member—be established. Your Reference Committee agrees that this is a wise suggestion, for the reasons ably set forth by the Chairman of the Committee on Membership. No members appeared at the hearing in opposition to this . . .

The motion to adopt this recommendation of Reference Committee E has the effect of creating the new class of membership if this can be done without amending the constitution or bylaws. Otherwise, it has the effect of advising the membership that an amendment to this effect is desired and should be drafted.

If a reference committee is created long in advance, and has the reports to work on long in advance, it is a study committee rather than a reference committee. A study committee often holds hearings. A reference committee may be set up in advance of the convention, but does not ordinarily receive its documents until the opening of the annual meeting.

Reference committees may be identified by name, by letter, or by number. For example, here is one possible pattern:

Reference Committee A considers the report and recommendations of the Executive Committee.

Reference Committee B considers the reports and recommendations of the Officers.

Reference Committee C considers the reports and recommendations of the Standing Committees.

Reference Committee D considers the reports and recommendations of the *ad hoc* committees.

Reference Committee E considers motions and resolutions introduced as new business on the floor.

Here is another possible arrangement:

The Reference Committee on Internal Affairs will consider the reports of the Committees on Finance, Constitution, Building and Grounds, and Publication.

The Reference Committee on Community Contacts will consider the reports of the Committees on Legislation, Publication, and Awards.

The Reference Committee on Officers' Reports will consider the reports of the Officers.

Here is a third pattern:

Reference Committee Number 1 will consider reports of Officers.

Reference Committee Number 2 will consider reports of all Committees concerned with finance.

Reference Committee Number 3 will consider reports of all Committees concerned with internal operations other than financial.

Reference Committee Number 4 will consider reports of all other Committees.

Reference Committee Number 5 will consider resolutions and motions presented from the floor other than proposed amendments to the Constitution and Bylaws.

Reference Committee Number 6 will consider proposed amendments to the Constitution or to the Bylaws.

1039. Committee Departments

As indicated in paragraph 1036, it may be desirable to group committees into a few "departments." The funds might be allocated to the "department" ("committee group"), and the chairman could report to his group director (department chairman), and the latter would consolidate all these reports. Then at the general meeting, instead of listening to twenty-five or thirty-five committee reports, the assembly would hear from only three or four group chairmen or department directors.

Most of the grouping is done in connection with the technical (idiomatic) committees, where logical subject matter divisions suggest themselves. Thus, in a civic society, all committees concerned with schools could constitute one group; all concerned with sidewalks, zoning, and land use another; all concerned with taxes and government a third, and so on. In a medical or dental society, or in an association of lawyers or chemists, these idiomatic committees could be grouped by subspecialties.

The universal committees might be grouped in some such pattern as this:

Finance Group: Committees on Auditing, Budget, Investment, Finance, and Ways and Means

Housekeeping Group: Committees on Building, Grounds, House, Library, and Personnel

Public Relations Group: Committees on Ethics, Grievances, Publicity, Public Relations, and Legislation

Internal Operations Group: Committees on Arrangements, Program, Hospitality, Publication, and Membership

Certain committees might be exempted from the requirement of reporting through a department chairman or group director. An executive committee or nominating committee, for example, deals with material that goes directly to the general membership. This system of committee grouping is not used as widely as it could be. In these days of increasingly complex organizations, some such departmentalization appears to be necessary.

11

Second Thoughts: The Motion To Reconsider

1101. Reasons for Moving To Reconsider

There are two reasons for moving to reconsider previous action; and there is a type of motion for each reason.

(a) The two reasons for moving to reconsider are:

1. Belief that the action was hasty or impulsive and that if the group would listen again they might be talked into reversing their previous stand. This calls for a motion to reconsider *now*.

2. Belief that the group at this meeting is unrepresentative; with a conviction that if a larger (or more representative) group were present this action would never be taken. So the hope is that if the matter were reconsidered at the next meeting, the action will be reversed because more members would attend. This calls for a motion to reconsider *later*.

(b) If a member wants to reconsider because of Reason 1 above, he moves that "We *now* reconsider our action with respect to XYZ," or words to that effect.

(c) If a member wants to reconsider because of Reason 2 he moves to reconsider *later*. He makes the motion *now*—but the actual decision as to reconsideration is voted on at a subsequent meeting. The typical form is: "I move that at the next session (or at some specified early date) we reconsider our action with respect to XYZ."

(d) The latter motion—the one to reconsider *later*—is listed in some parliamentary manuals under the confusing title of "Reconsider and have entered on the minutes" (see 1109).

1102. Who May Move

The motion which a member wants to reconsider is the "basic" or "primary" motion. The actual motion to reconsider is the secondary motion. Any member who, on the primary motion, voted on the prevailing side, may make the secondary motion to reconsider. He may even change his vote to make himself eligible, provided he changes it before the chair announces the result of the vote on the primary motion.

For example, a member *opposed* to a primary motion hears a loud chorus of "ayes" and knows that this motion is going to pass. Hoping he can get the action reversed later, he immediately says, "I'm voting 'aye' too, Mr. Chairman." This places him on the prevailing side, so he can move to reconsider. Or, a person strongly *in favor of* a motion hears only a few "ayes," including his own. He immediately says: "Mr. Chairman, I am withdrawing my favorable vote." He then joins in with the "noes" thus siding with the majority. This puts him in position later to move to reconsider.

This applies only when the voting was by an unwritten method. That is, it applies to a rising, standing, roll-call, show of hands, or voice vote (see Chapter 6). It does not apply when the primary motion was disposed of by secret written ballot. Under those circumstances, any member may move reconsideration (otherwise, the secrecy of the written ballot would be destroyed).

1103. Seconding the Motion

The motion to reconsider must be seconded. It may be seconded by any voting member, regardless of how he voted on the primary motion.

1104. When Motion May Be Made

It must be made after the primary motion has been voted, but before adjournment of the meeting. If the organization meets once a week or once a month or three or four times a year, then each meeting consists of only one session. In that case, the motion to reconsider must be made on the same day as the primary motion.

However, if the meeting consists of a two-day or three-day or five-day period which includes several sessions, then the motion to reconsider may be made any time after the primary motion has passed (or failed) but before the *sine die* adjournment of the entire meeting (see Chapter 12). A recess does not impair the right to make a motion to reconsider. To illustrate:

1. A society meets monthly. At one meeting, a motion is made to do XYZ, and this passes. An hour later, a member moves "to reconsider our action with respect to XYZ." This is in order, if the member had voted *for* XYZ earlier. However, if no motion to reconsider is made, then a motion to reconsider *cannot* be made at the next month's meeting.

(A motion to *rescind* could be made then—see 1111; or a neutralizing motion could be made then—see 1115; but not a motion to reconsider.)

2. An annual convention runs for four days, with a business session on Monday morning, Tuesday afternoon and Thursday morning. On Tuesday afteroon, the convention rejects a motion to do ABC. It is then in order for a member (who voted "no" on ABC) to move to reconsider on Thursday morning, even though the adjournment (of Tuesday's session) had intervened. However, it is not proper at next year's convention to introduce a motion to reconsider something done at the previous year's convention. A motion to rescind may be made instead (see 1111).

3. An all-day session is interrupted by a recess for luncheon. A primary motion, disposed of in the morning, can be reconsidered in the afternoon. A recess is not an adjournment.

4. An executive board (house of delegates, board of trustees, council, or similar body) holds a two-day meeting every spring. It starts Saturday afternoon, has a morning session Sunday, and a final afternoon session on Sunday—in other words, the meeting consists of three sessions, separated by adjournments. A primary motion disposed of at one ses-

sion may be reconsidered at a later session of the same two-day meeting. But it may not be reconsidered after the *sine die* adjournment of the last session.

1105. Passed Motions Which Cannot Be Reconsidered

The following motions, once passed, cannot be reconsidered, for the reasons indicated under *rationale* below:

1. To adjourn
2. To recess
3. To lay on the table
4. To take from the table
5. To suspend the rules
6. To rescind a previous action
7. To nominate or appoint someone
8. To elect someone to membership or to office or to higher grade
9. To approve a contract after a commitment has been made or funds encumbered
10. To reconsider

Rationale. If (1) or (2) is passed, the motion executes itself and thus prevents reconsideration. There is no reason to reconsider a motion (3) *to lay on the table* because the same effect is achieved by passing a motion to take from the table. By voting to (4) *take from the table,* the group have indicated that they want to dispose of the matter now and should not have to vote again by reconsidering. If the meeting votes to *suspend the rules* (5) to permit immediate consideration, then obviously that is what they want and they should not have to vote again on reconsideration. So with a motion *to rescind* (6). This is, in itself, a species of reconsideration and the group should not be harassed by being, in effect, asked if they want to reconsider a decision to reconsider. *Elections* to office or to membership (7) (8) are not reconsiderable for obvious reasons. A *partly executed matter* (9) cannot be reconsidered because of legal difficulties. And finally, it would be absurd to reconsider a motion *to reconsider* (10) since this would permit an endless chain of motions on the same point.

1106. Motions Which, if Defeated, Cannot Be Reconsidered

(a) With certain exceptions, practically any motion, once defeated, can be *renewed* after some other business has intervened. If a motion can be renewed, there is no need to ask for reconsideration after its defeat. A renewed motion does just as well. For example:

While subject A is under debate, a member moves that we adjourn. This is seconded, but defeated. Subject A is disposed of, then subject B is introduced. The impatient-to-go-home member may now move that we adjourn. He is simply renewing his previously defeated motion, which is his right. There would be no sense to his doing it in the two-stage form of first moving to reconsider the defeat of his first motion (to adjourn); then, if reconsideration is voted, his moving to adjourn again. So it is with many other motions. Substitute them for the "motion to adjourn" in this example—and it will be apparent why a renewable motion, if defeated, cannot be reconsidered.

(b) A primary (main) motion, if defeated, can be reconsidered. If some other business has intervened, the motion can more easily be renewed (repeated) than moved for reconsideration, since this would require only one vote, whereas a motion to reconsider requires two votes: (1) the decision to reconsider; (2) the actual revote on the primary motion. However, if no other business has intervened, a defeated motion cannot be renewed. And in that case, a motion to reconsider is the proper one. If a motion to lay on the table has been defeated, it can be renewed as soon as some additional discussion has taken place, so there is no need for a motion to reconsider. If appropriate, when a member moves to reconsider a defeated motion, the chair can say: "I will not recognize the motion to reconsider, since you can accomplish the same effect by simply making your original motion again." The one exception is: if no business or debate has intervened since the motion was lost, it cannot be renewed; and therefore a motion to reconsider is in order.

1107. Parliamentary Limitations

(a) The motion to reconsider may *not* be amended, postponed, referred to a committee, nor (if recently defeated) may it be renewed. In private, voluntary, and professional organizations, the motion to reconsider may not be laid on the table. See 1107(d) below for a note on this point.

(b) The motion to reconsider is debatable if the primary motion was debatable. Debate is not permitted on a motion to reconsider an undebatable motion. A motion to close debate (on a motion to reconsider) is in order.

(c) If amendments are attached to a primary motion, the motion to reconsider should state clearly whether the member proposes to reconsider only the amendment, or the entire motion as revised, in the form passed; or, if the primary motion was defeated, whether the reconsideration applies only to the amendment or to the motion as amended.

(d) In legislative assemblies (but not in voluntary organizations and societies) a motion to reconsider may be laid on the table. This is very much in the public interest, but the reasons do not apply to a voluntary, nongovernmental, scientific, civic, or technical organization. What happens in certain legislatures is this: a bill passes; a legislator favorable to the bill moves to reconsider. This is seconded. Another legislator, favorable to the bill, moves to lay on the table the motion to reconsider, and this passes. The effect is to seal up the bill itself. It cannot be reconsidered because a motion to reconsider has been laid on the table. And in legislative, unlike private assemblies, a bill is killed when it is laid on the table. This serves the public interest, because it is desirable to have stabilized laws, not laws which might be reconsidered with every temporary change in the composition of the legislature.

In a private or technical organization, this factor does not operate. Since any motion laid on the table can be taken from the table at any time, it would mean constant uncertainty if a motion to reconsider were laid on the table. The officers would hesitate to carry out a motion, if at any time the reconsideration could be taken from the table and voted on, and the motion completely nullified. Hence in voluntary assemblies a motion to reconsider must be disposed of: voted either favorably or unfavorably, and not left hanging in uncertainty.

1108. Motion To Reconsider Now

The member says: "I move that we now reconsider our recent action with respect to ABC" (or "reconsider our approval of . . . ," or "our defeat of the motion to . . . ," or words of like effect). This must be seconded. Someone can challenge the right of the moving member if it is thought that he voted with the minority at the time the primary motion was passed (see 1102). If the primary motion was debatable, this motion to reconsider is debatable. And debate can be shut off by a motion to that effect. After discussion, the chair calls for a vote. If more vote "aye" than "no," the chair says: "The 'ayes' have it, and the motion is now to be reconsidered. This was the motion on ABC. Is there any further discussion on the matter of ABC?" The entire issue is reopened to discussion, and, when debate ends, the primary motion is put to vote in the same manner as if it were first before the meeting. (If the motion to reconsider is defeated, the minutes reveal that fact, and no further action is taken.)

1109. Motion To Reconsider Later

In some parliamentary manuals, this is called the motion "to reconsider and have entered on the minutes."

(a) Even before it is voted on, this motion has the effect of suspending action on the primary matter as soon as it is seconded. Action on the main matter then cannot be taken until the motion to reconsider is disposed of or until the right to reconsider lapses. The eligibility requirements for making this motion and its parliamentary limitations are those described above for the regular motion to reconsider (see 1102, 1103, 1104, and 1107). The member says: "I move that at 8 p.m. (or at tomorrow morning's session) we reconsider the action just taken with respect to XYZ." When this is seconded, it is opened to limited debate (assuming that the primary motion was debatable). Since no vote is going to be taken at this time, debate is limited to the question of whether it is safe to postpone implementing the motion. The chair then says: "Further debate at this time is out of order, as the subject will be discussed more fully at (stating time). This matter is now placed on the agenda for that meeting. No action will be taken on the primary matter until the reconsideration is disposed of."

(b) This suspension of action must be understood. Suppose a motion was passed to authorize purchase of a new desk for the executive secretary. A motion to reconsider later would mean that no one could actually go out and buy that new desk until the reconsideration was disposed of. Or, perhaps a motion was passed to place the association on record as favoring Senate Bill Number 13. If a motion to reconsider this later is made and seconded, no publicity about the association's stand can be released until the reconsideration is disposed of.

(c) A motion to reconsider later does not survive the end of the meeting (as distinct from session). Thus, suppose the meeting is a four-day convention. A primary motion is passed or defeated on Tuesday. A member then promptly moves that this be reconsidered on Thursday. If this motion is seconded, no action can be taken to implement the primary motion until Thursday. If by the time the convention adjourned *sine die* (probably on Friday) the reconsideration was never "called up," the motion to reconsider then lapses, and the primary motion goes into full effect. The same would be true if the motion to reconsider *were* "called up" and defeated. Consider the following example:

At the Monday session of a three-day convention, a motion is made and passed protesting a recent decision of the State Commissioner of Highways. Shortly after this is passed, one member moves, another seconds, a reconsideration of this, the reconsideration to be at the Wednesday meeting. Until Wednesday, the association cannot release its protest. No action can be taken to implement the motion. However, on Wednesday the motion to reconsider should be called up. If it is not called up, then the *sine die* adjournment of the convention on Wednesday evening kills the motion to reconsider. Such a motion cannot survive a *sine die* adjournment. Then the original motion goes into effect and the protest can be published. If the motion to reconsider *is* called up on Wednesday, it is voted on. If it is defeated, the original motion goes into full effect, and the protest is published. If the motion to reconsider passes, then the original matter (about the Commissioner's decision) is on the floor for debate and final decision.

(d) A motion to reconsider later is out of order at a one-session meeting. Thus, if a society meets once a month, a motion to reconsider *now* may be made and voted on at once; but a motion to reconsider *later* would be futile, because the adjournment of that meeting would destroy that motion. But at a two-day executive board meeting it would be possible to move in the morning that we reconsider something in the afternoon, or on the next morning.

(e) A motion to reconsider later must specify the time or the day or the session at which reconsideration will be called up. And this specified time must not be beyond the anticipated adjournment *sine die* (see 1204) of the present meeting series. A motion to reconsider later cannot, therefore, be made during the final sitting of a meeting A motion to reconsider *now* would be in order.

(f) At the time specified for calling up the deferred motion (to reconsider), the secretary will remind the chair: "There is to be called up now the motion to reconsider our decision (when?) on the matter of XYZ." The chair will announce that this is pending, and add: "Does any one wish to call this up?" Any member may call it up, and no second is necessary. If the chair fails to remind the assembly, then any member may rise to say: "Point of order. We should be considering now the motion to reconsider brought up yesterday. I call this up for discussion now." Thus the reconsideration is brought before the meeting.

(g) If no one wants to call it up, the motion to reconsider lapses. Then the primary motion, if it had been passed, is unlocked and may be implemented.

(h) When the motion to reconsider is called up, it is open to debate (if the primary motion was debatable). After discussion is concluded, the chair says "Shall the favorable (or unfavorable) action taken (date) on the matter of ABC now be reconsidered? All in favor of reconsidering say 'aye.'" If more vote "aye" than "no," the chair says: "The 'ayes' have it, and the matter of ABC is now before you again." If more vote "no" than "aye," the chair says: "The 'noes' have it. The motion to reconsider is defeated, and the original action is in effect." If the vote is a tie, the motion to reconsider is defeated, and the original action stands. Of course, the chair might (if he had not voted before) break the tie by voting "yes," and then the motion to reconsider would pass.

(j) If a motion to reconsider is passed, this does not, of itself, reverse the previous primary action. It merely brings it back to the floor for review. The primary matter is then open to discussion (if debatable) and is voted on just as if this were its first appearance on the floor.

(k) The minutes should show clearly the course of the primary motion and the motion to reconsider.

1110. Action When Reconsideration Is Out of Order

A member may feel strongly that certain action was wrong and desire a review. If there has been a *sine die* adjournment since such action, a motion to reconsider is not in order. And, as indicated in 1105 and 1106, motions to reconsider may be out of order for other reasons. In those circumstances, the member can ask that an unwise or injudicious action be rescinded; or, if the original (primary) motion had been defeated, the member can simply renew it; or he can introduce a neutralizing motion (see 1115).

At its January meeting, the Kenosha Society of Podagra Specialists adopted a motion to retain a public relations expert to promote public interest in podagra. This was done over the resistance of a vigorous minority of those present. They felt that if bad weather had not kept dozens of members away, this motion never would have passed. A motion to reconsider at the same meeting was voted down. A motion to place this on the agenda for reconsideration at the February meeting was declared out of order—and properly so, since the adjournment of the January meeting would have lapsed any motion to reconsider later.

In the interim it appeared that many of those absent at the bad-weather meeting in January were disappointed at the action at that meeting. And at the February meeting, practically every member was present. At this meeting, a motion to reconsider would have been out of order, since the contract had been let, the work started, and an adjournment had intervened.

Two measures of relief were available: A motion could be introduced as follows: "Whereas the public has now been made fully podagra-conscious, and whereas this was due to the skilled public relations work of the POH Company, and whereas this company's mission has been accomplished, therefore be it resolved that the podagra educational program has now come to an end, and the POH Company be relieved of its assignment with the thanks of this Society." This would have been, in effect, a motion to neutralize the primary motion.

A second method would be a motion rescinding the January action. See the next four sections.

1111. Requirements for Motion To Rescind

If advance notice is given that a motion to rescind will be submitted, that motion is passed by a majority of those voting on it. If no advance notice had been given, the motion requires either (1) a two-thirds vote (see 614), or (2) an absolute majority of all the members of the society. This is necessary because of fluctuations in attendance. One small group, attending the later meeting, might (if no advance notice had been given) reverse the action of a larger group at an earlier meeting, and then another group might rescind the reversal and so on, *ad nauseam.* Hence the requirement of "notice." If everyone knows that a motion to rescind a certain action is coming up, then those who want to protect their prior action can come to the later meeting and vote down the proposed rescission. If, in spite of this, more vote "aye" than "no" on the rescission, it is apparent that there has been a genuine change of heart. If it is not practical to give advance notice, then a matter cannot be rescinded unless twice as many want to rescind it as want to retain it.

1112. Motion To Rescind: Form

Any such wording as the following is acceptable: "I move that we rescind our action with respect to XYZ"; or ". . . that we rescind our decision to do thus and so"; or ". . . that our action of (date) on (subject) is hereby rescinded." The member may also add, ". . . and that we expunge it from the records." The motion to rescind is then voted on in the form submitted (simple rescission; or rescind and expunge from the records), or in the form as amended. A motion to rescind could be amended by the addition of ". . . and expunge from the records."

1113. Expunction from the Records

If the vote is to expunge from the records, the original memorandum in the minute book is crossed out by lines drawn diagonally through the paragraph. Then a marginal note is inserted reading: "Expunged (date) by order of . . . ," using the correct name of the council, association, convention, society, board of trustees, or whatever the group may be. Printed versions and extracts then make no reference to the matter expunged. If possible, all reference to the primary motion is omitted from printed matter. It is as if the primary motion was never made. If material was already printed but not yet released, expunged matter may be blacked out. The point is that, so far as anyone outside the voting group is concerned, the record should not indicate that the primary matter was ever even considered. But for private use within the voting group, the official transcripts should show, by lining out, what material was expunged. As used in this paragraph, the phrase "voting group" means the persons eligible to vote at the session which adopted the primary motion.

1114. Parliamentary Features of the Motion To Rescind

(a) A motion to rescind may be made by any member regardless of how he voted on the basic motion. It must be seconded. It enjoys no special parliamentary privilege and cannot be made while someone else is speaking. It might be made a special order (see 307) or a general order (see 308) and often is, in connection with the notice given in advance. The motion to rescind is debatable, amendable, and committable (that is, can be referred to a committee). It may be postponed and it may be laid on the table. If passed, it may be reconsidered. If defeated it may be renewed at another meeting. A successful motion to rescind cannot itself be rescinded (the chain must stop somewhere) but the primary matter (the matter that was nulled out) could be reintroduced as new business later.

(b) "To annul" is about the same as "to rescind." Technically, an officer's action is annulled, whereas a motion (or resolution) is rescinded. It does not really matter which word is used. For a hair-splitter, the word choice would follow this pattern:

The primary motion was: "That this Society go on record as supporting the candidacy of Rufus Q. Thistlebottom for Vice-Constable."

After this motion was passed, after the meeting adjourned, some one reminded the members that our society is nonpartisan and that supporting one candidate is a breach of our own rules. Thus it becomes necessary to rescind the motion. This motion to rescind could take either of these forms:

1. To rescind our action of October 20 which supported Mr. Thistlebottom for Vice-Constable
2. To annul the action of the secretary in sending out a newspaper release indicating our support of Mr. Thistlebottom

The motion to rescind (or annul) requires a two-thirds vote for passage unless advance notice was given; then it requires only a majority vote (see 614). If an absolute majority of the entire membership wants to rescind, then the rescission is effective even if no advance notice had been given.

1115. Neutralizing Motion

(a) It is sometimes possible to draft a primary motion in such language that it cancels out or neutralizes some previous action. While this is *in effect* a motion to reconsider or a motion to rescind, it is *in form* a new primary motion and has that status. For instance, if a contract runs at the pleasure of either party, then the society could vote to terminate the contract at any time. In effect, this is a rescission of the motion to award the contract. But it is perfectly proper to introduce it as a primary motion. It is passed by simple majority vote without advance notice, provided that there is no legal impediment to canceling the contract that way.

(b) An association has an executive officer or other salaried employee, retained on an indefinite basis. A motion to separate the executive officer from service with the society is, in *form,* a new primary motion. In *effect,* it is a rescission of the motion to employ him in the first place. Unless the contract of employment required advance notice, a two-thirds vote, or some other procedural formality, such a motion would be proper even if passed only by a bare majority and without advance notice having been given.

(c) The association might have condemned a bill before the state legislature. Perhaps an amendment has made the bill palatable; or perhaps, for tactical reasons, it now appears wise to support the bill. Ordinarily this would require either a reconsideration of the previous action or a rescission of it. However, it is not difficult to draft a resolution which will, in effect, neutralize the previous action without explicitly rescinding it. For example:

WHEREAS, This Society has gone on record as condemning House of Burgesses Proposal 606 because it would furnish free milk for all children at public expense regardless of ability to pay; and

WHEREAS, The Whitten rider to Proposal 606 now provides that the milk be furnished gratuitously only when such children are in families on the welfare rolls; therefore

Be it resolved, That HB Proposal 606, having been purged of its unAmerican features, is now acceptable as a forward-looking health measure; and be it further

Resolved, That this Society endorse HB Proposal 606 as revised and that our Committee on Public Information clarify our position on the proposed legislation.

This resolution becomes a primary motion, and need not be governed by the traffic rules applicable to motions to reconsider or motions to rescind, even though it has the effect of such motions.

(d) Here is another example: The Contrary County Medico-Legal Society adopted a code of ethics which included the canon: "It is unethical for a doctor to accept a medicolegal case with the understanding that his fee will be contingent on the outcome of the litigation." Before the month was out, it was apparent that this canon was wreaking a hardship on injured indigent persons who could not afford to pay medical bills, and who, by operation of this clause, could not get any doctor to testify on their behalf. A motion to rescind this clause would have been awkward because it would have removed a single paragraph out of the middle of a long ethical code. No provisions for repealing or amending had been written into the code. (This is a common error by drafters of ethical codes. Assuming that ethics are immutable, they fail to provide for any way of amending the code.) So the following primary resolution could be offered:

RESOLVED, That the Contrary County MedicoLegal Society interprets canon number 13 as banning contingent fee agreements when patients can well afford to pay for care; and be it further

RESOLVED, That true to the centuries-old tradition of humanitarian service and free care to the indigent, nothing in canon number 13 is interpreted as barring a physician from gratuitously examining and freely testifying about the condition of an indigent patient; but be it further

RESOLVED, That, on collecting monetary damages, such a patient be no longer considered indigent; and be it further

RESOLVED, That under those circumstances, such a patient being no longer indigent should be expected to pay his medical bills.

This could be passed as a primary motion. Without rescinding the questioned item, it will effectively neutralize it.

12

Adjournment
and Recess

1201. Sessions and Meetings

In the ordinary organization, the shortest period of sitting
down together to do business is called a *sitting;* a part of a
meeting which is held all in one day is a *session;* and a series
of sessions closely following each other within a short block
of time is a *meeting.* Thus, in the usual professional, scientific,
or trade association, there is one annual meeting a year. This
"meeting" is made up of several sessions; and any session may
be interrupted by a recess so that a session might consist of
two or more sittings.

These uses of "meeting" and "session" are the opposite of
the meanings in legislative terminology. Some parliamentary
authorities base their terms on Congressional procedure and
thus present the words in reverse. A Congressional *session*
consists of a number of *meetings.* This, however, is peculiar
to legislative semantics. Among professional, civic, trade, community, and scientific organizations, the other usage is commoner: A meeting is a series of sessions; the individual unin-
terrupted, all-in-one-day sitting is a "session." This is reflected
in the phrase "annual meeting" for a series of sessions.

To sum up: a session is part of a meeting. A sitting is part
of a session.

1202. Meaning of Adjournment

To adjourn is to discontinue a session or meeting. A brief interruption (as, for example, to have luncheon) is a *recess*, not an adjournment. An adjournment *terminates* a session or meeting. The adjournment of the last session of a meeting is a *sine die* adjournment (see 1204) which also terminates the meeting.

1203. Adjournment *Cum Die*

Strictly speaking, a meeting must be adjourned *to* some particular day, since that word ("day") is the *jour* in *adjourn*. A stickler for technicalities would say that "I move we adjourn" is bad English, because we must adjourn *to* some day, whether it be tomorrow, or next year, or Friday. If we just adjourn, the *jour* in the word is left in the air. But this is being finical to the point of folly. Everyone knows what is meant by the word "adjourn" even without a date specified.

In actual practice the simple rule is this: an adjournment is *sine die* if the next session will not be held until three months or more have elapsed, or if no date has been set for the next session. If the next session is scheduled to start within three months, then the adjournment is *cum die*.

1204. Adjournment *Sine Die*

The phrase *sine die* means "without a date being set for the next session." In modern practice it means that the next session is either (1) not definitely scheduled or (2) definitely scheduled for a date more than three months hence. A society that meets once a year in annual convention will hold several *sessions* during that week. Each session (except the last) is adjourned *cum die* to the next session. The last *session* terminates by an adjournment *sine die* because it terminates the entire *meeting* as well as the last session, and because the organization will not reassemble for a year. As explained in 1210, a pending matter carries over a *cum die* adjournment, but lapses if not disposed of before a *sine die* adjournment.

1205. The Motion To Adjourn: When in Order

Since no one has the right to keep an assembly in session against its will, the motion to adjourn has a high priority. A member cannot make this motion unless and until he is recognized. He cannot make it:

1. While someone is speaking
2. If a motion to adjourn has just been defeated and no other business has intervened
3. If a motion to fix the time or place of the next meeting is on the floor
4. If a vote on something else is being tallied
5. While an answer is being given to a member's point of order, inquiry, or privilege

Except under these five conditions, the motion to adjourn is always in order, provided that the maker of the motion can get the floor.

1206. Wording of Motion To Adjourn

In practice, almost any chairman will accept the motion in the form of "I move that we adjourn." Strictly speaking, this is incomplete, because it does not carry a date. A chairman obsessed with correctness would insist that the motion be worded something like this: "I move that we adjourn to next Wednesday," ". . . adjourn to meet again at the call of the President," ". . . adjourn *sine die*," or ". . . adjourn to meet at the call of the Executive Committee."

1207. Debatability of Adjournment

Ordinarily the motion to adjourn is not debatable, and the chair calls for a vote on it as soon as it is seconded. The purpose of giving the motion a high rank in the first place is to protect the assembly's right to quit whenever it wants to. Endless debate would nullify that right. There is, however, one exception to this rule, as follows:

(a) If the motion is made at a time when no other business is pending, then it is in itself a primary (main) motion and is subject to debate like any other main motion. This usually is signalled by the chairman's saying "There seems to be no other business (or we have reached the last item on our agenda) and the Chair will now entertain a motion to adjourn." Under conditions like this, the motion to adjourn *is* debatable.

(b) If the motion is made when something important still has to be done, the chair may so advise the assembly. He would then say "Will the maker of this motion withdraw it to permit us . . . ?" If the maker refuses to withdraw the motion, then it is voted on without further debate, beyond the chair's explanation of why it is untimely. If it passes, the session adjourns.

(c) If any member has something important requiring action at this meeting, he may informally ask the maker of an adjournment motion to withdraw it; or he may advise the chair that this other matter must be disposed of. If the chair accepts this, he will ask that the motion to adjourn be withdrawn, explain why, and call for a vote on it if the maker refuses to withdraw the motion.

1208. Motion To Adjourn: Announcement of Result

The vote on the motion to adjourn must be concluded and clearly announced before the chair says "The meeting stands adjourned," or words to that effect. Members remain seated until the chair has received the votes of those who voted "no" on the motion to adjourn, and until the chair says, "The 'ayes' have it, the motion is carried and the meeting stands adjourned."

1209. Motion To Adjourn: Amendments, Reconsideration, and Renewal

(a) A motion to adjourn now and *sine die* cannot be amended; a motion to adjourn at or to some specified time may be amended with respect to the time.

(b) A motion to adjourn, having been disposed of (passed or defeated), cannot be reconsidered. If the motion is defeated, however, it can be renewed. It cannot be renewed until some other business has intervened. If a member keeps repeating the motion to adjourn every time he gets the floor, and if it is apparent that this is a harassing or obstructive tactic, the chair will stop recognizing this member after he has renewed the motion a few times. This refusal to recognize the obstructionist member is, of course, subject to appeal.

(c) A motion to recess (see 1211) may be substituted for a motion to adjourn if appropriate.

1210. Adjournment: Effect on Pending Business

(a) *An adjournment cum die* (see 1203) places all pending and unfinished business on the agenda for the next session, where it is considered under the heading "old business" or "unfinished business." Thus any matters pending at the time of adjournment get a high priority for consideration at the next month's meeting. To enjoy this high priority, the matter must actually have been pending or on the floor at the time of adjournment. For example:

On the agenda is Item 6. Action on proposed XYZ law
Item 7. Group insurance policy
Item 8. Publication of membership directory

When Item 6 came up, a motion was made and seconded to express approval of the proposed law; but before this came to a vote, a motion was made, seconded, and carried, referring it to a committee for study and report. Next, Item 7 was presented in the form of a motion that the association make a contract with the Perforated Shield Insurance Company to buy a special group policy. The motion was seconded. In the course of a discussion, a motion was made to adjourn, and this was seconded and carried.

Now at the next session (assuming this was a *cum die* adjournment), what happens to Items 6, 7, and 8 above? Item 6 had been disposed of: it was referred to a committee. The report of the committee comes up under the agenda heading for committee reports. Item 7 was pending at the time of adjournment. Indeed, it was actually on the floor, when discussion was terminated by the motion to adjourn. Item 7—the one on group insurance—therefore comes up under "unfinished business" or "old business" at the next session. It is heard *after* minutes have been read and committee reports received; but *before* any new business is considered. Not only that, but the actual motion is revived and pending. No one has to make the motion again. Debate continues on that specific motion. Item 8, however, gets no priority. In one sense, perhaps, it was "pending" at the earlier meeting: but as used here "pending" means that it was on the floor. Item 8 (the Membership Directory) had not yet been reached. It was not pending or on the floor at the time of adjournment. At the next session it is still new business, not old business; it may get a high position on the agenda, but it cannot be reached until committee reports have been received and old and unfinished business has been disposed of. (Note that a reassembling within three months means, as a rule, that the adjournment was *cum die*.)

(**b**) *An adjournment sine die* terminates all pending matters. Matters under discussion, motions made but not yet voted on, and other unfinished and pending matters, all come to an end. They have to be introduced as new business with no special priority at a subsequent session. Reassembling within three months is generally treated as a *cum die* adjournment, and not as a *sine die* adjournment. So if the organization meets within three months, pending matters can be carried over with high priority to the adjourned meeting or session.

(**c**) A recess has no effect on the agenda. Everything pending at the time of the recess is simply restored to its previous posture when the meeting reassembles. The agenda proceed just as if there had been no interruption.

(**d**) When a body consists of persons elected to represent a constituency, the effect of adjournment depends on whether there has been any significant change in the composition of the group. For instance, a board of trustees, house of delegates,

179

executive board, council, executive committee, or other representative assembly may undergo a marked change in composition between sessions. If pending matters retained a high priority, the new members would not have heard the earlier discussion. It is, therefore, a sensible rule that where in the interim the composition of a representative body has undergone substantial change, all pending matters are terminated by the adjournment even if the interim period is less than three months. A fair interpretation of "substantial change" would be: where more than a third of those at the present meeting would not have been entitled to participate in the immediately preceding session.

1211. Recess

(a) A recess is a short interruption in a session, a brief intermission for the purpose of rest, relaxation, eating, comfort, or attendance at some other function. The motion to take a recess must state the duration of the recess, or the time for reconvening. A simple "motion that we take a recess" cannot be accepted because it does not indicate time. A motion for a "ten-minute recess" would be in order, as would a motion for a "recess until after luncheon," or "recess until 2 P.M.," or a recess while the tellers count the ballots, or a "recess until the conclusion of the special film exhibit." A motion for recess may be amended as to the duration or time of reconvening. The motion to recess is in order whenever a motion to adjourn would have been in order (see 1205). Unless some other time was specified, the motion takes effect as soon as it is passed.

(b) A motion to recess made while some other matter is pending is a privileged, therefore a nondebatable motion. Made when nothing else is on the floor, it is a debatable primary motion.

(c) The chair has no right to order a recess except in emergencies. However, in civic or technical societies he often says: "If there is no objection, we will now take a 15-minute recess for the purpose of *ABC*." If in fact no one does object, the recess is granted by silent assent.

(d) Sample forms of the recess motion would be:

I move we recess until the count of ballots has been concluded.

I move that at 11:45 A.M., regardless of business pending, we take a sixty-minute luncheon recess.

I move we recess now and reconvene at 10:10 A.M.

I move a five-minute recess.

Dr. X has just come in and will deliver his address in the Rose Room. I move a recess so that we may hear this address and that we reconvene five minutes after the conclusion of Dr. X's talk.

(e) Sometimes a recess is announced in a prepared program; for example, the schedule for a scientific assembly may have the printed word "recess" or "intermission." Under these circumstances, the chair calls the recess at about that time without asking for any motion.

(f) The fractions of a session which are separated by recesses are called "sittings."

(g) At an annual convention, the usual practice is to consider all the activity on one day as a single session. The parts of the day separated by interruptions for meals and so forth are "sittings" separated by recesses. However, the group could, if it wished, adopt a motion to adjourn after the morning session and reconvene in the afternoon as a separate session, and thus use adjournments rather than recesses to separate parts of the program. If different chairmen preside, or if different kinds of activities are scheduled, it is better to consider each part of the day a separate session and the interruption an adjournment; otherwise, they should be considered sittings interrupted by recess.

1212. To Fix the Time to Which To Adjourn

Under certain circumstances, this is the most highly privileged motion in the book. An organization usually does have some automatic provision for reassembling. Either the bylaws set a fixed and regular meeting date or the power to call the meeting is vested in the chair or in some high authority body. It is rare, in modern organizations, for the general membership to determine by vote when to hold the next meeting. However, it is legitimate to do so.

(a) There is no need for a motion to fix the time of the next meeting if everybody knows when the organization is meeting again. It might, however, be desirable to determine, by motion, the place or the exact hour. This is, in effect, a motion to change the hour, or a motion to change or fix the place of the next meeting. This is an ordinary main motion. It has no special privilege. It is amendable, debatable, and reconsiderable. It would, however, be self-stultifying to refer it to a committee.

(b) If the next meeting is scheduled and a member wants to change that date, then the motion is either privileged or a main motion, depending on whether something else is pending. This works as follows:

1. Suppose nothing is pending, everyone is quiet, the chair has asked if there is anything else. A member now rises and says that since our next meeting is scheduled for November 11, and since this is Veterans Day, we ought to meet on November 18 instead. So he moves that our next meeting be on November 18 instead of on November 11 as scheduled. (Technically, the form is: ". . . that when we adjourn, we adjourn to November 18.") This is an ordinary, main motion. It has no special privilege. It belongs on the bottom of the list in 204. This motion is debatable and amendable. Of course if it is tabled, committed, or postponed, it is in effect killed. But the members may dispose of it that way if they prefer to do so in this more delicate fashion. (It is assumed that there is no constitutional mandate fixing the date. If there is—and this is bad constitution writing—the motion is out of order because it would breach the constitution.)

2. Suppose some other business (perhaps even a motion to adjourn) is pending. A member suddenly recalls that if we meet as scheduled on November 11, we will be in conflict with a civic celebration. He demands the floor, and says "I move that we hold our November meeting on the 18th instead of the 11th to avoid conflict with Veterans Day." (A stickler for form would require him to phrase it: ". . . that when we ad-

journ, we adjourn to November 18.") The member whose motion is on the floor may object to this rude interruption. But the chair would have to say that this motion (to set the date of the next meeting) has top privilege. It does. It is, indeed, the Number 1 motion in the hierarchy (see 204). However, if the motion is privileged, then it is *not* debatable, though it *is* amendable with respect to time. The reason it is nondebatable is that, being the absolutely top privileged of all motions, debate could continue forever. No motion to close debate, table, commit, or postpone could ever be in order. So when the mover claims this top privilege, he necessarily sacrifices the right to debate.

(c) If there is no generally agreed-on or known date for the next meeting, then the motion to set the time for the next meeting is a necessary one, or the organization may adjourn itself out of existence. If no other business is pending, the motion is an ordinary one, as explained in 1212(b)(1) above. If a member interrupts other business to set the time for the next meeting, then it is a privileged motion, and, as detailed above in 1212(b)(2), it is not debatable.

(d) Technically, the proper form is: "I move that when we adjourn, we adjourn until 8.30 P.M. November 18." However, any language which clearly states the intent and effect of the motion is acceptable. Thus, there can be no misunderstanding if the mover says: "That we hold our next meeting at 8.30 P.M. November 18," and this is in order.

(e) This is *not* a motion to adjourn. Sometimes—particularly if the "proper" form is used—members assume that it is. The motion "that when we adjourn, we adjourn to November 18" does sound like a motion to adjourn now. And if the chair says "passed, and when we meet again, we meet on November 18," the confusion is understandable. A careful chairman, therefore, explains, as he calls for a vote, that the meeting will continue regardless of how the vote turns out.

(f) If a motion to adjourn has obviously passed by voice vote, and someone suddenly recalls that there is no date for the next meeting, there is still time to call "I move that we meet again on November 18." Until the chair has actually said, "The meeting stands adjourned," the session is in business. And this motion to fix the date does take precedence over a motion to adjourn.

(g) This motion should not be confused with the infrequent motion to fix the time of adjournment (see 1213).

1213. To Fix the Time at Which To Adjourn

This differs from the preceding motion in this respect:
1. The motion which fixes the time *to* which to adjourn sets the date of the next meeting.
2. The motion which fixes the time *at* which to adjourn determines when *this* meeting will come to an end.

(a) The motion may be made whenever no other business is pending. It is not limited to the "new business" part of the agenda, but may be made at any time providing no other motion is pending, and provided that the mover can get the floor.

(b) The motion is phrased thus: "I move that this meeting adjourn promptly at 9.00 P.M. tonight."

(c) If the mover simply wants a brief interruption to permit some other activity, he should call for a recess, thus: "I move that at 4.15 P.M. we recess for fifteen minutes so that we may all see the running of the Kentucky Derby on this television set."

For the parliamentary features of a recess, see 1211.

(d) If a motion to adjourn at a specified time (see 1213(b)) is passed, the chair must declare the meeting adjourned as soon as practical after that time. Suppose the motion had been to adjourn at 9 P.M. What happens if something is pending when the clock strikes nine? Here is what happens:

1. There is no interruption if any of these things are under way: a vote is being counted or taken; an answer is being given to a point of order, inquiry, or privilege; a motion to fix the time of the next meeting is pending; a report is being read. The chair waits until this is concluded, and then takes the action indicated in 1213(e).

2. Except as indicated in (1) above, the chair interrupts what is going on—even cutting into the debate or discussion—and says "It is 9 P.M. and we must now adjourn." But see 1213(e).

(e) When the time comes, the chair says: "It is now 9 P.M. and, in accordance with the motion which you earlier passed, I must declare the meeting adjourned." He pauses briefly, and if no one makes a legitimate call, he drops the gavel and says "The meeting stands adjourned." The only legitimate interventions at this time are:

1. A motion to fix or change the date of the next meeting (see 1212).

2. If a member has an important matter that must be considered, he moves to suspend the rules so that his matter may be taken up before consummating action on the adjournment. The procedure is outlined in 306(b). In this situation, it shapes up as follows:

MR. A: Mr. Chairman, please, just a minute . . . I move to suspend the rules that interfere with the consideration of the report of the program committee.

MR. B: Point of order, Mr. Chairman. A is out of order because we have just decided that we are to adjourn at 9 P.M., and it is after that already.

CHAIR: No, because a motion to suspend the rules, if adopted, would change the order of the agenda. The adjournment was on the agenda for 9 P.M., it is true. But a suspension of the rules would change that. However, we cannot suspend the rules without a two-thirds vote. Mr. A has moved that we suspend the rules that interfere with consideration of the program report. Any second? Seconded by Mr. C. This is not debatable so we vote at once. Raise your hands, since a two-thirds vote is required. All in favor of suspending the rules—that is, temporarily suspending this adjournment—so that we can consider the program report, raise their right hands . . . all opposed raise their right hands. Fifty-four ayes and eighteen noes. The ayes have it by more than two thirds. We suspend the adjournment and proceed at once to the consideration of the program report.

(Once that is disposed of, the suspended adjournment comes into being and the members stand adjourned.)

13

Hints on the Construction of a Constitution

FORM

1301. Principal Divisions

A constitution is divided into units called "Articles," usually assigned roman numerals, as Article I, Article II, and so forth. Each long article is subdivided into sections or into paragraphs (or both) to which arabic numerals are assigned. Citations follow this pattern: Article III, Section 4; or Paragraph 3b of Article VII; or "Constitution, III,4."

1302. Omission of Details

A constitution is short and compact. It is general rather than detailed. For instance, the constitution might mention something about the frequency of meetings ("at least five meetings a year," or "a regular annual meeting in the spring"). It does *not* specify dates ("the second Friday of each month"). The constitution may indicate who appoints committees but

186

does not include a detailed list of committees. It mentions membership and nominating committees, if any, since these are necessary to the continued life of the organization. The constitution confers authority to impose and collect dues and tells what to do about delinquent members. It does not specify the amount of dues.

1303. Minimum Structure

The *minimum* structure of a constitution is:

Article I.   Name and object.
Article II.   Membership eligibility and selection.
Article III. Officers—titles, duties, term, how elected.
Article IV.   Meeting frequency.
Article V.   Right to assess dues and what to do about delinquents.
Article VI.   How to amend the constitution.

1304. Reference to Committees

The constitution may also include general references to committees—how appointed, distinction between standing and special committees, and so on. Usually, though, this is done in bylaws. The membership and nominating committees—and in some organizations a program committee—may be mentioned specifically in the constitution. Other committees need not be named. Even if the constitution is silent about committees, the society can always create them and the president may nominate committee personnel. This derives from the common parliamentary law that confers such authority on all societies and all presidents, unless there is some specific provision to the contrary.

1305. High Authority Bodies

If the society has an executive board, council, board of trustees, executive committee, house of delegates or other high authority body, it is mentioned in the constitution. This may be included in the same "article" as the other officers, or it may have an article of its own. The body is named, the composition is indicated, and its authority made clear.

1306. Nonduplicating Language

Legal language is not used in the constitution of a professional, scientific, civic, or technical organization. Lawyers use duplicate words with slightly varying shades of meaning in order to plug up every possible loophole; hence they use such expressions as "cease and desist," "null and void," "give and bequeath," "agree and covenant," "confirm and ratify," and many other pairs. There is no need for such doubletalk in the constitution of a body that has no law-making powers. Compare these versions of the same idea:

Jargon: This Constitution or any article, section, or paragraph thereof, may be amended, altered, revised, rescinded, or repealed, by a vote of the members to that effect, provided that two thirds or more . . . .

Common Sense: Any part of this Constitution may be amended by a vote of the members to that effect, provided . . . .

As a practical matter, there is no chance that the shorter version will be misunderstood and no chance that the society would allow a stubborn member to get away with a pretended misunderstanding. The stilted and confusing legal jargon is unnecessary. Here is another example:

Jargon: A person having been successfully elected to membership shall not be enrolled until and unless he shall have signed a statement to the effect that he promises, covenants, and agrees to abide by and conform to all the rules and regulations of this cooperative . . . .

Common Sense: By accepting membership in this cooperative, each person agrees to abide by its rules. Each new member will sign a statement to that effect.

The duplicate phrases, "unless and until," "covenants and agrees," "abide and conform," and "rules and regulations" are, perhaps, necessary in a document that has the effect of law; but they are unnecessary in the internal literature of a voluntary organization. The second version, above, is not only shorter but is actually clearer than the elegant jargon of the first version.

1307. Verb Tense Usage

A constitution is written in the simple future or simple present tense, and not in compound or auxiliary ("shall") form. For example: "Duties of the President are . . ."; or "An applicant *becomes* a member on payment of . . ." (illustrating simple present). The simple future is illustrated in "The duties of the President will be . . ."; or in "An applicant will be enrolled as a member upon payment of . . ." The legalistic auxiliary "shall" is best avoided in Constitutions. Compare 1, 2, and 3 below.

1. No candidate shall be entered on the rolls until he . . . .
2. No candidate is entered on the rolls until he . . . .
3. No candidate will be enrolled until he . . . .

Form 3 is best here because what is desired is to express simple futurity on the pattern of "the sun will rise tomorrow." But in expressing a present and continuous state, the future tense is *not* used. To illustrate, compare the three forms below for expressing a present and continuing state of facts:

1. The duties of the President shall be to preside at meetings . . . .
2. The duties of the President are to preside at meetings . . . .
3. The duties of the President will be to preside at meetings . . . .

Form 2 is best. It is simple and direct. It is also shorter than the other forms. The saving of a word or two in every paragraph makes an appreciable difference in the length of the constitution. Where possible the simple present is used. (Note that I did not write, "The simple present tense *shall be* used.")

The verb "will" means that it must be done. "A member will be expelled for nonpayment of dues" (or "A member shall be expelled . . . ,") means that the delinquent member *must* be expelled. However, "A member may be expelled for nonpayment . . . ," means that the society (or its appropriate tribunal) may or may not expel the delinquent member, according to their judgment or to the circumstances of the case. For these reasons, optional choices are indicated by "may" rather than by "will" or "shall."

The editor of the draft of the constitution is urged to review the semifinal copy and to replace all "shalls," "wills," and futures with the simple present wherever it can be done without impairment of sense. Thus "Elections shall be held at the January meeting" is better expressed as "Elections will be held at the January meeting." In this case the simple present is not sensible, since "Elections are held at the January meeting" does not convey the idea of an instruction but rather the idea of a reported fact. Consider:

1. No successful candidate for membership shall be entered on the rolls until he shall have paid his first year's dues.
2. No successful candidate for membership will be entered on the rolls until he has paid his first year's dues.
3. No successful candidate for membership is entered on the rolls until he has paid his first year's dues.

Form 3 is the best as well as the shortest. The entire document may, in this manner, be screened for unnecessary "shalls" and unnecessary use of the future tense or complicated future perfect forms ("shall have paid").

1308. Sample of Short Constitution

It is possible to draft a workable constitution that will cover only a single typewritten page. For example:

ARTICLE I

1. The name of this Organization is XYZ.
2. Its purposes and objects are ABC.

ARTICLE II

1. Every adult person residing in the DEF area who is sponsored by two regular members is eligible for membership on payment of entrance fee; and remains a member so long as he resides in the DEF area and is not delinquent in the payment of dues, unless expelled from membership in accordance with Section 3 below.

2. A former resident of the DEF area may, on request, and on approval of the Executive Committee, become an Honorary Member.

3. A person found unworthy of membership may be expelled on recommendation of the Executive Committee, and on approval of that recommendation by two-thirds of the members attending a regular meeting. However, the Executive Committee will not make such recommendation until after the member has been advised that he will be given the opportunity of being heard by the Committee.

4. An honorary member is not eligible to vote, nor to hold office; and is not liable for the payment of dues.

ARTICLE III

1. The officers are a President, a Vice-President, a Corresponding Secretary, a Recording Secretary, and a Treasurer.

2. Their duties are the ones usually associated with those titles.

3. These officers (Paragraph 1 above), together with the last three surviving of the most recent ex-presidents, constitute the Executive Committee. The Vice-President is Chairman of the Executive Committee.

4. The Executive Committee has all the powers of the Association in the intervals between meetings. This Committee will meet on call of its Chairman, or on the request of any three members of the Committee; and in any event will hold at least one meeting in every period of six consecutive weeks.

5. Elections will be held at the Annual Meeting. Candidates will be nominated from the floor. If there is more than one candidate for a vacancy, the office will be filled by written ballot. The candidate receiving the largest number of votes is elected.

6. Each successful candidate assumes office on the first day of the month which next follows the month during which he was elected. He serves until his successor is installed.

ARTICLE IV

1. Regular meetings will be held on dates fixed by the Executive Committee. At least four regular meetings will be held during each calendar year; and one of these will be in December and will be the Annual Meeting. The Corresponding Secretary will notify each member of the date and place of the next meeting, such notices being sent out at least three weeks prior to the scheduled meeting date.

2. Special meetings will be held on call of the President.

3. Any twenty members may, by signed petition, instruct the President to call a special meeting, indicating in the petition the reason therefor. On receipt of such a petition, the President will call the special meeting.

ARTICLE V

1. The amount of dues and the entrance fee will be determined by the Bylaws and may be changed from time to time by adoption of a new Bylaw.

2. No candidate for membership is entered on the rolls of the Association until he has paid his entrance fee.

3. A member a full year in arrears of dues is suspended from the privileges of membership, and is dropped from the rolls if all dues then owing have not been paid within ninety days after the date of his suspension.

ARTICLE VI

1. The Association may adopt new Bylaws by affirmative vote thereon, provided that no Bylaw is in effect until passed by two separate meetings. The affirmative vote of a majority of those present will be sufficient to pass a Bylaw.

2. A Bylaw may be repealed by passing a Bylaw to that effect.

3. This Constitution may be amended by the affirmative vote of two thirds of the members in attendance at a meeting, provided that no vote will be taken on the proposal to amend the Constitution unless notice thereof was given in advance.

1309. Essentials of a Viable Constitution

Analysis of this brief constitution lights up certain aspects of constitution drafting. This is not a model document. It is too short and requires too many bylaws. However, it does assure a viable organization, because it provides for these bare essentials: a method of admitting new members, of expelling unworthy or delinquent members, of electing officers, of assuring that a minimum number of regular meetings will be held, of assuring that the members can insist on a meeting even if the officers don't want one; of setting up an instrument (here an executive committee) to maintain continuity of authority in the intervals between meetings, of assuring that officers will continue to function even after their terms have expired and until their successors are installed, and of amending the constitution. The duties of the officers are not spelled out, since everyone knows what a president or treasurer or secretary is supposed to do. Nor is any detailed grant of power given to the executive committee. It is provided, however, that this committee is the heir of all the society's powers in the intervals between meetings and provides a check on an arbitrary or dictatorial president (see 1318).

1310. Provision for Amending Bylaws

The bylaws contain the organizational details omitted from the constitution. Bylaws should be easier to amend than the constitution. This requirement is met by requiring only a majority vote to amend a bylaw (or enact a new bylaw) whereas a two-thirds vote would be required to amend the constitution. To prevent capricious changes in standing rules, it is well to require that advance notice be given before amending the bylaws. This may be done in either of these ways:

1. By requiring that, in advance of the meeting, notice be sent to all members telling them of the proposal to amend the Bylaws
2. By requiring that the proposal be passed at two consecutive meetings before being effective—the reading and debate at the first meeting being, in effect, notice that it will come up at the second meeting

1311. Contents of Bylaws

(a) Proper subjects for bylaws include: order of business; dates of meetings; places of meetings; lists of committees; the quorum rule; provision for representation or affiliation; amount of dues; amount of entrance or initiation fee; details as to method of becoming a member; procedural details with respect to nominations and elections; instructions about the receipt of, depositing of, vouchering of, expenditure of, and auditing of funds; parliamentary procedure, either by citation of an authority (such as this book), or by actually including the major rules of debate, motion-making, precedence of motions, and voting on motions; filling of vacancies when an officer dies, resigns, or becomes disabled; and the like.

(**b**) The bylaws should also indicate if a "majority" means something more than a majority of those voting. If the bylaws are silent on this, then a motion is passed if more vote for it than vote against it. If a hundred members are present, and three say "aye" while one says "no," a motion is passed, even though only three in the hundred voted for it. If this is considered undesirable, the bylaws may specify that "majority" means something other than its normal meaning in the common parliamentary law. For example, a bylaw might read:

> No motion is passed unless a majority of those present vote for it, and then only if a quorum be present. If by the common rules of order a motion requires a two-thirds vote, then that two thirds will be measured as that fraction of those present regardless of the number actually voting.

(**c**) The same effect may be achieved in fewer words (but a bit obscurely) by the following bylaw: "In counting votes on any motion or resolution, the votes of those present who remain silent, will be counted as 'no' or negative votes."

Or it may be expressed this way: "If a member, while present, does not vote, his vote will be tallied in the negative."

Any of these wordings will produce the desired effect, and change the rule so that a motion cannot pass unless a majority of *those present* vote for it. Unless some such rule is spelled out, the standard ruling will apply and a motion will pass if more vote for it than against it—blanks and nonvotes being ignored.

As a general rule, the standard (common parliamentary law) is adequate for ordinary voluntary (nonlegislative) societies and clubs. This means that, if a member sits silently by and lets a motion pass or fail without his vote, he has no right to complain later that the action was taken by only a small fragment of the quorum.

1312. Form of Bylaws

Bylaws are sometimes set up in articles and sections, following exactly the same format as the constitution. However, this is confusing. Most members ignore the difference between the two. When they cite Article II, Section 1, it is hard to know whether the reference is to that part of the bylaws or that part of the constitution. To avoid this ambiguity, the drafter of the bylaws may do one of these things: (1) divide the bylaws into chapters instead of articles, i.e., Chapter 1, Chapter 2, and so on, (2) number the bylaws with arabic numerals and identify the subdivisions with letters—thus, the reference would be to Bylaw 2A instead of Article II, Section 1, or (3) divide the constitution into articles and *paragraphs,* while the bylaws could be divided into *sections.* Then, a reference would be "according to Section 4 of the bylaws," whereas, for the constitution, the citation would be to Article IV, Paragraph 2.

CONTENT

1313. Purpose

The purposes or objectives are stated rather broadly in the constitution. If too narrow or too specific, some member may challenge the right to use the organization's funds for some special purpose, arguing that it is not in line with the objectives of the organization. Hence the "purpose" clause should include vague and flexible verbs such as "enhance," "improve," "promote," "protect." If the immediate purpose seems narrow, the stated objective should include matters which might *indirectly* affect that purpose. For example, if the avowed aim of the society is to study ways of preventing juvenile crime, it would be unwise to limit its objective so sharply in the constitution. Perhaps more playgrounds will reduce delinquency. But some member will argue that the relationship between playgrounds and crime is not established and that it is an illegal use of the society's funds to divert any of it to promoting new playgrounds. The objective should have been written as "To advance the welfare of children in XYZ" rather than "to prevent juvenile crime," the general rather than the specific aim. If it must be stated so narrowly, then a loophole should be drilled into it by some such phrase as: "To study all factors which directly or indirectly promote or contribute to crime among juveniles and to stimulate the community to adopt such measures as may, directly or indirectly, immediately or in the future, prevent juvenile crime or reduce its frequency or seriousness." Here the words "indirectly" and the phrase "in the future" open the door to almost anything. This tautologic sentence is justified because the purpose of this paragraph is to assure a broad and diffuse grant of power.

1314. Membership

(a) If the organization is selective (that is, if members must be *elected* to it rather than become members as a matter of right), the constitution should provide, in general terms, for the membership election process. This is usually done through a membership committee. The composition of that committee, its method of appointment, its term of office, and its function should be written into the constitution. Details may be reserved for the bylaws. For example:

A Membership Committee of six members is hereby established. Each member of this committee will serve thereon for two years. Terms will be so arranged that two seats will become vacant each year. The President in office when a vacancy occurs will name a member of the Society to fill each vacancy on that committee. Every application for membership will be forwarded to that committee, which will report to the Executive Board on the acceptability of each candidate for membership. If the Board and the committee concur in disapproving an application, that application will be rejected and the sponsor of the applicant so notified. If the Board and the Committee concur in approving an application, or if they disagree about a member's acceptability, the name of the applicant will be transmitted to the general membership at the next meeting for dispositive action thereon.

The appropriate bylaw could include such details as how long the membership committee may hold the application before relaying it to the board; what forms the applicant fills out; what references or sponsors he needs; what to do if further inquiry is ordered; how the general membership votes (open or closed ballot); what vote is required to elect an applicant (majority, two-thirds, or unanimous), and so on.

(b) In implementing this (whether in the constitution or bylaws) the following points should be considered. It is unwise to require a written secret ballot on all applicants. It may seriously and unnecessarily slow up business to go through the form of distributing and counting ballots if the custom is to accept anyone approved by the membership committee. The best rule is to provide for a voice vote ("All in favor say 'aye' ") unless two or more members demand a secret written vote. (This detail belongs in the bylaws, not in the constitution.) A majority of those *voting* (not a majority of those present) should be sufficient to elect the candidate and the constitution should so specify. Otherwise, a situation will commonly arise where 90 per cent of those at the meeting pay no attention to a routine procedure like this, and no applicant can ever get a vote from a majority of those present. In some organizations it is practical to vote by mail. Under these circumstances, most members will not return their ballots at all. The rule should be that the applicant is accepted if a majority (or two thirds or three fourths) of the returned ballots favor his election to membership.

1315. Voting for Office

(a) It sounds democratic to require the nominating committee to bring in at least two candidates for each office, and to require voting by written ballot. However, in most organizations these are unwise provisions. If it is required that at least two persons be nominated for every office, then there must always be a contested election. This often provokes bitterness and is always embarrassing. Furthermore, many a superior member will refuse to risk the loss of face that goes with defeat and therefore will not run in a contested election. It is better to have the provision read:

The Nominating Committee will present a panel of candidates, at least one for each vacancy . . . .

The democratic process is preserved by the rule that nominations may also be made from the floor.

(b) The election itself should be by plurality. If an absolute majority is required, some provision must be made for repeating the ballots and reducing the slate. Otherwise a meeting may last all night. A better form is shown on the next page.

If there is only one candidate for any vacancy, the Chairman will declare him elected, and no ballots will be distributed or counted. If there are two or more candidates for any vacancy, election will be by written ballot. The candidate for any vacancy who receives the largest number of votes for that office will be elected.

This is short, simple, and lucid. If it seems necessary to have an absolute majority to elect, then provision must be made not only for multiple balloting but also for the disqualification of low-vote candidates. Two methods are available: (1) the runoff ballot, or (2) the repeated ballot with shrinking panel. The constitutional provision would be:

A majority of all ballots cast (not counting blank or defaced ballots) is required to elect a candidate.

(c) This is implemented by a bylaw detailing either the (1) runoff ballot or (2) the repetitive ballot system as follows:

1. Runoff ballot:

A majority of all ballots cast (not counting blank or defaced ballots) will be required to elect a candidate. If no candidate receives a majority on the first ballot, then all except the top two candidates are forthwith disqualified. And a second election is then held (same day? next meeting? by mail?) limited to the two top candidates. The one receiving the most votes therein is elected. If this second election results in a tie, a third election is held.

2. Repetitive ballots:

A majority of all ballots cast (not counting blank or defaced ballots) will be required to elect a candidate. If no candidate receives a majority on the first ballot, the results are announced in open meeting, and a second ballot with the same candidates is then held. If no candidate receives a majority on the second ballot, that candidate who received the smallest number of votes is disqualified. Any or all candidates receiving no votes are considered as having received the "smallest number" and are disqualified. If every candidate (at any ballot) received some votes, then the one who received the smallest number is disqualified from receiving votes in the next ballot. And in this manner, additional ballots are taken, each time dropping from the panel the candidate who received the smallest number of votes. This continues until some candidate receives an absolute majority of all legally marked ballots. If on any ballot the smallest number of votes was received by two or more candidates, this tie is disposed of as follows:

a) If by disqualifying the low-vote tied candidates there still remain two or more qualified candidates, then the tied candidates are all disqualified.

b) If by disqualifying the low-vote tied candidates there remains only one candidate, then none of the tied low-vote candidates are disqualified at this ballot.

c) If all candidates received exactly the same number of votes, none is disqualified at this ballot.

1316. Nominating Methods

The method of nomination need not be included in the constitution, but should be mentioned in the bylaws. Three methods are available:

1. Nomination from the floor
2. Nomination by petition
3. Nomination by committee

(**a**) Unless elections are by mail, the bylaws should always permit nominations from the floor, even if nominations are also being made by petition or by committee. For method of nominating from the floor, see 621. The bylaws should state whether nominations and elections take place at the same meeting, or whether the nominations are made at one meeting and elections are held at a later meeting. It is the practice of nearly all organizations to require that a nomination must be seconded to be officially received. (This refers to nominations from the floor only.) If the society prefers to follow the obsolete rule (that nominations need no second), the bylaws should state that "nominations will be received from the floor and require no second."

(**b**) If nominations are by petition, the bylaws indicate the minimum number of signatures and state that no member may sign petitions for more than one candidate for the same office at the same election. A timetable for the issuing and return of petitions is found in the bylaws.

(**c**) If a nominating committee is used, the constitution (not the bylaws) indicates how the nominating committee is selected. Presidential appointment is the common method.

This may be abused, permitting a president to select his own successor by packing the nominating committee with persons committed to his choice. Candidates suggested by the nominating committee are elected about 99 per cent of the time. To discourage this possible abuse, other methods of selecting the nominating committee are available: (1) named by president, but must be confirmed by an executive board or even by the general membership; (2) selected by an executive board, board of trustees, or other high authority body; (3) choice limited by certain geographical or official considerations; as, for example, that the nominating committee include only (or a certain number of) ex-presidents; or that it include representatives from specified geographic areas or affiliated institutions, agencies, or organizations; (4) election of the nominating committee by general membership. This raises the question of who nominates nominees for the nominating committee. It is usually done from the floor.

(d) The bylaws include a timetable for the nominating committee, showing date on which they must report. The requirement should be "at least one candidate for each vacancy." It is amateurish to require two candidates, since many excellent members will refuse to participate in a contested election. So long as additional nominations may be made from the floor, this is not a steam-roller provision.

Sample provisions:

1. *For nominations from the floor:* Nominations for office will be made from the floor at the last regular meeting prior to the Annual Meeting. Elections will take place at the Annual Meeting from among candidates nominated at the preceding meeting.

2. *For nomination by petition:* Starting ninety days prior to the Annual Meeting, the Secretary will make available forms for the nomination of candidates. Each form will indicate the office to which the candidate aspires and the date of the election. Any regular member may sign a form, and by so doing becomes a sponsor of the candidate named therein. No member may sponsor more than one candidate for the same office at the same election except when the first-sponsored candidate has withdrawn, thus releasing his sponsors. Signed petitions will be filed with the Secretary not later than twenty-one days prior to the Annual Meeting. If the petition bears the valid and non-duplicated signatures of five per cent or more of the members, the candidate will be

declared nominated and his name will be placed on the ballot. If the Secretary rules that a petition is invalid because of insufficient signatures, late filing, or illegal signatures, the sponsors or candidate may appeal to the Executive Board for final ruling.

3. *For nomination by Committee:* Prior to September 1, each year, the President will send to the Executive Board the names of six members as proposed personnel for the Nominating Committee. Two of these will be ex-presidents; and of the other four, no two or more will reside in the same parish. The Executive Board will determine whether these names are acceptable, and if so, they will become the Nominating Committee. If any nominee is not acceptable to the Board, the Board will elect a member of the Society in his stead, maintaining the distribution of two ex-presidents and members from four different parishes. The Nominating Committee will be furnished with a roster of all members and of all current and past officers, including dates of office and expiration of terms. The Committee will select its own Chairman, Vice-Chairman, and Clerk. The Committee will, by November 15, present a panel of candidates, at least one for each vacancy. This will be announced in the *News-Letter* or otherwise made known to all members. At the Annual Meeting, a representative of the Nominating Committee will announce the panel of candidates, and then the meeting will be open to nominations from the floor. And after nominations for President have been closed, a President will be elected. And in like manner the meeting will proceed to the nomination and election of other officers. If for any office or any vacancy there is only one candidate, the Chair—after allowing sufficient time for nominations from the floor—will declare that one candidate elected, without distributing or receiving ballots.

1317. Meeting Frequency

Neither meeting dates nor the exact frequency of meetings should be written into the constitution. Circumstances may make it impossible to adhere to any rigid schedule, and swift amendment of the constitution is rarely possible. But it is important to provide for at least a minimum frequency of meetings, and to write in some arrangement that makes this independent of the whim of the president. Otherwise a president could, by failing to call a meeting, maintain himself in the chair indefinitely. A high authority body such as an executive board may likewise prefer to carry on the association's affairs by themselves without being answerable to the general membership at frequent meetings. Accordingly the constitution should include provision for (1) a minimum number of meetings which must be called, and (2) a way of by-passing the officers and calling for a special meeting on petition of members. Sample provisions for (1) and (2) are:

1. Meetings will be held on call of the President, or on dates set by the Executive Board; and in any event there will be at least one Annual Meeting and two other regular meetings each calendar year.

1. The general membership will convene in Annual Meeting once each calendar year on a date in April selected by the Board of Directors. In the event of war or other national emergency, when, by proclamation of the President of the United States, travel is restricted, the Board of Directors may prorogue the Annual Meeting for that year; and in that case, the Board will submit to the membership for mail ballot and referendum all elections and major resolutions that would have been on the agenda of the Annual Meeting; and will be bound by the results of such ballots.

1. (This for Bylaws, not for Constitution) The Association will meet on the second Thursday of January, March, April, October, and December, unless, because of holiday or by reason of conflict with another meeting, such a date be considered by the Executive Council to be inappropriate: and in that case, the Executive Council will select another meeting date for that month, not more than ten days earlier or later than the regular meeting date. The Association may also meet in regular session during other months on call of the President or by decision of the Executive Council; and may meet in special sessions as provided in the Constitution.

2. The President will convene a special meeting whenever (1) he receives a petition signed by twenty or more members requesting a special meeting, or (2) he receives from the Board of Trustees a resolution to that effect, or (3) in his own judgment such a special meeting is necessary. A petition or resolution requesting a special meeting will indicate the topic for disposition or the reason for the special meeting and will also indicate the date and place. And the President will be bound thereby.

2. Regular meetings will be held on call of the President. The President will call such meetings whenever requested by the Executive Committee, or on his own motion. He will also call a regular meeting, if none has been held for 30 days and none is scheduled within the next 30 days, if he receives a petition, signed by five per cent (or more) of the members requesting that such a meeting be called.

1318. Provisions for Continuity of Control

Since general membership meetings are held sporadically, some provision must be made for operations control in the interval between meetings. A society that engages in no activities of any sort between meetings does not need any such provision. But a society that has a program operating between meetings, or that may have to make public statements or issue newspaper releases between meetings, must have some instrument for maintaining operations in those intervals.

(a) If the organization has one or more staff persons on salary, the usual arrangement is to let the senior staff (salaried) official conduct the administrative operations and make public statements or issue newspaper releases that accord with previously established policy. If prior policy does not cover an emergency situation, the staff official consults with the president, the secretary, or the executive board before issuing the statement, making the decision, or taking the action. This is usually *not* spelled out in the constitution or bylaws. It is good practice to include in the constitution some authority for some person or groups of persons to make statements in the name of the society in emergencies. Samples of such clauses are given below, in 1318(f) and 1318(h).

(b) If the society has no salaried staff personnel, a decision must be made as to whether emergency and *ad interim* authority will reside in the president or in a body such as an executive board, council, executive committee, or board of trustees (directors). This is often dramatized as the "strong president vs. weak president" controversy. In practice, control vests in the person or group who can handle it, regardless of the formal architecture of the organization.

(c) A "strong president" structure gives the president authority to (1) name and remove all committee personnel, (2) assign chores to committees and transfer assignments from one committee to another, (3) preside at meetings of the executive board (council, board of trustees, executive committee), (4) speak for the association when a matter comes up between meetings, (5) represent the association before other groups or other agencies. The president's control over the society under this arrangement lies in two factors: he can shape all committees to his way of thinking, and thus translate his own ideas into committee recommendations; and by speaking in the name of the organization he can effectively commit it to his own policy. See 1318(e) for the defects and advantages of this plan.

(d) A "weak president" structure assigns no duties to the president except to preside at meetings, and, possibly, authority "to appoint all committee personnel whose appointment is not otherwise provided for in this constitution or in the bylaws." Since under this structure members of major committees are not appointed by the president, the latter's committee-appointing authority is very limited. The president will have *pro forma* or ceremonial authority, but day-by-day administrative control vests in a board, committee, or council: perhaps an executive committee, a board of trustees or directors, a council, or an executive board. Indeed, the board may even make all committee appointments. No one—not even the president—is authorized to speak in the society's name without approval of this board. Whether the president appointed committee members or not, he cannot remove them without approval of the board. Committees are answerable to the board, not to the president. See 1318(e) for the defects and virtues of this plan.

(e) The advantages of the "strong president" plan are: concentration of responsibility, concordance of power with responsibility, opportunity for swift action, reasonable certainty that there will never be any doubt as to the stand of the society's leadership or any slowness in rising to meet the need for leadership. The disadvantage is that it may make the entire society the captive of a strong president. Similarly the advantage of the "weak president" structure is that it prevents one-man control and assures a more democratic leadership. (A board, however, may fall under the spell of one member and be just as arbitrary as a single officer; and it may become self-perpetuating.) The disadvantage is that it is sometimes hard to fix responsibility when decisions are made by many voices.

(f) For a "strong president" structure, the following constitutional provision is typical:

The President is the chief executive officer and chief administrative officer of the Society. He presides at all meetings of the Society and at all meetings of the Board of Directors. He appoints all committee personnel and designates all committee chairmen. He assigns projects to appropriate committees and may reassign or transfer such projects if, in his judgment, such a transfer is desirable. He speaks on behalf of, and in the name of, the Society whenever a matter in the Society's field of interest is raised and requires presentation of the Society's point of view. He is the Society's official representative at meetings of co-operating and affiliated organizations. He calls all regular and special meetings, fixing the date and place thereof, except when calling such meetings pursuant to membership petition. He is an ex officio member of all committees. All employees and committee members are responsible to the President for the proper performance of their duties.

(g) For a "weak president" structure, the following constitutional provision is typical:

The President is the ceremonial and parliamentary head of the Society and presides at general membership meetings. He appoints committee members except when other provision for the selection of such committee personnel is laid down in this Constitution, in the Bylaws, or in the resolution creating the committee. He serves as a voting member of the Board of Directors but may not serve as Chairman of that Board. He signs the call for Annual, Regular, and Special Meetings when directed to do so by the Board. He is not authorized to commit the Society to any course of action, policy, or point of view without prior authority from the Board. In emergencies where the Society's point of view must be promptly expressed, he is authorized to convene a meeting of the Executive Committee of the Board and to take action in conformity with their decision.

(h) In such a constitution it would be necessary to detail the powers of the board, and in consonance with the above, the following would be typical:

The Board of Directors will consist of the elected officers plus seven Directors specially elected for seven-year terms, one from each District. The Board each year will select, from one of the specially elected Directors, a Chairman. The Board has all the powers and authority of the general membership in the intervals between meetings. There will also be selected, from the Board, an Executive Committee to consist of the President of the Society, the Treasurer of the Society, the Chairman of the Board, and one other Director appointed to the Executive Committee by the Chairman of the Board. The Chairman of the Board will be Chairman of the Executive Committee. The Board of Directors will have the authority below recited; and in intervals between meetings of the Board, its Executive Committee will inherit such authority:

To prepare the call for and the agenda for each Regular and Annual Meeting; to appropriate whatever funds are needed for the operation of the Society; to determine the amount of dues and assessments and methods for collecting and depositing the same; to hold title to all of the Society's assets; to employ whatever staff are in its judgment needed, to fix their salaries, and determine the conditions of their employment; to publish all the Society's publications, naming the editors thereof and determining the publication and editorial policy of each; to elect members of the Nominating Committee, Program Committee, Membership Committee, and Auditing Committee; to sit as an Ethics Committee, and hear charges against members for unethical conduct; to bond the Treasurer; to fill vacancies in offices; to determine the policy of the Society in answering communications or issuing publicity releases; to make public statements in the name of and on behalf of the Society. All officers, staff personnel and committee members are responsible to the Board for the proper performance of their duties.

A board commissioned in this way can do almost anything; and that, indeed, was why the grant of power was made so broad. Every power listed above must, explicitly or implicitly, reside somewhere within the society. A small organization that meets frequently would reserve most of that authority to the general membership. A larger society, and one that meets fewer than three or four times a year, has to make some provision for continuity of this type of control.

1319. Constitutional Booby Traps

Before submitting its final draft, a constitution committee had better review the following check list to make certain that they have not set any booby traps in the society's course:

1. The term of each officer extends until his successor is installed.

2. Provision is made for filling vacancies in the event that an officer dies, resigns, or becomes disabled prior to the regular end of his term.

3. Election of officers is by plurality vote (whoever receives most votes is elected) and not by majority vote. Or, if majority vote is desired, the provision may be that the successful candidate needs a majority of the marked and undefaced ballots. Also, if this is done, that provision be made for runoff elections or for dropping the low-score candidate (see 1315(c)).

4. Meeting dates are not spelled out, but a minimum number of meetings is indicated.

5. Provision is made for calling a meeting by petition of a certain number of members if the officers fail to do so.

6. There is clear assignment of operational authority in the intervals between meetings.

7. A built-in method exists for amending the constitution. If the society meets more often than once a quarter, the time taken to amend the constitution should not exceed three months.

8. Provision is made for omitting an annual meeting or convention during war periods or other times when travel is difficult; with, perhaps, permission for necessary action by an executive body subject to postal ratification or instructions from membership by mail (see 1317).

9. The statement of the purposes or objectives of the organization is broad enough so that matters only indirectly related to it may be considered (see 1313).

10. A realistic quorum rule is adopted. Few organizations can expect more than forty or fifty at an ordinary meeting. If the membership roll includes a thousand names, a 10 per cent quorum rule (requiring an attendance of one hundred) would be unrealistic. Some sort of quorum rule should be written into the bylaws. If no rule is spelled out, the general parliamentary principle applies: a majority is a quorum. In many organizations, it is impossible to expect a majority of members to attend every meeting. Thus the organization would be paralyzed unless a workable quorum rule is detailed in the bylaws. For the executive board or similar body, a majority should be a quorum (see 111).

11. The draft has been fine-combed for the auxiliary verb "shall"; and the "shall" is removed wherever it can be de-

leted without threatening the sense of the sentence. See 1307 for examples of how this is done.

12. If no fixed meeting date is provided, the constitution (or bylaws) requires that notice of each meeting be sent to every member.

13. Provision is made for admitting new applicants to membership. The constitution or bylaws make some reference to eligibility requirements and the process of admission. A secret written ballot is not required routinely (see 1314(b)).

14. Provision is made for dropping a member from the rolls of the society for nonpayment of dues; and, under proper safeguards, for unworthy conduct.

15. The nominating committee, if any, is *not* required to nominate more than one candidate for each vacancy (see 1315 for the reason).

16. Authority is given somewhere in the constitution or in the bylaws for the hiring of salaried staff personnel.

17. Authority is given somewhere in the constitution or in the bylaws for some officer or group of officers to speak in the name of the society in emergencies.

18. Provision is made for some textbook or reference manual of parliamentary procedure as an authority on procedure or practice. For example:

In the absence of any bylaw or standing rule to the contrary, the practices described in the latest edition of Davidson's *Handbook of Parliamentary Procedure* (New York: The Ronald Press Co.) shall apply at all meetings of this organization and its committees.

or

The meetings of this association and its committees will be conducted in accordance wth the rules laid down in the latest edition of Davidson's *Handbook of Parliamentary Procedure* (New York: The Ronald Press Co.).

14

How Not To Get
Pushed Around

1401. The Rank and File Member

The rank and file member usually does not learn parliamentary procedure. He leaves that to chairmen, to ambitious members who aspire to office, and to natural-born hecklers. One difficulty with this passive attitude is that sometimes the ordinary member gets pushed around. This may be due to a dictatorial chairman, an aggressive minority group, or to the victim's unfamiliarity with parliamentary usage. This chapter reviews some of the ways in which a member may protect his rights.

1402. Rights that Should Not Be Protected

If the member wants to compel the group to listen all night to *his* views, let him read no further. This chapter will not tell him how to guarantee that right. If he wants to prevent the majority from carrying out their wishes, no matter how ill-advised, he will find no help in this chapter either.

1403. Right To Appeal

If the chairman rules against you, and if you honestly think he was wrong, you have a right to appeal (see 408(b)). Better have the documentation to support your contention. This or some other authoritative manual will do if you know how to find the citation in a hurry. You may even interrupt someone else to make this appeal, though it is discourteous to do that if it can be avoided. But your appeal must have a seconder. If there is not even one other member who agrees with you, yours is a lost cause. You may not use an appeal as a substitute for reconsideration or as a wedge for reopening a discussion on the merits. You use it when you sincerely think the chair has pulled a parliamentary boner.

1404. Right to an Explanation

If you think someone is pulling a fast one by double talk or jargon, you rise to a point of information (see 704). You are entitled to an explanation of the meaning of a motion, and you use the "point of information" to get it. Do not use a "point of information" as a platform for discussing the merits of a question (see 704(c) for an example). If you need explanation about a parliamentary or procedural point, you raise a "point of parliamentary inquiry" (see 705).

1405. Freedom from Insult

Unless you are the defendant in a formal disciplinary action, you are immune from charges of dishonesty, venal motives, stupidity, or disloyalty. If you are defamed, you may interrupt the speaker by rising to a "point of order" (see 706).

1406. Right To Have the Agenda Followed

A group may try to put something over by removing it from its place on the agenda and voting on it at a time favorable to them. They cannot get away with this if a few other members are alert.

The way to enforce this right—or get a clear statement from two thirds of the members that they don't want to enforce it—is by a call for "orders of the day." See 308(a) for the technique. If they want to, two thirds of the group can vote to suspend the rules (see 306(b) and 307(e)), and thus take something up out of order. And if two thirds of the group don't agree with you, you don't have many rights left anyway.

1407. Preventing an Unrepresentative Majority from Binding the Organization

If you think that a meeting is highly unrepresentative, you may prevent irrevocable action. You do this by a motion to reconsider later. In some manuals this is called a "Motion to Reconsider and Enter on the Minutes" (see 1109). You need a second, and the delay is only until the next meeting. But you may believe that (or see to it that) a more representative group will come to the next meeting.

1408. Right To Talk

This is a qualified right. If two thirds of those present want to stop debate they can do it by a motion to that effect (or by moving "previous question"). And when that is done you have no right to talk. If you made the main motion in the first place, you do have an absolute right to speak to it, provided you ask for the floor as soon as it is seconded, and provided the motion is a debatable one (also see 507). If someone who has already discussed a matter is again clamoring for the floor while you have not yet been recognized, you may rise to a point of order if the chair recognizes him and ignores you. As a general rule, a member is not permitted to talk a second time to a motion if a previously silent member is asking for the floor. If the chair refuses to recognize you, you may appeal (see 408(d)). Once you have spoken, however, the chair is within his rights in refusing to let you talk again if some previously silent member wants the floor. While talking, you may be interrupted by any member who raises a point of privilege (see Chapter 7) or who wants to appeal a recently announced decision. If you are the first speaker on the motion, you may be interrupted by an "objection to consideration" (see 116). Otherwise, no one but the chairman may interrupt you; and he may interrupt only if you are becoming tangential in topic, abusive in manner, or highly repetitive.

If the chair insists that you have talked long enough, or if he says your discussion is out of order for any reason, you must either conform to his request or ask for an appeal (see 408(b)).

1409. Right To Stop Someone Else from Talking

This is done by the methods listed in 505. If the speaker is really out of order, you may interrupt by a "point of order" (see 706). Otherwise you have to wait until you can get a word in and then make a motion to stop debate, to lay on the table, to refer it to a committee, or to adjourn. Any of these motions, if seconded, would have to be disposed of before debate on the primary motion could continue.

1410. Right To Reopen a Matter

A meeting cannot be compelled to act on the same subject time and time again just because a few members keep returning to it. However, most primary motions can be renewed if some other business has intervened, and any member who voted on the prevailing side may, under certain circumstances, move to reconsider action just taken. Read Chapter 11 (read it slowly—it is a complex matter) for discussion of this. A matter that was laid on the table may be started on the road to revival by a simple motion to take it from the table. This is explained in 806 to 810.

1411. Right To Exclude Outsiders

Sometimes a member feels tongue-tied in the presence of strangers, and wants to feel free to discuss a matter with only members in the room. This is done by moving that we go into executive session (see 105).

1412. Right To Have Your Motion Seriously Considered

A member cannot resent his motion's being defeated; he recognizes that the majority has that right. But he resents a maneuver which keeps the group from clearly voting on his motion one way or the other. The devices to prevent your motion from reaching a clean decision are:

1. Objection to consideration: see 116 and 1413
2. Laying on the table: see 801(a), 802 to 805, and 1414
3. Postponing indefinitely: see 801(c), 812, and 1415
4. Postponing to a definite time: see 801(b), 811, and 1416
5. Referring to a committee: see 1005 and 1417
6. To attach a stultifying amendment: see Chapter 9 and 1418
7. To adjourn: see 1205 to 1208 and 1419

1413. When Objection to Consideration Is Raised

This motion is not in order if debate has gotten beyond the first speaker. If the "objection" is then raised, and if the chairman entertains it, the maker rises to a point of order and suggests that the motion is out of order (see 116(a)). If the motion is made in good time, there must be a vote on it. But it takes a two-thirds vote to kill the matter (see 116(d), 116(e), and 116(f)). If two thirds of the voters want to take the matter off the agenda, there is nothing the maker of the motion can do about it at that time. After some other business has intervened, he may move to reconsider the vote which withdrew his subject from the floor. To make such a motion (to reconsider) he must have voted with the two-thirds majority in the first place (see Chapter 11).

1414. When Matter Is Laid on the Table

Someone hostile to your motion may move to lay it on the table. If seconded, the motion to lay on the table is immedi-

ately (without debate) voted on. If passed (and a majority
vote is sufficient) the matter is put on the shelf. What you
can do, as soon as some other business has been disposed of,
is to move to take the matter from the table. See 806 to 810
for description of this process. You may *not* move to reconsider a vote to lay on the table. You achieve the same effect
by moving to take from the table.

1415. If Indefinite Postponement Is Moved

If this motion passes, your subject is practically dead; debate stops, and you cannot revive the matter at this meeting.
As the motion (to postpone) has low rank, here is what you
can do. *First,* you can debate it fully, and perhaps convince
the group to defeat the motion to postpone indefinitely; *second,* you may move to refer the matter to a committee. This
is in order. If it passes, then you have at least kept the matter
alive and can appeal to the committee for favorable action.
If this fails, your *third* device (before the meeting votes on
the indefinite postponement) is to move to postpone to a definite time. If this passes, it assures that the matter will come
up again at the time specified (see 811). If that fails, the
fourth possibility (if you can get the floor that often, or have
a friend who knows the ropes) is to move to lay the whole
matter on the table. If that passes, you can, when the group
is more sympathetic, move to take it from the table (see 806
to 810). Finally, if all this fails, your *fifth* and last course is
to let the motion (to postpone indefinitely) pass, voting for
it (that is voting for the postponement) yourself; and then,
as soon as you get the floor thereafter, moving to reconsider
(see 1107(b)). This is debatable and gives you another opportunity to convince the brethren of the error of their ways.

1416. If Motion Is Made To Postpone
to a Definite Time

It is usually good tactics to let this motion take its course.
If the motion passes, it means that, at this session, the majority
is hostile to the primary matter; so it is just as well to have it

come up again at a later meeting. If the motion fails, your position is improved. You can get more control over the revival of the matter by moving to lay it on the table. Such a motion takes precedence over a motion to postpone, so the motion to table is voted on first. If this passes, then you can recall the original matter later or at a subsequent meeting by moving to take from the table (see 806 to 810).

1417. If Matter Is Being Committed

Whether referring a matter to a committee is or is not a consignment to the graveyard depends on the practices of the association. In most organizations, a commitment is simply a temporary shelving, not an early demise. A committee that holds the matter too long can be discharged (see 1017(b)). If the maker wants to prevent his motion's being sent to a committee, he can, in order (1) debate it and try to persuade the meeting to defeat the motion to commit; (2) if it looks as if that will not work, he can make a motion to postpone to a definite time. This *is* in order while a motion to commit is pending (see 204) and by making the "definite time" a convenient one, the maker assures some control over the motion. If that fails (3) he can move to lay it all on the table, and then revive it at a more propitious time by a motion to take from the table (see Chapter 8).

1418. When Faced with a Stultifying Amendment

It is possible, by amendment, to make a motion so unpalatable that its original sponsors denounce it. This can be done by offering a crippling amendment which does not seem to neutralize the motion. Chapter 9, and particularly 911, should be reviewed here. If an unacceptable amendment is made and seconded, the sponsor of the original motion may take the following steps to protect his original interest: (1) protest to the chair that the motion is out of order because its effect is to neutralize or negate the primary motion (see 911(a)). If the chair overrules the protest, and if the member believes that the chair was wrong, (2) he may appeal the decision of the chair (see 408). If the action of the chair is sustained, the first sponsor (3) may move an amendment to the amendment which restores the motion to its original vigor. If this is not possible, the sponsor of the initial motion then (4) debates the amendment, urging that the amendment be defeated; and if it looks as if the amendment may pass, then the sponsor must make a rapid choice: is it better to gain time by referring the whole matter to a committee, or to try for a clean decision now? If the former seems wise, he (5) moves to refer the whole matter to a committee. This may be effective if it passes because, away from the heat of debate, the committee may bring in a recommendation favorable to the motion in its original form. If the sponsor decides to fight it out on the floor, he (6) speaks and votes against the amendment. If the amendment passes, the sponsor then must decide whether he wants his motion as amended, or prefers no motion at all. In the latter case he (7) indicates by debate that he wants his friends and supporters to vote against the primary motion. If the primary motion (as amended) is thus defeated, the entire matter may be renewed at a more favorable time.

1419. When Threatened with Adjournment

If the organization really wants to adjourn, you can't stop it. They won't adjourn simply to avoid action on one little motion, as a rule. If the matter is really urgent, you may rise to a point of privilege, and tell the chair that something desperate will happen if they adjourn. See 1207(b) for the method and disposition. If, in spite of all this, the motion passes, then—if it is a *cum die* adjournment (see 1203(b)), your motion gets a priority position at the next meeting as explained in 1210(a).

1420. Right to an Honest Vote

If you think the chair is not honestly appraising the vote or the sense of the meeting, you may call for a "division" or ask for an appeal (see 612 for division, 408 for appeal). You do not even need a second to call for, and get, a division, provided you don't keep calling for division all the time just to harass the meeting.

1421. Right to a Secret Vote

If you represent a group of members, you have no right to a secret vote. If you are a member of an executive board, a delegate, a trustee, or belong to any other body with a constituency, your vote cannot be kept secret. Your constituents have a right to know how you voted. However, at a general membership meeting you have a right to keep your vote a secret on at least two occasions: (1) on voting for office, and (2) on voting on disciplinary matters. In many organizations, the vote on an applicant for admission to membership is also secret. A motion to make the (secret, written) vote unanimous is not in order if it would compel you to show your hand, and you can insist on that (see 617(c)). A motion to vote by roll call at a general membership meeting is never in order. This would make your vote a matter of permanent record and you can insist that such a procedure is improper (see 607). You may, on any matter, ask for a secret, written vote, though you have no right to insist on it if the majority prefer an unwritten vote (see 602(b), 602(c), and 608).

On a motion to increase or decrease the salary of an employee, good taste requires a secret (written) ballot.

1422. Right To Change Your Vote

Any member may change his unwritten vote up to the time the chair announces the result. For details, see 615.

1423. Right to a Recess

Sometimes it appears that, given a recess, a breathing space, a chance to talk things over informally, you might win converts. You have a right to ask for, but not to insist on, a recess. The motion must be seconded. If nothing else is pending, it is a debatable motion. If some other motion is pending, the

217

recess is voted on first and is undebatable (see 1211). It is effective if more vote for a recess than vote against it.

1424. Right To Disinter Something Buried in Committee

Sometimes a committee hangs on to a matter, and apparently intends to kill it. Under such circumstances any interested member may move to discharge the committee from consideration of that item. See 1017(b) for method. In voluntary organizations, there is no way of compelling a committee to report, but it can be compelled to disgorge the topic by a motion to discharge it from consideration of a subject. Majority vote is sufficient, as explained in 1017(b).

1425. How Not To Get Pushed Around

This chapter has listed the ways in which an unsophisticated member may be deprived of some of his parliamentary rights, and points up the methods for meeting this challenge. If the meeting is overwhelmingly determined to deprive the member of a right, they can do it, by simply sustaining the chairman; and, short of an appeal to the courts, there is nothing the member can do about it. Usually, however, it is a matter of unfamiliarity with the procedure rather than deliberate malice. Hence a copy of this or of some other authoritative manual of procedure should be at hand. And the member who expects to have to defend his rights aggressively will thumb over the book in advance of the meeting so that he can find his citations in a hurry.

15

How To Handle a Heckler

1501. The Psychodynamics of Heckling

Even the most decorous of organizations may be cursed with a few members who seem determined to torture the chairman. They demand divisions or roll calls for trivial reasons. They are always protesting the chair's decisions and frequently insist on a formal appeal. They keep repeating previously rejected motions. They volubly demand their rights. If the chair does not maintain control over the meeting, he is a failure as a chairman. The heckler is a serious threat to that control.

The chairman ought to understand the kinds of hecklers and the factors that provoke their badgering. To be sure, the chair is presiding at a meeting, not operating a mental hygiene clinic. However, if he can understand why the heckler acts as he does, he may be better prepared to cope with him. For example, it is helpful to know whether the heckler is acting in good faith or is being malicious; whether he is sincerely trying to put across a constructive idea, or is interested only in protecting his rights; or whether he is powered by the negative aim of embarrassing the chairman.

Hecklers fall into five overlapping classes:

1. The crusader
2. The crotcheteer
3. The exhibitionist
4. The paranoiac
5. The psychopath

1502. The Crusader

This is the man with a mission—the member who has a torch to carry which, he honestly believes, will bring light to the world. Nothing at any meeting is as important as his crusade, and all other subjects are forced to be related to it. At one civic association, a member has dedicated himself to a crusade against comic strips in newspapers. Here, he feels, is the cause of all delinquency, crime, truancy, drug addiction, industrial strife, and low morale. So to every resolution he wants to tack on an amendment condemning comic strips. Although free of malice, he heckles the chairman by (1) insisting on amending every motion or resolution even though the amendment, being irrelevant, must be ruled out of order; (2) appealing from such a decision; (3) refusing to believe that his motion or amendment was defeated, so (4) demanding "Division" at every voice vote; (5) talking at great length, often without relevance to the topic; (6) refusing to stop talking when told that he is irrelevant; and (7) demanding that his pet subject be made a special order.

1503. The Crotcheteer

The crotcheteer operates much like the crusader. However, his crotchets are variable rather than fixed, and there is a greater element of perverseness and whimsy in the crotcheteer than there is in the crusader. He may, for example, ride a particular parliamentary hobbyhorse and demand that the chairman follow exactly some obscure and unimportant fragment of parliamentary usage. In the sense that he is sincere, he approaches the crusader, but, since there is a strong tincture of vanity in his behavior, he also approaches the exhibitionist. He develops whims, fancies, vagaries, and caprices, and seeks to stop the forward march of the meeting's business while he airs his crotchets.

1504. The Exhibitionist

Here is the well-meaning, bumbling, somewhat inadequate or insecure member, who compensates for his inadequacies by getting his name in the minutes. If he can't make the motion, he will loudly second it. If no one else will discuss the matter, he will. He delights in pointing out trivial defects in resolutions which everyone wants passed at once. If the wheels seem greased to effect the passage of a motion—even if it is only a *pro forma* motion, he rises to ask a question. He does not even like to have the minutes accepted as read, though he may have trouble finding any error in them. His cry of "Mr. Chairman" may come from any corner of the room, at any moment—usually it comes when everybody is set to dispose of a matter smoothly. If he learns a bit of parliamentary procedure, he goes out of his way to air it, even if he has to manufacture an occasion. One exhibitionist stumbled on the fact that there was such a thing as a motion to reconsider. It delighted him hugely. He made a motion to reconsider anything and everything in order to get himself noticed. And it worked. His name was spread all over the minutes. Influential members pleaded with him to keep quiet.

1505. The Paranoiac

With this character, we cross the border from benign hecklers to malignant ones. A paranoiac is a person with a fixed delusion, usually a delusion of persecution. What characterizes the paranoid state is the existence of an ever spreading, incorrigible, intelligent-sounding and well-organized delusion. Paranoiacs are suspicious of the motives and behavior of all of the society's officers. They see conspiracy everywhere. They look behind even the simplest of motions, seeking some underhanded or cabalistic reasons. Frequently the paranoiac can assemble a company of followers, who soon form an indigestible mass within the society, not fully accepted by it, not entirely outside of it. The paranoiac is a great petition circulator and a writer of long letters (often of open letters) with much capitalization and underlining of words. He is a maker of impassioned speeches. He likes to take profuse and detailed notes of whatever an officer says, and later to analyze each word and confound the officer with his own remarks. Because he soon becomes such a destructive force, the officers have to conspire to manage him in some way, and this, in turn, gives verisimilitude to his delusion that he is the victim of a conspiracy. While the paranoiac (unlike the psychopath) is not basically malicious, he soon comes to identify his opponents with the forces of evil, and then he considers no measure too unfair in attacking them. As a result, the paranoiac in operation seems to act in bad faith.

1506. The Psychopath

A psychopath is a man without a conscience. Unlike the paranoiac, he has no real delusions; unlike the crusader, he has no sincere goal. He is exhibitionistic, opportunistic, and trouble-making. His basic motive is a problem for a psychiatrist. He is recognized at meetings by the fact that he enjoys making trouble, does so for no apparently sound reason, does not mind embarrassing or even degrading himself so long as he *can* harass others. He is usually intelligent, and by definition he is sane. His perversity is incurable; his forte is mischief.

1507. The Heckler's Armamentarium

The heckler torments the chairman by such devices as demanding roll calls, shouting "point of order," insisting on a division of the house, renewing rejected motions, shouting "question," and demanding this serve to choke off all debate, refusing to yield the floor, appealing from the chair, and firmly misquoting the rules of parliamentary procedure. The five devices on which he leans most heavily are (1) speaking out of turn, (2) making dilatory motions, (3) making repetitive motions, (4) appealing, and (5) refusing to yield the floor. Here is what the chair can do.

1508. Speaking Out of Turn

(a) When the heckler speaks out of turn, the chair can refuse to recognize him. If asked why, he can explain that the heckler's point is not in order, or that he has already had ample chance to be heard, or that the matter has been settled. If the heckler appeals (see 408), the chair asks if anyone seconds the appeal. (An appeal from the chair, unlike a point of order, must be seconded.) If it is not seconded, the chair explains that, for want of a second, the appeal cannot be entertained. If there is a second, the procedure of 408 (particularly 408(c) *et seq.*) is followed.

(b) Usually this kind of appeal is *not* subject to debate or discussion. The rule is that, when the matter touches on decorum, courtesy, or priority, the appeal is not debatable, and that is usually the situation. The chair will have to be arbitrary here and rule out the debate, explaining that it is contrary to parliamentary procedure to permit debate on this kind of appeal, but adding that the chair's decision, while not debatable, is reversible. It would be absurd to allow debate on this, because the ruling was intended to prevent endless debate in the first place. The appeal is phrased, "Shall the decision of the Chair be sustained?" If more vote "no" than "yes," the heckler wins. Nearly always, the chair will be sustained. A tie vote sustains him. The member can then be told that he has been found out of order not only by the chairman but by the society, and he should also be told that this bars a repetition of the point already disallowed even if presented in different form.

1509. Making Dilatory Motions

A heckler may try to destroy a matter or try to impede the progress of the meeting by moving to postpone, commit, or table a proposal, and by repeating the motion over and over again. See Chapter 8 for a general discussion of this; also see 1414 to 1423.

1510. Repetitive Motions

(a) As a general rule, a motion cannot be renewed at the same meeting after it has been rejected, postponed, tabled, or referred to a committee. This extends to motions which, in effect, are the same even though worded somewhat differently. A member does have a right, under certain circumstances, to ask that a matter be *reconsidered* or *rescinded* (see Chapter 11). He can ask to have a negative vote as well as a positive vote reconsidered. In other words, a member may ask that a rejection be reconsidered under the ground rules detailed in Chapter 11. But he has no right to keep renewing a matter previously disposed of. This refers to primary motions (see 202) only, but it is with primary motions that hecklers wreak most of their mischief. A secondary motion (such as a motion to table, close debate, or refer to a committee) *is* renewable if some other business has intervened since it was last rejected.

(b) If a member keeps renewing a previously rejected primary motion, the chair rules it is out of order and does not entertain any second. He explains that a primary motion, having been disposed of, cannot be renewed. If the member appeals, the procedure of 408 and 1508 is followed. If, on a point of parliamentary inquiry, a question is raised about whether a rejected matter can be reconsidered, the chair points out that it can and explains the conditions (see Chapter 11).

(c) If the member is unable to bring the matter back to the floor by a motion to reconsider, the chair thereafter peremptorily rules him out of order when he tries to revive the same rejected matter. He points out that it cannot be revived because it has already been rejected, and that this is doubly true if the society has rejected a motion to reconsider.

1511. Appeals from the Chair

See 408 and 1508.

1512. Refusing To Yield the Floor

(a) In most American assemblies, a chairman is more likely to let irrelevant debate continue than he is to cut off appropriate debate. However, debate must be germane to the topic. The chair may interrupt a speaker by saying "The relevance of this to the matter under discussion is not clear," or words to that effect. The chair may then, at his own discretion, rule that the discussion is irrelevant and therefore out of order. The speaker at this point must either (1) return to the mainstream of the subject, or (2) appeal the decision of the chair, as in 408, or (3) sit down. If the discussion *is* germane but if it is so long-winded that everyone is becoming restless, the chair may interrupt by stating that the speaker has already consumed more than a fair share of the time, and that "I believe I speak for most of the members when I now ask the speaker to resume his seat." If the speaker refuses to do that, the chair then says: "The speaker's refusal to abide by the chair's instruction is, in effect, an appeal. I therefore ask the members to vote on it. I have asked Mr. X to terminate his debate. Shall this request of the Chair be sustained? All in favor of inviting Mr. X to sit down, please say 'aye' . . . ," or words to that effect.

(b) Sometimes the chairman has a good friend in the audience who knows what he, as a rank and file member, can do to help. The member simply rises to a point of order, interrupting the speaker. The chair asks the interrupting member to state his point of order. The member states that he believes that the speaker is out of order because the debate is irrelevant, disorderly, abusive, or obviously designed solely for the purpose of wearing everybody out (as the case may be). The chair says that the point is well taken and instructs the speaker to sit down. This is, of course, subject to an appeal (see 408).

(c) The chair has a right to maintain decorum. If the speaker is abusive, defamatory, noisy, insulting, or manifestly irrelevant, the chair will rule him out of order. In this connection see 706.

1513. Sublimating the Heckler

Surprisingly, the heckler is often tamed by being put to work. The chair might, for instance, appoint his most persistent heckler to serve as chief teller for a written ballot. This drains off some energy and gets him out of the room for a little while to count ballots. He can ask the heckler to serve as a member of (but not as chairman of) a committee. He might ask him to distribute literature within the room or assist in the display of charts or in preparing a collation. He might ask the heckler to retire in order to draft a proposed resolution which would require great care in composition. The meeting could then proceed while the heckler was engaged in the throes of creative labor, in some quiet anteroom.

This tactic must not be carried too far. The heckler should not be named as a delegate, representative, or observer; nor to a publicity or public relations post; nor as chairman of a committee. He is a poor spokesman for the society and should be kept away from any position in which he might appear to be a spokesman. Furthermore, he might sabotage a program if he has the power to do so, and is therefore a poor committee chairman.

16

The Society's Budget:
Its Form and Its Function

1600. Authorization of Bills

A small society often meets its expenses on an off-the-cuff basis. When a bill arrives, the treasurer sends out a check. There is no advance planning and sometimes even no provision for validating a bill or authorizing payment. Other societies use a budget. Here expenses are estimated and allocated in advance. Then there is specific authorization for most of the bills which the treasurer has to meet, and it is possible to plan to meet all bills, to determine in advance which categories of expense will have priority, and to correct in future years any errors of estimate made last year.

1601. What Organizations Need a Budget?

As a general rule, a predetermined and officially adopted budget (particularly an expense budget) should be on record for any organization which:

1. Spends more than $500 a year
2. Uses tax money
3. Vests all financial authority in a group less than its own general membership

4. Derives income from business operations, publications, sales, or rentals

1602. Who Prepares a Budget?

A budget may be prepared by one individual (a budget officer) or by a committee. The budget officer may be a non-member employed for this purpose, or a member specially designated by the executive committee or other high authority body. More commonly, budget drafting is the work of a committee—usually a special committee on budget having no other function. This committee may be appointed by the president, elected by the general membership, or designated by an executive committee or other high authority body. The committee should be small. It is important that there be some overlap of members each year, since it would be hard for a totally inexperienced committee to tackle the job cold. A committee of three each serving three years, with one term expiring each year, is a good pattern. The chairman should be one of the members who has had previous service on the committee.

1603. What Is a Budget Year?

A budget is prepared for a one-year period, except for certain national, international, or governmental bodies, where general assemblies are held only once in two years. A biennial budget would then be offered. In nearly all voluntary organizations, the budget period is one year.

(a) There are, in any organization, six possible meanings to the word "year."

1. *Calendar year:* January 1 to December 31.

2. *Program year:* In many organizations, all activities are suspended during the summer but continue without interruption during the winter. The program year thus might begin and end in July or in September. An organization that is coordinated with a school or college (a Parent Teachers Association, for example) would have a program year corresponding to the school year.

3. *Administrative year:* This is the period during which one person remains as president. It may be identical with a program year or a calendar year; or it might be figured from a different base. Thus, one society elects its officers at the December meeting and installs them at the January meeting, which is on the second Thursday in that month. The calendar year begins January 1, but their administrative year begins January 8 or January 14, or on some day between. When the administrative year begins in September, it usually coincides with the program year.

4. *Fiscal year:* This is the period by which or for which accounts are recorded. In the United States Government the fiscal year ends on June 30 and the next one begins on July 1. In most voluntary societies the fiscal year is the same as either (1) the administrative year, so that accounts can be transferred to the new treasurer at the end of the fiscal year, or (2) the budget year.

5. *Dues year:* This is the period during which a member would remain in good standing (is considered nondelinquent) on the basis of the payment of a year's dues.

6. *Budget year:* This is the period planned for in the expense budget and covered in the income budget. This often begins several weeks after the beginning of the fiscal year, as explained in (c), below.

(**b**) Each organization determines and definitely records the period covered by the budget—that is, the budget year. If the organization meets only once a year, this may pose a problem. Suppose the organization holds its convention annually in September. The treasurer wants to present a report for a period ending as close to the meeting date as possible. He would like to say "Here is the state of your treasury as of August 31, only a few weeks ago." This would mean that the *fiscal* year would have to end August 31. But to do this he could not close his books until September 1, which would leave him very little time before the convention. If the fiscal year ended on June 30 he would have all summer during which to prepare his report. But then the report on September 15 would not reflect summer income and expenses, and it would be almost three months old when presented.

(c) The task of the budget officer or budget committee is somewhat different. The budget should not be prepared until the officer or budget committee has heard from the society's officials, boards, committees and so forth, about their needs for the coming year. The obvious time to hold such hearings is during the annual convention when there is a concentration of members in one place. However, if the budget officer or budget committee does not make its decision until the close of the convention, then the budget year will have to start a little later. So, this hypothetical society (see 1603(b)) might logically have a budget year beginning October 1, though its fiscal year would begin July 1 or September 1.

(d) The association should, after weighing these factors, determine on a specific period to represent the budget year. If the organization meets monthly, this period could be identical with the administrative year or fiscal year. If the organization covers a compact geographical area so that officers can assemble easily at any time, the budget year could be almost any period—probably the administrative year would be best. But if meetings are infrequent and the membership is widely scattered, some kind of compromise must be reached.

1604. Major Headings of a Budget

Ordinarily a budget is divided into two major headings: an income budget and an expense budget. Since the budget reflects the flow of liquid funds into and out of the treasury, it does not usually list capital assets. However, a statement about the reserve fund and capital assets might well be included as an addendum to the budget, for the information of members.

The expense budget would be divided into several accounts or subaccounts such as president's office, committees, secretary's office, publications, and so forth. Each account would be further subdivided into lines, such as a "mailing and postage" line under secretary's office, after which would be written the amount allotted for postage and mailing out of that office.

For further details of the budget breakdown see 1607.

1605. Assembling of Budget Data

The two principal sources of data are (1) review of records of previous years, and (2) requests of officials this year, together with their supporting arguments.

(a) In preparing the expense budget, the budget committee or budget officer reviews actual expenses in previous years to obtain a base line. There are then two ways of proceeding:

1. The departmental budget. Under this system, each officer, committee chairman, and policy-making employee writes to or personally appears before the budget committee or budget officer. Each officer indicates how much money he will need for his activities next year, and answers questions about this. Rank and file members who object to appropriating too much money for one activity or another are usually permitted to appear before the budget officers to oppose certain appropriations. The budget committee then recommends an over-all expense budget to the fund-appropriating body of the society. This may be the executive committee, the entire association, or a board of trustees. As a rule, under this system, an official, employee, or committee chairman who feels that his budget has been unfairly reduced can then plead directly before the fund-appropriating body.

2. The executive budget. This is used only in a very large, highly departmentalized organization with a strong president responsible for the entire program, who has authority commensurate with that responsibility. He appoints one or more budget advisers. Every officer, committee chairman, official, and policy-making employee presents his needs to this budget adviser, who prepares an over-all budget. When the president approves, this over-all budget is submitted to the fund-appropriating body. Under this system, individual officials do not appear before that body, since the president assumes full responsibility for the amounts requested.

1606. Order of Preparing Budget

Two methods are used:

(a) *Fixed Income Method:* The income budget is prepared

first, based on reasonable expectations of income for the year. The budgetary requests of the officers, chairmen, officials, and employees are then totaled and, probably, found to exceed the anticipated income. Each budgetary item is then reduced—not necessarily pro rata—until the anticipated expenses aggregate no more than the expected income. If this proves impossible or undesirable, authority is obtained for making up the deficit by dipping into reserves or by borrowing. The essence of this method is that the income budget is prepared before the expense budget is started.

(b) *Adjusted Income Method:* The expense budget is prepared first in the manner described in 1605 above. Income from all sources except dues is then calculated and the total subtracted from the anticipated expenses. The remainder is divided among the number of members, thus fixing the annual dues. Or, the remainder is set up as a "total income from dues" account, and the annual dues are adjusted so as to bring in this amount.

(c) The *adjusted* income method is possible only if the dues can be easily changed. If dues are fixed by constitutional provision, or if it is awkward to make any change in the dues, then the fixed income method must be used. An organization which has taxing power can, of course, use the adjusted income method much more readily than an organization which lacks such power. By "taxing power" here is meant not only the normal governmental taxing function, but also the right to impose a serious sanction on a member who fails to pay his dues. For example, a physician by forfeiting membership in the medical society might lose his hospital affiliation; a laborer by losing his union membership might lose his job; a "mutual" corporation or a church where the assets are owned by all the members has a sanction for enforcing dues payment, in that loss of membership may mean loss of a capital holding. In all such organizations, where membership is a valuable property in dollars-and-cents terms, the fund-appropriating body can raise the dues to whatever level is needed to carry out its program without much fear of mass resignations. But where the bond which holds a member to the organization is a less material one, the budget officer cannot recommend expenses seriously in excess of ordinary income, and expect to make up the deficit by raising dues.

1607. Accounts and Lines in the Expense Budget

(a) The expense budget is broken down into several major headings. These may be labeled by letters or by words, such as:

> President's Account
> Membership Committee Account
> Secretary's Office Account
> Annual Convention Account.

Or, instead, they might be called simply Account A, Account B, and so forth.

(b) Each account is further broken down into lines. When a check is drawn or a bill paid, a note is made of the line from which the money came. That is, a separate account is maintained, on paper, for each line. Every time a bill is paid, the amount available on that line is reduced by that extent. For example, suppose the office of the secretary account is called Account S. The budget for this might read:

S. OFFICE OF THE SECRETARY .... $4,605.
1. Office rent .... $ 600.00
2. Postage stamps 20.00
3. Telephone 120.00
4. Stationery 75.00
5. Clerical assistance 3000.00
6. Heat and light 240.00
7. Janitorial services 200.00
8. Office supplies 250.00
9. Petty cash 100.00
$4605.00

When, each month, the treasurer mails a check of $50 for rent, he endorses on the counterfoil "S.1," meaning Account S, Line 1. In his books, the first month, he subtracts $50 from Line 1 in Account S, showing that this line now has $550 left in it. These are treasurers' operations, not budget officers' duties. However, this operation is described to show the reason for the nomenclature of "account and line."

1608. Transfer of Budget Allocations

Each association decides for itself whether it will permit transfers of unexpended funds from line to line or from account to account.

Within one account, a single officer is usually responsible for the entire amount, and therefore it is customary to allow the officer freely to transfer items from one line to another in the same account. In the example given above, if the secretary finds that he is using the telephone much less than anticipated but that he is spending more for supplies, he could simply transfer $50 from Line 3 to Line 8. To transfer from one *account* to another, however, usually requires permission of the executive committee or some other high authority body (except in societies where an executive budget, as explained in 1605(a)(2) is the rule. In those organizations, the president is usually allowed to transfer freely from one account to another). Otherwise it would lead to raids by one official on another's appropriations. For instance, the speakers' bureau might have an unexpended allotment of $200, while the convention committee is desperately in need of that. There must be some orderly way in which the chairman of the convention committee should be permitted to persuade a budget agency to transfer $100 from the speakers' bureau to the convention account. But there must also be some orderly way in which the chief of the speakers' bureau may resist such a transfer.

1609. Committee Budgets

An organization sometimes gets into difficulties because it fails to make provision for committee expenses. Several methods are available:

(a) Each committee can be expected to handle all its own expenses. No association funds are then made available to committees. This is appropriate in a small organization concentrated within a compact geographic area where committee work can be done largely by telephone or mail, with each member paying for the stamps or phone calls out of his own pocket.

(b) A coordinator or a committee on committees is designated. A lump sum is appropriated for all committees in the aggregate. Then each committee chairman has to persuade the coordinator, or the chairman of the committee on committees, to release funds for his own operations. Typically the committee on committees is made up of all committee chairmen, plus a neutral person (usually an ex-president) as chairman. At the start of each budget year, this committee on committees allocates about 75 per cent of the moneys appropriated to it, allotting so much to each committee. This is done at a conference at which all committee chairmen are present. The other 25 per cent is retained by the committee on committes as a reserve fund, or for emergencies. This system is appropriate in large, highly departmentalized organizations, where committees vary considerably in the amount of money they need and where committee operations are essential to the program of the association. Sometimes the treasurer or the president serves as coordinator, but it is generally better to name an impartial senior member to this post.

In some associations, there is a variation of this system. Committees are grouped into three or four categories, and sums are appropriated for each category of committees rather than for individual committees. Two obvious categories are (1) committees concerned with the internal affairs of the association: housekeeping committees; and (2) committees concerned with external relations: public affairs committees. For instance, included within the first (housekeeping) category would be committees on membership, constitution and bylaws, nominations, budget, resolutions, arrangements, and so on. An ethics committee and a program committee might be placed in either housekeeping or public affairs categories, depending on the weight of their activities. Obviously classified in the public affairs category would be committees on legislation, public relations, public education, publicity, and the like.

235

Under this plan, each group of committees would have its own coordinator, and one appropriation would be made for the public affairs group of committees, while another appropriation is made for the housekeeping group. The coordinator would then allocate funds within each bracket.

A civic association might set up three categories of committees: one concerned with relations with the city and state government, a sort of "government" group of committees; another concerned with voluntary neighborhood activities; and a third concerned with the internal affairs of the organization. Examples would be: a committee on zoning (related to the city zoning authority); a committee on publicity (related to the local newspapers); and a committee on constitution and bylaws (an internal or housekeeping committee). Each category could have its own appropriation and its own coordinator.

(c) A separate budgetary allotment could be made for each committee. Except in associations with only a few committees, this is an exceedingly unwieldy method. It has the further disadvantage that slight errors in estimate are multiplied if there are many committees. For instance, an association has twenty committees. An effort is made to estimate the expenses needed by each. This is in error by $20 each a year—not a large error—but for all twenty committees, the estimate is off by $400. It is likewise time-consuming for a budget officer or budget committee to scrutinize the activities of twenty committees and listen to the pleas of twenty chairmen, all clamoring for a greater share of the society's treasury. If an association has only four or five committees, or if it has many committees which need no funds at all, this method might work well.

(d) Each committee is invited to voucher its bills to the treasurer directly for payment out of a reserve or contingent fund. If a committee is forbidden to encumber the association's funds in advance, this system might work provided that experience has shown that, in the past, committee activities have not been a substantial drain on the treasury. This is handled in the budget by setting aside a reserve committee fund for this purpose.

(**e**) A combination of methods (c) and (d) above. Certain essential committees which require substantial sums of money are included in the budget. The others have to obtain authorization prior to each expense. For example, a committee on arrangements for the convention, or the committee which publishes the society's magazine, has to have funds. These could be included in the budget on separate lines. But a committee on nominations might transact its business by mail or, in the case of a city or county society, by a meeting at one member's home. So the committee on nominations could ask for a few dollars to pay for its small expenses, when those expenses accrue. There would be no need for a separate budget line for the nominating committee.

1610. Income Budgets

The income budget is usually fairly simple, consisting of a few lines, with indication of expected income on each line. If the only source of funds is membership dues, the income budget is nothing but an estimate of the average number of dues-paying members during the following year together with their expected payments. Following are possible sources of income for a voluntary organization. A society that has two or more of such sources will set up an income budget showing the anticipated amount from each.

INCOME BUDGET. ESTIMATED INCOME, YEAR ENDING_____, 19__

	...... $00,000.00
A. Membership dues	$
B. Rental of booths at convention	$
C. Subscriptions to our magazine	$
D. Advertisements in magazine	$
E. Subscriptions to our dinner-dance	$
F. Speakers' fees paid to our officers	$
G. Interest on investments	$
H. Sale of publications	$
J. Subleasing of desk space	$
K. Registrations at convention	$
M. Grants, bequests, donations	$

No one organization is likely to have all eleven of these sources of income. If it has more than two or three, the income budget is set up in this form. Each line could be a separately lettered "Account" (as above) or simply a numbered "line." Then, on the treasurer's books, any item of income would be recorded as "Account B" or "Line 2," as appropriate. An additional line for miscellaneous or sundry income is desirable.

Certain items represent expectations from income-producing activities, such as the convention or a magazine. Some societies prefer to set up completely separate budgets for these activities. See 1612 and 1613.

1611. Special Accounts and Dedicated Funds

It may be expedient, or legally necessary, to set up special funds, on both the income and expense side, which—on paper —are not to be mingled with the general treasury of the association. These fall into two categories: (1) grants of money from outside the association intended for specified purposes; and (2) parts of the association's own treasury segregated for bookkeeping purposes. The former are "dedicated" funds; the latter are "special accounts."

(a) Examples of dedicated funds: a member dies and leaves a sum of money to the association with the provision that it be used to make a cash award each year to the member who has done most to advance the cause. The capital sum and the income from interest on it must not be mingled with the association's general treasury or used for general operating expenses. This is dedicated money and must be earmarked for the purpose for which it was intended. In practice the money may be mixed with the society's general funds in one bank account. But separate books must be kept for this dedicated account to show the status of every dollar ever placed in it. This is handled as indicated in 1614.

1612. Convention Budgets

The association may, for accounting purposes, set up a special account for its monthly magazine or for its annual convention. This would show income from advertising, subscriptions, booth rentals, or registration fees, and anticipated expenses under various categories. If the budget shows an expected deficit, the income side would have to show a transfer of funds from the association's treasury to balance that deficit. If the special account budget showed an expected surplus, the surplus would either be transferred to the general treasury (and appear as anticipated income in its budget) or remain in the special account as a reserve, according to predetermined policy. For example, suppose that it was anticipated that an annual exhibit or convention would be operated at a loss this year but that the magazine would bring a profit. The committee would calculate the deficit in the convention or exhibit account and add to this account's income (as in Line CI.4 below) that amount as a transfer from the general treasury. Thus:

C. CONVENTION BUDGET

CI. ANTICIPATED INCOME

CI.1. Booth rentals	$ 900.
2. Registration fees	350.
3. Sale of banquet tickets	1000.
4. Transfer from general funds	270.
	$2520.

CE. ANTICIPATED EXPENSES

CE.1. Rental of ballroom for exhibits	$ 800.
2. Rental of auditorium for general session	350.
3. Travel for distinguished speakers	300.
4. Tips for certain hotel personnel	50.
5. Expense of annual banquet	800.
6. Printing of daily convention news	220.
	$2520.

These totals ($2520) are the same simply because, in operation, there was expected to be a $270 deficit (the difference between the $2520 anticipated expenses and the $2250 anticipated income), and that sum ($270) was transferred as indicated in Line CI.4 above. In the general budget for the association, there will be a line reading: "Convention, deficit . . . $270," balancing Line CI.4.

1613. Magazine Budgets

Assume the society issues a magazine on which a profit is anticipated. Let this be Budget M. The budgetary posture of the profit depends on the society's policy. Will the magazine be permitted to retain this profit in its own account? Or will it revert to the society's general treasury? In the latter case, the over-all budget for the association should show this profit in the income account. The magazine budget, here called Budget M, might look like this:

M. MAGAZINE BUDGET

MI. Anticipated Income from Magazine ($24,250)

MI.1.	Subscriptions, 4100 @ $3	$12,300.
2.	Advertising income	10,700.
3.	Sale of reprints	500.
4.	Reimbursement for picture cuts	750.
		$24,250.

ME. Anticipated Expenses for Magazine ($21,700)

ME.1.	Printing and binding	$ 9,700.
2.	Mailing	1,300.
3.	Engraving cuts and plates	1,000.
4.	Office salaries	9,100.
5.	Office operating expenses	600.
		$21,700.

MR. Recapitulation of Magazine Budget

MR.1.	Anticipated income	$24,250.
2.	Anticipated expenses	21,700.
3.	Anticipated surplus	$ 2,550.

If this reverted to the general treasury, the over-all budget would show an item of $2550 on the line "Profit from Magazine."

If it remained in the magazine account (or in the budget of the editorial or publication committee) it would appear in the treasurer's report as an expected increment of $2550 in the capital or reserve account for the magazine.

In this budget, Line MI.1 represented subscriptions at $3 a year. It may be the society's practice to give a free subscription to every member as one of the privileges of membership. If the dues are in excess of the subscription fee to nonmembers, the budget is drafted as indicated above. Suppose, for example, that nonmembers could subscribe to the magazine at $3 a year; but that members pay $10 a year dues and are entitled to a free subscription. This is usually set up in each member's statement of dues as:

General dues per year .... $ 7.00
Subscription to magazine 3.00
                                        $10.00

This is to comply with the requirements for entry as second class mail in the post office. Second class (magazine) rates are lower than third class (merchandise) rates. But magazines given away free are not eligible for entry as second class matter. Hence the books of the association should show clearly that each member does pay a reasonable subscription fee. It would not be honest to indicate this on the books without actually crediting the magazine with that amount of subscription money—hence the entry on Line MI.1 above.

If the magazine is distributed as third class mail, there is no postal regulation concerning subscription rates. Under those circumstances, the breakdown of dues would be unnecessary and the magazine budget might show no income from subscriptions.

1614. Budget for Dedicated Funds

When money is granted or bequeathed for a specific function, it is earmarked for that purpose. This must be shown clearly in the budget. Unless the donor specified otherwise, any profit from dedicated funds must remain in that account. It cannot revert to the association's general treasury. Whether the association is willing to lend or give money to make up a deficit is a matter for policy determination.

(a) In the first example below, it is assumed that the association has received a grant of $1000 from the American Land Use Association to study zoning problems in Contrary County. The treasurer's books will show the remaining surplus as an asset but will also show that the money there cannot be tapped for general use. The budget, however, need not show this. It will account for all dollars put into and taken out of the account. For example:

Z. SPECIAL ZONING ACCOUNT

ZI. INCOME FROM SPECIAL ZONING ACCOUNT ($1060)
ZI.1. Grant from ALU Association $1000.00
2. Interest earned from deposit of ZI.1 .... 60.00
3. Income for Special Zoning Account $1060.00

ZE. EXPENSES TO BE CHARGED TO SPECIAL ZONING ACCOUNT
(Anticipated: $632.50)
ZE.1. Rent of desk space in state office .... $ 480.00
2. Clerical assistance 120.00
3. Purchase of Master Map of Contrary County 7.50
4. Miscellaneous office expenses 25.00
5. Anticipated expenses .... $ 632.50

ZR. RECAPITULATION (Anticipated surplus: $427.50)
ZR.1. Anticipated income for Account $1060.00
2. Anticipated expenses 632.50
3. Anticipated surplus .... $ 427.50

This surplus is dedicated and is not available for general use of the association. It is available for continuing the project in its second year.

(b) In the following example, it is assumed that Uplift Elevator Company has granted the association the sum of $5000 to make a psychological study of why people push elevator call bells more than once. It is anticipated that this sum will not be sufficient to pay for the project for the year but that the Association, in view of the gravity of the problem, is transferring sums from its own treasury to meet the deficit.

X. ELEVATOR CALL BELL ACCOUNT

XI. INCOME
XI.1. Grant from Uplift Elevator Company $ 5000.00
2. Anticipated interest .... 150.00 See Note A.
3. Anticipated outside income .... $ 5150.00
4. Donation from Association .... 5425.00 See Note B.
$10,575.00

XE. EXPENSES (Anticipated for year)
    XE.1. Rent of special office (one year).. $ 1200.00
      2. Salary of psychologist (half time).   4800.00
      3. Salary of clerk-stenographer 4000.00
      4. Charts, graphs and record paper ..   75.00
      5. Office operating expenses 500.00
      6. Anticipated expenses $10,575.00

XR. RECAPITULATION
    XR.1. Anticipated expenses $10,575.00
      2. Anticipated outside income 5150.00
      3. Deficit to be made up ....   5425.00 See Note B.

NOTE A. Since about half of the grant will be liquidated at once for immediate expenses, the amount remaining on deposit and eligible for interest will be only about $2500.

NOTE B. This donation from the general treasury is needed to neutralize the anticipated deficit; that is, the difference between lines XR.2 and XR.1.

In this case, the over-all budget of the association will show, on the expense side, a line representing $5425 as "deficit on Elevator Call Bell Project."

1615. Sample Expense Budgets

The heart of the budget is the "expense" side of the account. This, in the long run, determines the amount of dues. It yardsticks the extent of the association's program. Intelligent budget drafting requires that the expenses be broken down into sufficient detail so that the members understand where the money is supposed to go, and areas of excessive cost can be spotlighted. On the other hand, an excessive pettiness of detail makes the budget incomprehensible to the average member. Below are several suggested patterns for the expense budget, varying with the size and commitments of the organization.

(a) A small neighborhood association with no business office which hires a hall for a monthly meeting, and without paid employees. See 1616.

(b) A state-wide organization with a half-time clerical employee. The society meets every month in a community hall for which janitorial expenses are paid. It has a monthly newsletter but no printed magazine, no conventions, and no business office. See 1617.

(c) A state-wide organization holding only one general meeting a year, usually in the state capital or in a resort area. It has a business office in rented quarters in the state's metropolis, with a monthly magazine which accepts advertisements and a staff of three full-time employees. See 1618.

(d) A national organization which owns its own headquarters building, holds an annual convention, operates a magazine, has a large staff of employees, and renders numerous services to members. See 1619.

In these samples, amounts are not inserted. The purpose is simply to show typical patterns for breaking down an expense budget.

1616. Small Neighborhood Association

This small neighborhood association has no major expense except its meeting hall. Its expense budget is presented as several lines, coded for the purpose of charging each expense item to the proper heading.

ANTICIPATED EXPENSES, YEAR ENDING_____, 19__

ACCOUNT

R. Rental of meeting hall, ten meetings at $15 . . . . $
P. Postage, printing, stationery, office operations . . . . $
M. Membership in League of Neighborhood Associations . . . . $
D. Donation to Neighborhood Christmas Decoration Fund . . $
X. Miscellaneous expenses . . . . $
        Anticipated expenses for the year . . . . $

1617. Small State-wide Organization

An organization that meets every month, but has no convention and no printed magazine, can also present its expense budget in the form of a few lines. Grouping by categories is scarcely necessary. For example:

Account

S. Salary of clerk-secretary .... $
J. Janitorial expenses of meeting hall .... $
N. Reproducing and mailing the News-Letter .... $
P. Other postage, printing and mailing expenses .... $
E. Operating expenses of office, not otherwise classified ..... $
L. Special appropriation for committee on legislation .... $
X. Miscellaneous and sundry expenses .... $

Anticipated expenses for the year .... $

1618. Larger State-wide Organization

Whenever an association publishes a magazine, rents quarters, and holds an annual convention or exhibit, it is necessary to departmentalize its expense budget. In this hypothetical organization, the expenses are set up under six headings as follows:

A. Operation of the Executive Office
B. Operation of the Magazine
C. Arrangements for the next Convention
D. Officers' Expenses
E. Committee Operations
F. Miscellaneous Expenses

Account A. Operation of the Executive Office

A.1. Salaries .... $
2. Rent .... $
3. Heat, light, and janitor service .... $
4. Postage, mailing and stationery .... $
5. Travel of (salaried) Executive Officer .... $
6. Office supplies .... $
7. Telephone and telegraph .... $
8. Expense account of Executive Officer other than travel .. $
9. Social Security and other taxes .... $
10. Other office operating expenses .... $
11. Total anticipated expenses for Account A .... $

ACCOUNT B. OPERATION OF THE MAGAZINE (See 1613)

B.1. Salaries of editor and his secretary .... $
  2. Printing and binding the magazine .... $
  3. Mailing the magazine .... $
  4. Cuts, plates, and engraving .... $
  5. Reprints for official use .... $
  6. Editor's travel and expense account .... $
  7. Postage, other than for the magazine .... $
  8. Telephone and telegraph .... $
  9. Other office operating expenses .... $
  10. Commission to advertising solicitor .... $
  11. Copyright and other legal fees .... $
  12. Sundry expenses not otherwise classified .... $
  13. Total expenses anticipated for Account B .... $

ACCOUNT C. THE NEXT CONVENTION (or Annual Exhibit)

C.1. Hotel bill for officers .... $
  2. Hotel bill for distinguished guests .... $
  3. Rental of ballroom for exhibits .... $
  4. Rental of auditorium for general session .... $
  5. Flowers for wives of distinguished guests .... $
  6. Gratuities to waiters and others .... $
  7. Gross cost of annual banquet .... $
  8. Printing of daily Convention news .... $
  9. Transportation for distinguished guests .... $
  10. Printing the programs .... $
  11. Special expenses, Committee on Arrangements .... $
  12. Miscellaneous Convention expenses .... $
  13. Total anticipated expenses for Account C .... $

NOTE: See paragraph 1612 for other aspects of a convention budget. If income from sale of banquet tickets is set up in an income budget, then the gross cost of the banquet would appear as Item C.7. If the tickets were sold at a profit to the organization, it would also be proper to omit Item C.7, and include only the net profit on the income side of the budget. If tickets were sold at a loss, it would also be practical to calculate the per capita loss and set up Item C.7 only as the net cost (deficit), omitting any reference to the income from tickets in the income budget.

ACCOUNT D. OFFICERS' EXPENSES

D.1. The President's allowance .... $
  2. Secretarial help for the Secretary .... $
  3. Bookkeeper for the Treasurer .... $

4. Postage allowance for the Secretary .... $

5. Postage allowance for the Treasurer .... $

6. Bank service charges .... $

7. Travel allowances for Secretary .... $

8. Travel allowances for Treasurer .... $

9. Allowances for the Vice-President .... $

10. Total anticipated expenses for Account D .... $

ACCOUNT E. COMMITTEE OPERATIONS

See 1609.

ACCOUNT F. MISCELLANEOUS

This is prepared by reviewing all expenses for the past several years, and allotting each item to an existing budget line. Items not classifiable under any of the above headings are regrouped into Account F.

1619. A Large National Organization Which Owns Its Own Headquarters

Typical headings for the expense budget might be:

A. Functional Operations at the Executive Office

B. Maintenance of Building and Structure at Executive Office

C. Budget for Next Year's Convention

D. Operation of Magazine

E. Budget for Trustees (Executive Committee)

F. Committee Operations

G. Officers' Expenses

H. Miscellaneous Expenses

ACCOUNT A. FUNCTIONAL OPERATIONS AT EXECUTIVE OFFICE

A.1. Payroll .... $

2. Executive Officer's travel .... $

3. Other expenses of Executive Officer .... $

4. Telephone, telegraph, postage, and mailing .... $

5. Operating office expenses .... $

6. Operation of special services .... $

7. Sundry expenses at Executive Office .... $

8. Anticipated expenses, Account A .... $

ACCOUNT B. MAINTENANCE OF BUILDING AND STRUCTURE

B.1. Taxes .... $

2. Heat, light, and janitorial expenses .... $

3. Interest on mortgage .... $

4. Amortization of mortgage ... . $
5. Repairs of building .... $
6. Fire insurance .... $
7. Liability and other insurance .... $
8. Miscellaneous maintenance expenses .... $
9. Anticipated expenses, Account B .... $

ACCOUNT C. ARRANGEMENTS FOR NEXT CONVENTION OR EXHIBIT

See Account C under 1618. Also see 1612.

ACCOUNT D. MAGAZINE

See Account B under 1618, and also 1613.

ACCOUNT E. BUDGET FOR TRUSTEES (Executive Committee or
other title)

E.1. Traveling expenses .... $
2. Rental of meeting rooms .... $
3. Stenographic or recording services .... $
4. Meals and incidental expenses .... $
5. Reserve fund for special projects .... $
6. Postage and office operations .... $
7. Anticipated expenses, Account E .... $

ACCOUNT F. COMMITTEE OPERATIONS

See 1609.

ACCOUNT G. OFFICERS' EXPENSES

See Account D under 1618.

ACCOUNT H. MISCELLANEOUS

This is prepared by reviewing expenses in all categories during the past
several years and noting which ones could not be classified in any of the
standard Accounts. These anticipated expenses are then grouped in
Account H.

1620. Public Relations and Legislative Expenditures

Public relations activities are generally entrusted either to
an information office or to a public relations committee. The
budget for the former would usually be on a line in the executive office account, though it could, of course, be set up in a
separate account. The budget for a public relations committee

would usually be part of the committee budget in general. See 1609. Money appropriated for legislative committee operations should be separately set up in budgets and separately listed in treasurers' reports. A donor may find that his contributions to an organization have lost their otherwise tax-exempt status if the organization devotes a significant part of its budget or its activities to the influencing of legislation.

1621. Allowances for President and Other Officers

Many organizations find it wise to allow the president a fairly substantial sum for miscellaneous expenses, clerical help, travel, and postage, and to include in that special allowance a sort of contingency or reserve fund which the president is free to expend, at his own discretion, in emergencies, for special projects or for public relations activities. It is also a good rule to place some funds at the disposal of the executive committee, board, or other high authority body. Situations develop at their sessions which might require expenditures of moneys that could not have been anticipated or that should not be publicly explained. Of course, if the executive board or comparable body has authority to appropriate funds from the treasury at any time this special provision is unnecessary.

17

Warehouse of Forms and Documents

1700. List of Forms

An inexperienced secretary is frequently puzzled about the exact wording of a credential to another organization; about the way in which to draft a certified copy of the appropriate portion of the minutes, needed to support a contract; or about the wording of a membership card. A treasurer may wonder about how to word his report or how to get to the bank the documentation needed to authorize him to sign checks. Scattered throughout this book are samples of the exact wordings of many of these documents. The following alphabetical list summarizes this; numerals indicate paragraph numbers in this book:

1701. Notice of Proposed Amendments

It is often provided that no proposal to amend the constitution or bylaws may be voted on unless members had received advance notice. If the proposals had been fully discussed at previous meetings or in NewsLetter or Journal issues, it is sufficient if the notice merely indicates what the proposal is about. For example:

Notice is hereby given that at the meeting on (date) two proposals to amend the Constitution and one to amend the Bylaws will be voted on. These propositions are:

No. 1. To amend the Constitution by creating a class of Emeritus Members.

No. 2. To amend the Constitution by abolishing the elected Board of Auditors and requiring that the Trustees employ certified accountants to audit the books.

No. 3. To amend the Bylaws by changing the Annual Meeting from June to May.

This notice complies with Art. V, Section 2 of the Constitution.

The notice can be printed on the announcement mailed to members or included in the NewsLetter or other publication, either as part of the publication or as an inclosure. Under certain circumstances, an announcement in a newspaper or a publicly displayed poster might be sufficient notice.

If the proposals had not been discussed before, members must have a chance to study them. In that case, the notice must include the verbatim text of the proposed amendment, thus:

Notice is hereby given that at the meeting on (date) the following proposal to amend the Constitution will be read and submitted to final vote:

That in Article II, Section 3, between the phrases "Junior Members" and "Inactive Members," there will be inserted the phrase "Emeritus Members" so that the section, if so amended, would read: "All persons of the membership will be in one of these classes: Senior Members, Junior Members, Emeritus Members, and Inactive Members."

That to the end of Article II there will be added a new section to be numbered as Section 9, reading as follows:

"9. An Emeritus Member is a former member who has remained in good standing for more than ten consecutive years and who has retired from active service or duty by reason of disability or age. An Emeritus Member will have the right to vote, but not to hold office, and will be exempt from the payment of dues."

1702. Petitions Proposing Amendments

In many societies, amendments to the constitution or bylaws are initiated by petition. A typical form for such a petition would be:

We, the undersigned, members in good standing of the XYZ Society, hereby propose that the Constitution of the Society be amended as indicated below. We ask that this proposal be submitted to the membership in accordance with Article V, Section 4 of the Constitution, and we pledge to vote favorably on such proposed amendment when submitted.

Proposal: That Article III, Section 1, be amended by striking out the phrase "Vice-president" and substituting therefor the phrase "President-elect"; and similarly that wherever the phrase "Vice-president" appears in the Constitution, the phrase "President-elect" be substituted therefor; and that Article IV, Section 2 be amended to read: "At each Annual Meeting a President-elect, Secretary, and Treasurer" will be elected; and that Article IV, Section 4 be repealed and in its place the following be substituted: "4. The President-elect, after one year of service in that office, will automatically become President at the Annual Meeting next following the meeting at which he was installed as President-elect."

1703. Letter of Appointment

Ordinarily a president appoints committee members, representatives, and so on, simply by delivering an oral message to that effect to the appointee and notifying the secretary to make a record of the appointment. However, it is well to put such appointments in writing (1) in large organizations, or (2) whenever the appointee has a specific grant of authority to encumber funds or speak in the name of the organization, or (3) whenever a letter of appointment could serve as a credential.

The letter of appointment may be stilted or informal, pompous or breezy, according to the temperament of the president. In any event, the letter should be typewritten, and two carbon copies made: one for the president's personal files and one for the general archives of the organization.

A letter of appointment is ordinarily addressed to the appointee. In some societies, the letter is of the "To Whom It May Concern" type, or it is a sort of open letter (See Sample 3.A below) addressed to no one in particular, but simply announcing the appointment. This is the kind of document which used to be called a "letter patent" and is now more generally known as a "warrant" or "commission." If the appointee is to serve as a delegate or representative, his document is a credential rather than a letter of appointment. See 1716 for sample credentials. He may, of course, have a letter of appointment by way of information to him, in addition to a formal credential to exhibit to the body to which he is accredited.

EXAMPLES OF LETTERS OF APPOINTMENT

Sample 1.A. An informal letter:

Dear Joe:

It would be a great boon to the organization if you would accept appointment as Chairman of the Program Committee. Pick your own members and let me know who they are. Three or four would be about right. Give me their names and I'll appoint them. Bill Evans, the last Chairman of Program, has a fat file all waiting for you to pick up. Thanks for your help.

(*Signature*)

Sample 2.A. A formal letter:

(SOCIETY LETTERHEAD)

December 15, 19—

Joseph Zilch
1492 Columbus Street
Arlington, N.J.

Dear Mr. Zilch:

You are hereby designated as Chairman of the Committee on Program of this Society. Your functions are those outlined in Bylaw No. 7. The names of the other members of your committee are listed below. The files of that committee are in the hands of Mr. William Evans, current Chairman, whose term expires on December 31. Mr. Evans will deliver the files to you at any time and place you designate. You will be Chairman of this Committee for the year beginning January 1 next.

Your assistance to the Society is appreciated.

Sincerely yours,

(*Signature*)

Members:

Arthur Andrews
Benjamin Barton
Carl Carlson

Sample 3.A. A warrant:

STATE SOCIETY OF SORCERERS

Be it known, that by virtue of authority vested in me by Article II, Section 3 of the Constitution of this Society, I, the President of this Society, hereby designate

JOSEPH ZILCH

to serve for one year, starting July 1, 19—, as
Chairman of the Committee on Necromancy.

Note that the reference to II, 3, of the constitution here is to the section which authorizes the president to name all committee personnel. If the office to which the member is appointed is a constitutional one, the warrant should also cite that, as, for example:

to serve for one year, starting July 1, 19—, as
Chairman of the Committee on Necromancy
and to perform the functions assigned to that Committee in Article V, Section 2 of the Constitution.

1704. Auditor's Report

At one time it was the common practice to elect auditors from the membership. With the development of the profession of accountancy occasioned by the increasing reach of the income tax, this practice has gradually changed. Today most organizations that audit their books at all engage professional auditors or commercial accountants. If this is done, the auditor will, of course, know the standard reporting form. If amateur auditors are still being used, an appointee may find the following sample helpful:

This is to certify that I have examined the books, accounts, and deposits of (fill in name), the Treasurer of the (name of organization). I find that these books are correct and in balance as shown in the attached treasurer's report. Total receipts during the period (indicate beginning and end of the period) in fact were (insert amount) and the records of the (name of bank) show that this amount was deposited in that period. Total disbursements during the year were (indicate amount) and there are on file vouchers for all disbursements except those below indicated. These vouchers total (amount), and the unvouchered expenses listed below total (amount). The unvouchered expenses during the year were:

Postage stamps purchased for cash	$3.15
Tip to taxi driver (date) (purpose)	.15
Bus fare for (purpose, date)	.20
Donation to Christmas Fund for building employees ..	5.00
	$8.50

(If expenditures exceeded receipts): Expenditures exceeded receipts by $aa.aa. On deposit at the beginning of the period (give date) was $bbb.bb. This amount was diminished by $aa.aa, the deficit of expenditures over receipts. There was also the amount of $c.cc as the bank's service charge, so that the amount on deposit at the end of the period was $dd.dd.

(If receipts exceeded expenditures). Receipts exceeded expenditures by $aa.aa. The bank service charge was $bb.bb. Subtracting this from $aa.aa, we find that the bank balance should have increased by $cc.cc. The amount on deposit at the beginning of the period (give date) was $dd.dd. The amount on deposit at the end of the period (date) was $ee.ee. This is correct.

(If there is a reserve fund, capital account, or endowment fund, the report should indicate what the audit of this showed.)

Respectfully submitted,
E. E. Eye, Auditor

1705. Bylaws

For examples of bylaws, see 1312. For a sample certification of an extract of the bylaws, see 1709.

1706. Budget

See Chapter 16.

1707. Membership Cards

A membership card serves two purposes: (1) a receipt for dues; (2) a means of identification. If the card serves principally as a receipt for dues, it is essential that some means be provided for indicating at a glance whether the member is paid up. The commonest method is to have a new card every year. Each year's card differs from the one of the previous year either by a change in color or by the placement of the year of expiration date in conspicuous type at an easily visible part of the card. Occasional organizations keep the same card for years, but have space on the back in which the Treasurer can indicate the date up to which dues have been paid.

This may also be done by small adhesive stamps affixed to

spaces provided on the back; or by spaces in which legends can be rubber-stamped.

If the card serves essentially as an instrument of identification, it is advisable to provide some means whereby the one presenting the card can prove that he is the person named thereon. The commonest method is to require each member to sign the card as soon as he gets it. Thereafter, he can satisfy a skeptical observer by reproducing the signature in the observer's presence.

A membership card should be from 3 to 3½ inches long; the best length is 3¼ inches. It should be 2 inches or, at the most, 2¼ inches wide. This size will fit into the standard wallet card space without the need for cutting off the margins or without subjecting the card to frayed edges.

In large organizations, where every member has an account number or an identification number, the cards should be numbered too. In smaller societies it is unnecessary to number the cards except as a measure of control or counting.

A facsimile officer's signature (printed, rubber-stamped, or otherwise mass produced) is usually sufficient. Individually signed cards are too much to expect except in very small organizations. If the organization has many local chapters, the signature of the national officer could be printed and that of the local (chapter) officer could be hand signed or hand stamped. The organization decides for itself whether the signature should be that of the president, the secretary or the treasurer.

If space is provided for the member's signature, a line along one margin (usually the left margin) running along the short side of the card is the commonest practice. Or the signature may appear on the back of the card.

Following are sample texts:

Sample 1

This is to certify that

JOSEPH ZILCH

is a member in good standing of
The Bethlehem Bird Observers Club
with dues paid for the year ending
June 30, 19—

Sample 2

NATIONAL NECROMANCY ASSOCIATION 19–

Oscar Arbeit

is hereby certified to be a member of the
Post Mortem Chapter of This Association
with dues credited for the calendar year
stamped above

Sample 3

OFFICIAL MEMBERSHIP CARD

19–

STATE SOCIETY OF FERRIS WHEEL MECHANICS

Name of Member: _____
Grade of Membership: _____
Dues paid until: _____

Sample 4

19– Membership Card
DogPatch Civic Association, Inc.

This certifies that the citizen whose name is
printed on the margin and whose signature appears
on the opposite side of this card is an

ADJUNCT MEMBER

of the Association with all the rights
and privileges thereunto appertaining

The seal of the organization may appear on the card, usually
near the upper right corner. The validating officer's signature
appears along the middle or right side of the lower edge of the
card.

The back of the card may be blank. It may carry a calendar
of the year, the seal of the society, information about the annual meeting (convention), an extract of the society's constitution (such as the list of aims or membership qualifications),
the member's photograph, description, and/or signature, or a
slogan descriptive of the society's activities.

1708. Certification of an Amendment

When the constitution or bylaws have been amended it may be necessary to issue a formal certificate to that effect. This may be simply a matter of information to members. Or it may be legally necessary to certify to such an amendment if it changes the officers who have authority to sign checks or makes any significant change in the society's jurisdiction. The secretary, as the custodian of the society's seal and records, is usually the certifying officer. But certification could be equally well effected if signed by the president and counter-signed by the secretary. When certifying the change to an outside agency (such as a bank) the short form, as in Sample 1, is sufficient. For information of members within the society and for the organization's own records, the long form (Sample 2) is better.

Sample 1

(SOCIETY'S LETTERHEAD)

I, Augustus Arcularius, Secretary of the (name of association) certify that on June 30, 19–, Article III, Section 2 of the Constitution was amended in accordance with the amending process laid down in Article V of that Constitution. As a result of this amendment, Article III, Section 2 of the Constitution now reads as follows:

2. Vouchers for the withdrawal of sums not in excess of fifty ($50) dollars may be signed by either the President or the Treasurer; and for sums in excess of fifty ($50) dollars must be signed by both of these officers.

This is certified to be a true copy of the section as now in force.
(*Signed*)

Sample 2

(SOCIETY'S LETTERHEAD)

I, Augustus Arcularius, Secretary of the (association) certify that on June 30, 19–, Article III, Section 2 of the Constitution of this Society was amended by a vote of 95 in favor of, and 6 opposed to the proposed amendment. The affirmative vote being in excess of two thirds of the votes cast, was declared effective and the proposed amendment was adopted and is now in operation. Prior to the adoption of this amendment, Article III, Section 2 of the Constitution read:

2. No sums shall be withdrawn from the treasury except on vouchers signed by both the Treasurer and the President.

This was repealed by the amendment, and the section now reads:

2. Vouchers for the withdrawal of sums not in excess of fifty ($50) dollars may be signed by either the President or the Treasurer; and for sums in excess of that amount, vouchers must be signed by both of these officers.

This is certified to be a true copy of the section as now in effect.

(*Signed*)

1709. Certification of Extracts of the Constitution or Bylaws

It is sometimes necessary to prepare extracts of the constitution or bylaws and certify that they are correct. This may be required on the society's membership application blanks; or banks may ask for such certificates when the society opens an account. The form is simply "I certify that the following is a true copy of (Article a, Section b) of the Constitution (or Bylaws) of the XYZ Association." It is signed by the secretary, or it may be signed by the president and countersigned by the secretary. The treasurer sometimes uses such extracts in reminding members of what will happen to them if they become delinquent in dues.

1710. Certification of Election Results

The certificate prepared by the tellers (see 1722) is usually sufficient for certifying a current election or referendum. In the society's own publications, or for legal reasons in apprising outside agencies of changes in office, it may be advisable for the secretary to issue a formal certificate. For example, if there is a new treasurer, the secretary could issue a certificate like this to send to the bank:

I, Georgia Georgesson, Secretary of the Perfume Testers Association of Oshkosh, hereby certify that at an election held on June 30, 19–, Mr. William Williamson was elected Treasurer of this Association. I certify that the election was held in the manner prescribed by the Constitution (or charter) of the Association.

A certificate of election could also be prepared by simply attaching a copy of the tellers' certificate (see 1722) to a letter of transmittal reading:

I, Herbert Brown, Secretary of the Brooktree Civic League, certify that the attached document is a true copy of the report of the Tellers concerning the election held at the meeting of that League on February 22, 19–.

1711. Certification of Minutes

An organization may authorize an officer or committee to negotiate for a group insurance contract, to withdraw deposits from the bank, or to engage in business with a corporation. The corporation or bank may ask for a certified copy of the minutes showing that the committee or officer was properly authorized to transact that business. Samples of such certificates follow:

Sample 1

I (name), Secretary of the (name of organization), certify that at a meeting of Society (Association) held on (date), the following named members were authorized to negotiate for a group accident and health insurance policy. A motion granting such authorization was unanimously passed together with a motion pledging the faith and credit of this Association in the fulfillment of any contract accepted by these members. The members authorized to accomplish these negotiations are (names)

(*Signature of Secretary*)

Sample 2

I (name), Secretary of the (name of organization), certify that the following is a true and accurate extract of a portion of the minutes of a regular (or special) meeting of the Society held at (place) on (date).

Mr. Argus moved that the Chairman of the Program Committee be authorized to sign checks on behalf of the Association, with respect to funds needed for the operations of that Committee.

Mr. Bertrand seconded the motion.

Mr. Charleton moved that the motion be amended by adding "not in excess of twenty dollars" after the phrase "sign checks."

Mr. Davis seconded the amendment.

After a short discussion, the Chair called for a vote on the amendment and it was passed without dissent.

The Chair then called for a vote on the main motion, and this was passed by a preponderance of the votes and was declared in effect at once.

(Signed)

Sample 3

I (name), Recording Secretary of the (name of organization), certify that the document attached to this letter, and bearing my signature, is a true copy of a portion of the minutes of a regular meeting of the (name of organization) held on (date) at (place).

(Signed)

Attached document:

Mr. Elias, Chairman of the House Committee, then reported that the ceiling of the ladies' rest room was cracking and in need of repair. He reported that his Committee had made contact with four building contractors, one of whom had declined to bid on the job. The B Company's offer was, in the opinion of the Committee, the most advantageous to the Society. This Company offered to repair the ceiling of the ladies' rest room in workmanlike manner, restoring its original condition, for $200. Your Committee recommends that this offer be accepted and that contract be awarded to the B Company. This is our recommendation, Mr. Chairman.

The Chairman called for a motion to adopt the recommendation. Such a motion was made by Dr. Ferguson and was seconded. After brief discussion, the Chair stated the motion as "That the B Company be authorized to repair the ceiling in the ladies' rest room under the terms of their letter of (date) and that the Treasurer be authorized to allocate $200 of Society funds for that purpose." In that form the motion was passed.

Certified True Copy

(Signature of Secretary)

1712. Certification of Resolutions and Motions

This is substantially the same as the certification of minutes detailed in 1711. When a resolution is certified, the exact text is included in the certificate. It is not necessary to name the member who seconded the motion, but the name of the member who made the motion or introduced the resolution should be listed.

1713. Charter to a Subordinate Body

A state society frequently charters constituent, component, or subordinate county or city societies; and a national organization often charters subordinate state societies. The charter should be suitable for framing. It may include the original officers (sometimes even all the "charter members") in the text; or it may charter the organization by designation without listing the names of the original officers. A charter may be issued to an existing organization, thus affiliating it with the parent body. Or, a charter may be issued to a few individuals as a warrant to start recruiting members of a still nonexistent satellite organization. In the latter case, the document is, strictly speaking, a warrant or commission rather than a charter. A group of members or of member-aspirants may petition for a charter for themselves; or a parent body may issue a charter to a group of its own members with instructions to establish the peripheral organization. These variations are all reflected in the form and wording of the charter.

Sample 1

AMERICAN ASSOCIATION OF TERATOLOGISTS

BE IT KNOWN that on the umpteenth day of upf, 19—, the
Executive Council of this Association chartered

263

THE NEVADA SOCIETY OF TERATOLOGY

As a Component Society of this Association, with all
the rights and privileges thereunto appertaining.
And in testimony thereof, there is hereby issued

THIS CHARTER

NUMBER 000

Sample 2

AMERICAN ASSOCIATION OF TERATOLOGISTS

Whereas Bylaw VII provides for the establishment of
Local Teratologic Societies, and

Whereas Xavier Xanadu, Yosef Young, and Zigmond
Zuckerman have met the requirements for the
formation of such a Local Teratologic Society,
Be It Therefore Known, that these three members are
hereby designated as the first members of the

WYOMING LEAGUE OF TERATOLOGISTS

And that that League is hereby chartered as an Affiliate
and Constituent Society within this Association.

Sample 3

AMERICAN ASSOCIATION OF TERATOLOGISTS

The general membership of this Association, in convention
assembled on February 31, 19–, have approved the
application of the

SOUTHERN NORTH DAKOTA TERATOLOGIC SOCIETY

for affiliation with this Association; and accordingly

THIS CHARTER

is hereby and this day issued to that Society.

Sample 4

AMERICAN ASSOCIATION OF TERATOLOGISTS

CHARTER NUMBER 23

Authority is hereby given to the members whose names
appear below to associate themselves together as the

NORTHERN SOUTH CAROLINA TERATOLOGICAL SOCIETY

which is hereby recognized as a constituent of this
Association; and in token thereof there is issued

THIS CHARTER

to be retained by that Society so long as they comply
with the Constitution, Bylaws, Resolves, and Enactments
of this Association.

Feb. 28, 19—

_____

President, AAT.

Charter Members February 28, 19—:

Arnold Arbutus	Frederick Frankfort
Benjamin Bernard	George Gorge
Carl Claptrap	Harry Horseman
David Dewey	Irving Igelfritz
Elmer Elias	Jon Jackson Jacques

1714. Committee Reports

See 1011 for more details. A sample repórt from a house
committee is given above as Sample 3 in 1711. A report from
a nominating committee is illustrated below in 1718. Here
are some additional examples.

Sample 1

The membership committee favorably reports the nominations of
Mr. X and Mr. Y to this Society, and I move that they be received into
membership at this time.

Sample 2

Your *ad hoc* committee to examine the kitchen wishes to report that
the hoods above the stove are in need of replacement. Repair would
cost about $90 and replacement about $150. Your committee is agreed
that it would be worth the extra $60 to get new hoods. We recommend,
and ask that this be considered a motion to authorize, appropriation of
$150 from the treasury; and we further recommend and move that the
Steward be authorized to arrange for replacement of the hoods and to
return to the treasury any unspent residue of that sum.

Sample 3

Your Committee appointed to investigate the matter of XYZ has concluded its work. Our findings are:

> *a)* . . .
> *b)* . . .
> *c)* . . .

Our recommendations are:

> (1) . . .
> (2) . . .
> (3) . . .

See 1013 to 1016 for further processing of this type of report.

Sample 4

The Committee on Social Events has decided, by a vote of 5 to 4, to recommend that we hold a cocktail party immediately prior to the annual meeting. This is the majority recommendation. The minority wish to make their views known. The majority prefer a cocktail party to a regular sit-down dinner first, because it is cheaper; second, because it is quicker; third, because it lends itself better to the informal character of the occasion. Mr. Wilson will, when requested, give the minority view.

Mr. Wilson: "The minority feel strongly that the occasion justifies a real sit-down dinner. A cocktail party is never satisfactory. People pass each other casually. The whole air is one of haste. A dinner can be leisurely. We are certain that most members will be willing to pay the small additional amount. We ask you to vote 'No' on adopting the committee report. If you reject the report, I will move that we hold a dinner prior to our annual meeting."

1715. Constitution

See 1301 to 1308 for the form of a constitution. See 1709 for the form of certifying an extract from the constitution.

1716. Credentials

When a member is sent as a delegate, observer, or representative to an outside body, or to a delegate body within the organization, he should carry with him an identifying document. Here are four types of credential documents:

Sample 1

This is to certify that Arthur Abeles is an official delegate of the Martinson Run Civic Association to the County Federation of Civic Clubs for the period ending June 30, 19–.

(*Signed by President and Secretary*)

Sample 2

(LETTERHEAD OF ORGANIZATION)

It is hereby certified that, at an election held on May 27, 19–, Mr. Benjamin Bernard was elected as first alternate of this Association to the Annual Meeting of XYZ.

Sample 3

The Contrary County Dental Society hereby designates Dr. Charles Carruthers as one of its delegates to the State Convention of County Dental Societies for the Annual Meeting during the month of June 19–.

Sample 4

(LETTERHEAD)

Pursuant to the authority vested in me by Article III, Section 1 of our Constitution, I, the President of the Hyperopic Bird Watchers Association of Coma County, have appointed the following as delegates and alternates to the Annual Convention of Bird Watchers Associations.

As Delegates: Mr. David Dawson of Denville
                            Mr. Elmer Effigy of Evanston
                            Mr. Francis Francis of Franktown

As Alternates: Mr. George Guenther of Grosses Point
                            Mr. Henry Harbeson of Harrisonville
                            Mr. Irving Irish of Irvington.

(*Signed*)

1717. Minutes

For suggestions as to the form of minutes, see 125. For the certification of the minutes, see 1711.

1718. Nominating Committee Report

A typical report would be:

Your Committee on Nominations, after carefully reviewing the field, hereby offer the following candidates:

For president: Mr. A.B.	For secretary: Mr. E.F.
For vice-president: Mr. C.D.	For treasurer: Mr. G.H.

For Board of Trustees:

> To fill unexpired portion of Mr. J's term, and to serve until July 1, 19—: Mr. K.L.
>
> For regular 3-year terms: Mr. M.N. and Mr. P.Q.

Respectfully submitted,

(Signatures)

Note that when the committee offers more candidates than there are vacancies (which is really not a good idea), the alternate names are presented alphabetically, as: For treasurer: Mr. William Jones and Mr. Maurice Stevenson; For Board of Trustees, three to be elected:

> Mr. Arthur Brown, Mr. Charles Davis,
> Miss Ethel Federici, Mr. George Gelber,
> Mrs. John Harbeson, and Mr. Louis Mountain.

1719. Nominating Petition

Sometimes instead of, or in addition to, nominations by committee and/or nominations from the floor, the organization permits nominations by petition. Each petition form contains a heading and space for eighteen or twenty signatures. The sponsor distributes the forms where he thinks they will do the most good and then collects them just before the deadline date. It is usual practice to require the addresses as well as the signatures of those who sign. In small organizations, there may be no need for listing the addresses. Here is a typical caption for a petition form:

We, the undersigned members in good standing, of the XYZ Association, hereby recommend to our fellow-members the election of Mr. Burton Thornwald of ABC as Vice-President of the Association. Each of us pledges to vote for Mr. Thornwald for that office if he is nominated. Each of us affirms that he has not, for this election, signed any still-valid petition, nominating any other person for the post of vice-president. In affixing our signatures, we offer in nomination the name of Mr. Burton Thornwald:

1720. Reports

For certain special reports, see the following:

Budget Officer	1718
Committees	1712
Minority	1723
Nominating Committee	1600
Tellers	1011
Treasurer	1015 and 1714

1721. Resolutions

For the form of a certificate detailing a resolution, see 1712 above. For the text and format of a resolution, see 120.

1722. Report of Tellers

Sample 1 shows a report of a double election: a primary ballot at one meeting and a runoff ballot at the next meeting. Sample 2 shows the report of a mail referendum on proposals to amend the constitution:

Sample 1

Your Tellers (or Board of Tellers) herewith submit a report of the election held January 3, 19—:

For President: Votes cast 2814
Necessary to an election 1408

Primary Ballot

Anslem Brown	982
Charles Carruther	777
David Dawson	641
Elmer Elias	298
Blank Ballots	90
Illegal Ballots	26

a) Illegible	3
b) For ineligible candidates	8
c) Defaced (voted for 2)	15

Result: No choice. Runoff Ballot between Messrs.
Brown and Carruther.

Runoff Ballot

Votes cast	2799
To elect	1400
Mr. Brown	1623
Mr. Carruther	1166
Blank Ballots	1
Illegal Ballots	9

(three defaced, two illegible, four
for nonrunning candidates).

Anslem Brown is elected.

(Signed by Tellers)

Sample 2

Submitted herewith is the report of the mail ballot held during the
month of November 19— on the three proposals to amend the Constitution.

Members of the Association	8765	
Minimum return to validate ballot	876	(10 per cent of members)

PROPOSITION 1. (To create a class of Honorary Members)

Ballots returned	4462
Two-thirds majority	2974
Returned in favor of Proposition 1	4145
Opposed to Proposition 1	307
Disqualified ballots	10

(9 failed to sign certificate; one defaced)

PROPOSITION 2.   (To increase the term of officers from 1 to 2 years)
Ballots returned 5120
Two-thirds majority 3414
In favor of Proposition 2 2559
Opposed to Proposition 2 2561
Disqualified .... none

PROPOSITION 3.   (To authorize the Executive Board to fix the dues)
Ballots returned 4848
Two-thirds majority 3232
Ballots cast in favor of Proposition 3 1699
Ballots opposed to Proposition 3 3048
Illegal ballots 101
    73 blank
     1 voted both "for" and "against"
    27 failed to sign certificate
    <u>101</u> illegal ballots

CERTIFICATION
Proposition 1, having received more than the required two-thirds majority, is adopted.
Proposition 2, having received a majority of less than two thirds, is not adopted.
Proposition 3, having received a minority of the votes cast is not adopted.
(signed)

1723. Treasurer's Report

The treasurer submits his report in two forms: (1) a compact and round-numbered form for oral delivery; and (2) a detailed, accurate-to-the-penny form for the record. The report as read aloud is short, and rounded off this way:

Amounts under $10 are stated exactly to the penny.
Amounts of $10 to $100 are rounded off to the nearest dollar.
Amounts in excess of $100 are rounded off to the nearest ten dollars; except that totals are rounded off to the nearest dollar.

As a result of this roundoff, the totals when given orally

may not come out right. For instance, there may be, in bills payable, the following items:

To X	$ 7.21
To Y	83.99
To Z	221.98
Total	$313.18

When the treasurer is giving his report orally, these odd cents are hard to follow. Rounding it off (on the principle above) he would say:

To X	$ 7.21
To Y	84.00
To Z	220.00
Total payable:	$313.00

The total of $313 was obtained from the actual total of $313.18 by rounding to the nearest dollar. If the sums as stated orally were added, the total would be $311.21, which would be misleading.

The written report is filed. It may be duplicated and handed out to each member as he enters the hall. It may be mailed to each member, printed in the society's magazine or NewsLetter, or stuffed into an envelope mailing. It may simply be filed with the secretary. In that case, the treasurer announces that the detailed report is available to anyone who wants to ask the secretary for it, or who wants to inspect it at the secretary's office.

The report—both the oral and the written one—must indicate exactly the time period covered and then must answer these questions:

1. How much cash was in the treasury when the period started?
2. How much money did we take in during the period?
   2.a. From what sources?
3. How much money did we pay out during the period?
   3.a. For what purposes?
4. How much balance does that leave in the treasury now?
5. How much do we owe now?
   5.a. To whom and why?
6. How much is owed to us?
   6.a. From whom and why?

7. What are our nonliquid assets (investments, buildings, supplies, endowment funds, dedicated funds, and the like)?

So long as the report answers these seven questions, with their four subquestions, it is a good and adequate report, regardless of form. Traditionally, the written report is set up in six schedules as follows:

Schedule A. Answers Questions 1, 2, 3, and 4.
Schedule B. Receipts. Answers Question 2.a.
Schedule C. Expenditures. Answers Question 3.a.
Schedule D. Accounts payable. Answers Questions 5 and 5.a.
Schedule E. Accounts receivable. Answers Questions 6 and 6.a.
Schedule F. General balance sheet. Answers Questions 4 and 7.

Here is a sample written report, arranged in that fashion:

TREASURER'S REPORT FOR THE PERIOD BEGINNING JAN. 1, 19— AND ENDING JUNE 30, 19—

SCHEDULE A. On hand, Jan. 1, 19— $5643.17
Received during the period (see Schedule B) .. 154.44
Total, on hand plus received $5797.61
Spent during period (see Schedule C) 212.31
On hand, June 30, 19— $5585.30

SCHEDULE B. Receipts during period
Received from dues $135.00
Sale of literature 15.00
Reimbursement 4.44
Total received $154.44

SCHEDULE C. Expenditures during period
Rent, heat, and light $120.00
Postage stamps 2.31
Janitor services 60.00
Subscription to Legislative News ... 5.00
Dues to National Federation 25.00
$212.31

SCHEDULE D. Accounts Payable
July rent, heat, and light now due ... $ 20.00
Janitor fee 10.00
Reimbursement of taxi for speaker ... 1.40
$31.40

SCHEDULE E. Accounts Receivable
Dues from 43 members $215.00
Advertisement in our NewsLetter ...   37.50
$252.50

SCHEDULE F. General Balance Sheet
One U.S. Bond, Series Z $1000.00
Office equipment; evaluation of 6/30/— 912.50
Accounts payable to us (Schedule E) 252.50
Cash in our reserve account 400.00
Interest earned on reserve account 8.15
Cash in our regular account (Schedule A) ...   5585.30
TOTAL ASSETS $8158.45
Liabilities (Schedule D) 31.40
Balance $8127.05

This kind of report, set up in six schedules, is easy enough
to follow if the member has it in front of him to study. But
when the treasurer reads his report, the figures lose all meaning. The oral report is simplified, rounded out, and colloquial-
ized. Here, for example, is how a treasurer might present
these six schedules in every-day language:

Fellow-members. The detailed treasurer's report, down to the last
penny, is being printed in our journal. And you can see it any time by
asking Mrs. Peeler, our secretary. She has a copy. In round numbers,
here is the story:

At the beginning of the year we had some $5600 in the bank and at
the end of June we had some $70 less than that. That was because
we took in only $150 whereas we spent over $200 during that period.
That is nothing to be alarmed at, because three fourths of our members
pay their dues in the second half-year. Actually we took in $154 during
the half-year, of which $15 was from the sale of literature and the rest
from dues, except for a $4 item which represented reimbursement.

As against an income of $154, we spent $212 during that period.
Rent and janitor service accounted for the bulk of that: $180 of it. Also,
our dues to the National Federation come due in April, so that was a
$25 expense that we won't have in the second half-year. And our sub-
scription to the Legislative News comes due in January so that accounted
for another $5 expense item.

Right now, we have more than $250 owing to us—most of it from
members whose anniversary fell during the first half and who should
have paid. There are 43 in that class, and if you are one of them please

leave your $5 with me before you go home tonight. And as you noticed, the May NewsLetter carried an advertisement from the University Book Store. They agreed to pay us $37.50 for that, and I'm sure they will pay later this month. When we get that $37.50 plus the $215 owed by you members, we'll have taken in $252 more and then our balance will be higher than it was at the start of the year. As against this anticipated and overdue income of $250 we have less than $32 in debts.

We still have our $1000 U.S. Bond. And we have not yet touched the $400 that we placed in the Old Dominion Bank five years ago as a special reserve, but the amount has increased during this period by some $8 worth of interest accumulation. If you include our office equipment, we now have assets of over $8000.

Glossary

Accept. To accept a report is to agree that its findings and facts are accurate. Acceptance does not necessarily mean endorsement of recommendations. A factual statement is *accepted*. A recommendation is *adopted*. See 1013(c), especially (c) (2) and (c) (3).

Ad Hoc. The phrase *ad hoc* means, in Latin, "for this case only." Thus, an *ad hoc* committee (as distinct from a standing committee) is appointed for a specific task (see 1037). An *ad hoc* action applies to the particular circumstance and is not a precedent.

Administrative Year. The period during which the same person remains as president (without need for re-election) is the "administrative year." It is contrasted with "fiscal year" and "program year" (see 1603(a)).

Adopt. To adopt a report is (1) to concur with the recommendations, and (2) to agree to implement them. It contrasts with "accept," which means only that the facts are acceptable, but which says nothing about recommendations.

The verb *adopt* is also used to mean "to pass a resolution." A lengthy resolution is read, or distributed in writing. Someone then moves "to adopt the resolution." This is the same as saying, "I move the following resolution," or "I move the adoption of the foregoing resolution."

Adjourn. Literally, to adjourn is to put off until another day. The "jour" in *adjourn* is the French word for "day." In parliamentary jargon, to adjourn is to terminate a session or meeting. Technically, it must adjourn to a certain time, or specifically adjourn without setting a day. But in practice many meetings just adjourn without specifying the next meeting time. Adjourn should be distinguished from "recess" (see 1211). See "Adjourn *Cum Die*" and "Adjourn *Sine Die*" below.

Adjourn Cum Die. If a day is fixed for the next session or meeting, the adjournment is *cum die*—that is, with a day fixed. If no definite date is set, the adjournment is *sine die*—that is, without a fixed day. While this is the literal meaning of those Latin phrases, there is a parliamentary convention to the effect that if the next meeting is not for three (or more) months, the adjournment is *sine die*. For example, an annual meeting (convention) terminates by a *sine die* adjournment even though a date is set for next year's meeting. In practice, therefore, to adjourn *cum die* means to terminate a session with a date for reassembling fixed for less than three months ahead.

Adjourn Sine Die. Literally, to adjourn *sine die* is to adjourn without fixing a day for the next session. In practice, if more than three months will elapse between meetings, the adjournment is considered *sine die* even though there *is* a date fixed for the next meeting. See 1204.

Agenda. Agenda is a collective noun meaning "things to be done." It is the plural of agendum, just as "data" is the plural of "datum." No one today speaks of "a datum" and hardly anyone today speaks of "an agendum." It would not be wrong to speak of "agendum" for a single item on the "agenda." The word "agenda" means the order of business, the society's docket, the roster of matters to be brought up, discussed, and disposed of (see 305). In some organizations "agenda" means the broad program of the society. Thus, a civic association might say "our agenda for the year include more playgrounds for our community." Generally, however, "agenda" means items on the program for the next or current meeting.

Amend. To amend an item is to change it by adding, substituting, or subtracting words (see Chapter 9) The verb "emend" is not used in parliamentary practice. It means to detect and rectify an error, whereas "amend" means to change a statement, not to remove error, but to alter the meaning.

Announcement. The "announcement" is the chair's statement of the result of voting. When he says, for instance, "the ayes have it and the motion is carried," the chair is making the "announcement." See 611 and 615. Announcement marks the point of no return when it comes to changing a vote.

Annul. To annul an action is to denounce it as unauthorized, or to take counterbalancing action to cancel it (see 1114 (b)).

Appeal. An appeal is a member's refusal to accept the chair's ruling unless the entire organization concurs. It is based on the challenger's belief that the chair made a parliamentary error. The word is also used to designate the process of asking a review of a disciplinary decision by a higher tribunal within the organization. Unless otherwise specified, "appeal" is used in its first sense (getting a review of the chair's ruling) rather than in its second.

Approve. In modern parliamentary practice, a report is rarely "approved." To approve a report is to accept the findings and also to concur in and implement the recommendations. Since these may be separate issues, it is commoner practice to "accept" facts or findings, and "adopt" recommendations. The verb "approve" is also used as a synonym for "ratify," which see. Also see 1013(c), especially (c) (5).

Assent. Assent is general concurrence. The chair may sense that everyone is in favor of a certain action. He says: "If no one objects, we will consider this approved," or words to that effect. If no one does object, this is adopted by "assent" rather than by vote. Another example: after hearing some discussion, the mover says, "I withdraw my motion." No one says anything, so the matter is dropped, the motion is withdrawn. Here, permission to withdraw was granted by *silent assent*. In the first example (no one objecting), the decision to take the action was made by *general assent*. See 123(a) and 603.

Board. In parliamentary practice, a board is a group of members (rarely including nonmember experts) appointed for a major long range or periodic task (see 1018). A board is like a committee except that its term is longer and it has more authority (sometimes autonomy) than a committee. (It may, for example, have money-raising authority.) In some organizations, an "Executive Board" may be the heir of the society's full authority in the intervals between meetings (see 1022).

Budget. A budget is an advance statement of anticipated income and expected expenses. It is sometimes used—rather loosely—to mean the monetary allotment for a specific item. See Chapter 16, particularly 1605.

Bylaw. A bylaw is a rule, adopted in advance, as a fixed part of the organization's operating code. It may be, in effect, something like a paragraph of the constitution. Usually, however, the constitution contains broad principles of organization and the bylaws spell out the details. (See 1302 and 1310.) If a local organization has a charter from a parent body, it may have bylaws without having any constitution at all. The phrase may be spelled bye-laws, by-laws, or bylaws.

Caucus. In a voluntary organization, a caucus is an informal session (off the record) of a group of members or leaders, held in advance of a regular meeting, in order to agree on tactics, candidates, or policies. In a legislative body, it refers to a meeting of representatives of a political party, called to agree on procedures, principles, or nominees.

Certification. Certification is the process of issuing a "certificate," that is, a formal document attesting to the accuracy of an extract of the minutes, a copy of a motion or resolution, or the report of an election. See 1708 to 1712 for examples.

Chair. The word "chair" means one of three things: (1) the presiding officer; (2) the authority of the presiding officer; (3) the actual piece of furniture in which he sits. Examples are: (1) "The Chair announced that . . ."; (2) "It is within the province of the Chair to determine whether . . ."; (3) "The officer must vacate the chair if he wishes to discuss . . ." See 401 and 402.

Charter. In a voluntary (nongovernmental) body, a charter is an authority to form a subordinate or component body. In government, it is a written document which gives legal right to exercise certain privileges or to do certain kinds of business. Even if a voluntary organization does not actually issue a piece of paper, the process of authorizing a subordinate or component society would be one of "chartering" that body (see 1713).

Commission. In its essential meaning, a commission is an authorization or instruction to one or a group of members to do something for the organization. The word is also used for a group of members with such authority. In the former sense (an authorization) a "commission" is about the same as a "warrant" (which see). In the latter sense, it is about the same as a committee. Both words (commission and committee) stem from the same Latin roots meaning "to send to" or "to send with." A commission usually has more autonomy than a committee, and its term of office is generally longer. In some organizations, a commission is called a Board (see 1018).

Commit. To commit a matter is to refer it to a committee or board (see 1005).

Committee. A committee is a group of members to whom a matter is referred (that is, committed) for deliberation, study, action, liaison, or recommendation (see 1001).

Committee of the Whole. A committee of the whole is a more or less informal meeting of all the members of the organization who happen to be present. It is the entire membership, assembling under a different chairman, for the purpose of informal (often off the record) discussion (see 1024 to 1032).

Constitution. In voluntary (nongovernmental) organizations, the constitution is the fundamental document which broadly outlines the purposes and structure of the association. If the organization is given its life by a "charter," the charter is, in effect, the constitution (see Chapter 13).

Constitutional. The word "constitutional" means in accordance with, deriving authority from, or not at variance with the constitution. Except by formal amendment, an association cannot suspend any part of its constitution and cannot adopt motions in conflict with it.

Constitutional Committee. A committee which is specifically mentioned in the constitution or charter is a constitutional committee. All others are "derivative" committees.

Convene. Originally the word "convene" meant simply "to meet together." It is the verb counterpart of "convention." All the time the members are meeting, they are necessarily convening. However, in parliamentary practice the verb has come to mean "calling the meeting to order," or otherwise formally opening the session.

Convention. A convention is a periodic meeting, either of all members or of their elected representatives. Usually a convention lasts for several days. It may have plenipotentiary powers.

Convocation. Originally a convocation was a meeting of an ecclesiastical or academic body. It is now used, by some voluntary organizations, to designate a ritualistic or ceremonial meeting.

Convoke. To call or summon a meeting is "to convoke" it. The term is usually reserved for formal occasions. See "convocation" above.

Credential. A credential is an identifying document which a member carries when he is named as a delegate, observer, or representative to a parent body or to another organization. See 1716. In a broad sense, the word "credential" could also be used to define any document which shows that a person holds office or membership.

Cum Die. If a day is fixed for the next meeting, an adjournment is technically *cum die*—that is, with a day fixed. However if that day is more than three months away, the adjournment is considered *sine die* (without a fixed day). See 1203 and 1204.

Debate. Open, on-the-floor argument for or against a motion is "debate" or "discussion." In a broad sense, any open talking at a meeting, unless it is to make or second a motion or nomination, is "debate." See 501.

Dedicated Funds. Allotments of money from outside sources are called "dedicated funds" if they are earmarked for special purposes (see 1611 and 1614). If part of the association's own treasury is set aside for a specific purpose, this is a "special account" rather than a dedicated fund. A grant of money, from an outside donor, is a dedicated fund.

Derivative Committee. A derivative committee is one that derives its authority from a motion or resolution rather than from the constitution. A derivative committee is a creature of the body which names it (see 1002(b)).

Dilatory. In its dictionary sense, "dilatory" is the adjective of "delay." A dilatory motion or tactic is a delaying operation. Originally "dilatory" was an invidious word for an obstructive, filibustering, or sabotaging maneuver. Older parliamentary manuals sometimes state arbitrarily that a dilatory motion is always out of order. However, time has mellowed the word. Today, the view is that a dilatory motion is a benign procedure, for it relieves the society of impulsively disposing of a matter when it does not want to. A motion to lay on the table, for instance, is a dilatory motion; so is a motion to postpone or even a motion to refer to a committee (see 801).

Discharge a Committee. A motion to discharge a committee is a motion to relieve it of a specific assignment, and not a motion to abolish the committee (see 1017).

Division of the House. Also called "division of the assembly," this is a tallied vote taken by actual count to verify the chair's previous announcement that a motion passed or failed by voice vote (see 612).

Division of a Question. It may be desirable to take a lengthy report, resolution, or motion and break it down so that its component parts may be separately considered. This is a "division of the question." See 618.

Ex Cathedra. *Cathedra* means chair. *Ex cathedra* means "based on the authority of official position." What the president says, as an official, may be different from what he says in his capacity as a private member. The former statement is made *ex cathedra*.

Executive Session. An executive session is one from which nonmembers are excluded. If a *committee* goes into executive session, then members of the parent association must leave unless they are also members of the committee. An executive session is often informal (see 104). But it is the exclusion of nonmembers rather than the informality that is the touchstone of the executive session.

Ex Officio. Entitlement to one position solely because of holding some other office is an ex officio entitlement. For example, it may be provided that the president is an ex officio member of the executive committee. This means that whoever is president is automatically a member of that committee. The one seat derives from the other (see 1004(g) and 1004(k)).

Expunction. The act of expunging is an "expunction." See "expunge" below.

Expunge. To expunge is to remove from the records by crossing out, tearing out, or inking out. It is actually accomplished today by drawing a line through the expunged material and indicating in the margin the date and authority for the expunction (see 1112 and 1113).

Fiscal Year. The financial year of an organization is its "fiscal year." It is the period between the opening and closing of the treasurer's books for the year, the period for which financial statements are issued. See 1603(a)(4). In modern accounting practice, the adjective "fiscal" means pertaining to organizational (or governmental) finances.

Floor. A *person has the floor* when he has the right to speak; no one else may speak until he yields the "floor," or until the "floor" is given to another. A *subject is on the floor* (or it is "before the house") when it is the issue on which action is to be taken before any other matter may be disposed of.

General Assent. General concurrence without the formality of a vote is "general assent" (see 123(a) and 603).

General Consent. Unanimous agreement is inferred from the fact that no one has objected. This is agreement by "general consent."

General Order. To make a subject a "general order" for tomorrow (or for next meeting) at 2:00 P.M. means that it will be taken up, regardless of agenda, at the time specified, as soon as the matter then on the floor is disposed of. If the topic is not taken up then, any member may call "General order!" or "Orders of the day!" This is a demand that the agenda be followed (see 308, particularly 308(b)).

Idiomatic Committee. An idiomatic committee is one that is peculiar to the particular kind of organization. Any society might have a program committee or a membership committee. Such committees are *not* peculiar to one kind of organization. But only a dental society would be likely to have a committee on mouth washes. Only a neighborhood merchants' association would be likely to have a committee on improper window displays. These committees are idiomatic to their respective types of organizations. A committee on constitution and bylaws would, by contrast, be a universal committee (see 1034).

Incidental Motion. An incidental motion is one made while another matter is pending, but which does not directly dispose of the main matter. For example, the budget is being discussed and a member moves to adjourn. This motion does not dispose of the budget: it is incidental to it. Again, the chair has ruled that a motion was defeated by voice vote. A member calls for "division." This division call is an incidental action, since it does not by itself affect the content of the motion or the actual result of the vote: it touches only on the method of voting. A few parliamentary authorities use "incidental" as a synonym for "secondary" or "subsidiary." By this definition, a motion to lay on the table (or to refer to a committee) would be an incidental motion even though it does dispose of the main matter. In this book, the more limited meaning of "incidental" is used (see 202, especially 202(c)).

Information, Point of. A point of information is a bona fide question, permitting a factual answer, concerning the content or background of a motion (see 704).

Inquiry, Parliamentary. A parliamentary inquiry is a bona fide request for information on a question of parliamentary procedure. If its purpose is to challenge the chair or another speaker, then it is not a legitimate inquiry and should be considered as part of debate (see 705).

Lay on the Table. The phrase "lay on the table" means the same as the verb "to table." To table a matter (i.e., to lay it on the table) is to suspend any further consideration of it. Later, when the organization does want to take it up, they simply vote to take it from the table (see 806). Earlier organizations had an actual table near the entrance. Members placed on this table documents which they wanted to consider. The secretary would take up each paper, read it, present it for disposition. The vote "to lay on the table" was a decision to put this proposal back on the table. There it remained until the organization voted to take it from the table (see 801(a) and 802 to 810).

Main Motion. A main (or primary) motion is one which, if passed, will commit the association to doing something or saying something. It is a motion which stands by itself, independent of any secondary motion. It has implications beyond the one meeting. A motion to lay on the table cannot be a main motion. It does not stand by itself. Some other matter is being laid on the table. So a motion to refer an item to a committee cannot be a main motion, because it applies to some other matter (see 202(a)).

Majority. Unless otherwise defined in a special rule, the word "majority" means "more than half of those who voted." Suppose one hundred attend a meeting: five vote yes; three vote no. A majority voted yes, because five is more than half of eight. The ninety-two nonvoters are not counted.

When a motion to rescind is being considered, the word "majority" means more than half of those present, and not simply of those voting (see 1114). Otherwise, "majority" means more than half of all legitimate votes cast, ignoring nonvoters and blanks. A quorum must be present: otherwise a majority vote is meaningless. Distinguish it from "plurality," which see.

Meeting. In loose usage, a meeting occurs whenever a quorum of members engages in parliamentary activity. If an organization holds a long "annual meeting" or "convention," the word "meeting" describes the whole series. A single sitting is a "session." If the association meets once a month, a few hours at a time, and never has a two-day meeting, then every meeting is a session and *vice versa* (see 1201). In the United States Congress, the terms are reversed. There a "meeting" is part of a session. In voluntary organizations holding annual meetings, the "meeting" consists of several sessions.

Minutes. The official record of a meeting or session is "the minutes." This is a plural word. Originally, a detailed instruction was called a "minute" because it was so detailed. The word was then extended to designate the record of the meeting at which such instructions were drafted; and finally to the record of any meeting (see 124 and 125).

Moderator. A moderator is a chairman of a session. The adjective "moderate" originally meant "not extreme" or "kept within bounds." A moderator was a person who kept the meeting within bounds. Originally the term was limited to town meetings and ecclesiastical assemblies. It has recently acquired popularity in America, particularly with respect to executive committees, boards, councils, and other high authority bodies. The word "moderator" carries overtones of temper-soothing, fair-play-observing activities rather than the implications of being an administrator or executive. Sometimes the moderator is an outside expert hired as a referee.

Motion. A motion is a proposal for action: the basic unit of parliamentary procedure. In a court of law, a motion is a request of the judge. In parliamentary practice, it is a proposal aimed at action. Until phrased by the mover, it is a *proposition*. After it is moved but until restated by the chair, it is a *motion*. Once restated by the chair, it is the *question* before the house. If adopted it becomes an order, instruction, resolution, or release, depending on form. A formally worded motion which is explicitly written out is called a *resolution*.

Old Business. A matter which was pending at a previous meeting, but not then disposed of, is now "old business." Nothing is "old business" unless it was actually pending when the previous session adjourned, or unless it had been laid on the table prior to that adjournment. A motion to take from the table may be heard either as "old business" or as "new business" at the option of the mover. A matter pending when the previous meeting stopped is revived during the "old business" part of the next session, unless a *sine die* adjournment had intervened. Old business does not survive a *sine die* adjournment (see 304 and 1210).

Order of the Day. The "order of the day" is the formal assignment of a matter to a specific hour, day, or place on the agenda. The call, "orders of the day," is a demand to consider what is scheduled for now. An order of the day cannot (without suspending the rules) be considered ahead of its scheduled time. It must be considered when its time is reached (see 307 and 307(f)).

Parliamentary Inquiry. A parliamentary inquiry is a bona fide request for information on a matter of parliamentary procedure. If its purpose is to challenge the chair or confound the speaker, it should be offered as part of debate rather than as a point of inquiry.

Plurality. The word "plurality" is used only in elections, and not in "yes" and "no" votes. Whatever candidate has most votes has a plurality. If 100 were present, and

> A received 44 votes
> B received 36 votes
> C received 20 votes

> then, A has a plurality.

But since more voted against him than for him, he does not have a majority. In determining a plurality (or a majority) blank and illegal votes are not tallied.

Each association decides for itself whether a plurality is sufficient to elect or whether a majority is necessary (see 1315(b) and 1315(c)). If there are only two candidates, the word "plurality" is not used, since the prevailing vote is a majority.

Point of Information. A point of information is a bona fide question, permitting a factual answer, concerning the content or background of a motion (see 704).

Precedence. In parliamentary law, "precedence" designates the "rank" of a motion. If Motion X is in order while Motion Y is pending, then Motion X has precedence over Motion Y (see 203).

Previous Question. In the United States (but not in Britain), "previous question" is a demand that debate be stopped and the matter put to immediate vote. If the motion is defeated, nothing happens: Discussion continues. If it passes, the talking ends and the voting begins at once. This is so confusing a procedure that in more sophisticated American organizations "previous question" is considered obsolete. Instead, the motion is "to close debate" (see 513).

Primary Motion. The phrase "primary motion" is used in two senses. When a motion to reconsider is made, the original motion (the one up for reconsideration) is the "primary" motion (see 1102). The more common usage of the phrase "primary motion," however, is as a synonym for "main motion." That is, a motion which, if passed, will commit the organization to doing something or saying something that has implications beyond this one meeting. See "Main Motion" in this glossary and 202(a).

Privilege. Privilege is the right to immediate consideration of a matter which affects the safety, orderliness, or comfort of the group, or which imminently affects the safety, comfort, or honor of an individual member.

Program Year. A program year is the block of time into which an annual program is fitted. It contrasts with "fiscal year" and "administrative year." See 1603(a).

Prologue. The "prologue" (or "preamble") of a resolution is the part beginning with "Whereas . . . ." See 120(b).

Proposition. In its restricted sense, a proposition is a suggestion not yet formally phrased as a motion or resolution (see 108). In a broader sense, any matter under consideration might be called a proposition.

Prorogue. To prorogue is to terminate a meeting prematurely through outside direction. Perhaps the executive committee has the right to "prorogue" a convention on its second day even though the members want to meet all week. Perhaps the national body can prorogue a meeting of one of its component state or county units. Usually a voluntary organization is sovereign so long as it breaks no law; hence no outside agency can (unless its constitution or charter says otherwise) prorogue a meeting.

Proxy. A proxy is a signed paper which authorizes a person (a surrogate) to cast the signer's vote. The word is also loosely used to designate the one who casts the absentee's vote. The surrogate should say "I hold Smith's proxy" rather than "I am Smith's proxy" because "proxy" is a paper, not a person. If the surrogate is told how to vote, serving simply as a messenger, he holds "an instructed proxy." If he is free to use his own judgment, he holds an "uninstructed proxy." See 620.

Putting the Question. The formal call for the vote is "putting the motion" or "putting the question." The form is "All in favor say 'aye,' " or words to that effect (see 604).

Quorum. A quorum is the smallest number (or proportion) legally capable of doing business (see 111). The word is a Latin genitive plural meaning "of whom." In seventeenth-century Britain, a writ was issued to a panel of justices of the peace, authorizing them to try certain cases. Some of these justices were learned in the law. Most were not. The writ indicated that the tribunal could not function unless some of the learned ones were present. So the writ might read: "A, B, C, D, E, F, and G are authorized to form a panel of five, *of whom* B and D shall be two." The idea was that the court should not do business unless at least these two learned ones were present. Apart from this, any five of the seven could sit. So the phrase *of whom* (Latin, "quorum") came to mean the indispensable minimum needed to do legal business.

Rank. The rank of a motion is its entitlement to right of way over another motion. Thus, a motion to adjourn may be made while a motion to table is pending. The motion to adjourn has a higher *rank* than the motion to table (see 201 and 203).

Ratify. To "ratify" is to give an act *post facto* approval (see 119).

Recess. A recess is an interruption (usually brief) in a session for the purpose of comfort, eating, rest, relaxation, or attendance at another function. It is not an adjournment. When the session resumes after a recess, all matters are in the same parliamentary position as just before the recess (see 1211).

Recognize. A chairman "recognizes" a member by indicating that he has the right to speak. The chair does this by calling out his name, pointing to him, nodding toward him, or otherwise signaling that he may speak (see 402(c)).

Reconsider. To reconsider is to review again a matter previously disposed of; to discuss it again (if it had been debatable), and to vote on it again (see Chapter 11).

Rescind. To rescind is to vacate, cancel out, or nullify a previous action. A motion or resolution is rescinded. An action taken is annulled (see 1111 to 1114).

Resolution. A resolution is a written motion: a proposal reduced to writing, phrased in formal style, and offered as a motion (see 120).

Resolving Clause. A resolution has two parts. The first (beginning with "Whereas") is the prologue. The second part (starting with "therefore be it resolved") is the resolving clause (see 120).

Rise. At the end of an ordinary meeting, a committee adjourns. At the end of its last meeting, it "rises." The rising of an *ad hoc* (special) committee has the effect of dissolving the committee. For any other committee, the "rising" signals the end of its annual period of service (see 1017(h)).

Rising Vote. A rising vote is one taken in response to the chair's request: "All in favor, please stand," or ". . . please rise." The convention is to use the phrase "standing vote" for ordinary or routine matters, and reserve the phrase "rising vote" for ceremonial, *pro forma,* or complimentary motions (see 605).

Second a Motion. To second a motion is to add one's voice to that of the mover by calling out "I second it," or words to that effect (see 118).

Secondary Motion. Any motion other than a primary one (see "primary" in this glossary) is a secondary motion. It is a proposal to do something to a main motion: to table it, postpone it, stop talking about it, refuse to consider it, or refer it to a committee (see 202 and 505(4)).

Select Committee. A select committee is one selected for a specific mission; an *ad hoc* committee. The latter phrase is now more popular than "select" or "special" committee.

Session. A session is a meeting terminated by adjournment *cum die.* Literally, the word merely means a "sitting" and could describe any sitting down together of members. If an organization never holds a convention or meeting that lasts more than a single day, every meeting is one session and vice versa. If the organization does hold a convention or "annual meeting," each separate sitting is a single session. Thus, there might be three sessions during the annual meeting. The Congress of the United States uses "session" in a different sense. There, the "session" is the entire term or season. In voluntary organizations, however, the session is a unit part of the meeting. The word "session" is also used to designate committee meetings (see 1201).

Session, Executive. An executive session is one from which nonmembers are excluded. If a committee goes into executive session, members of the parent association must leave unless they also happen to be members of that committee. An executive session is often informal (see 104). But it is the exclusion of nonmembers rather than the informality which characterizes an "executive session."

Show of Hands. Show of hands is a method of voting on motions. The chair says, "All in favor of this motion, raise their right hands." After this is tallied he asks all who are opposed to raise *their* hands (see 606).

Silent Assent. Silent assent is the assumption of general concurrence based on the fact that no one has objected (see 123(a)).

Sine die. Literally, *sine die* is to adjourn without fixing a day for the next session. In practice, if more than three months will elapse, the adjournment is considered *sine die* even if a date is fixed. An annual convention always terminates by *sine die* adjournment since, of course, its next meeting is more than three months ahead (see 1204).

Sitting. A sitting is the part of a meeting which ends with a recess (see 1201). If an organization has a judicial tribunal (such as a grievance committee or other body that holds hearings or trials), the meetings of that tribunal are also called sittings.

Speaker. A "speaker" is not one who talks, but rather one who serves as a spokesman. It has thus come to mean the presiding officer of a deliberative assembly. In voluntary (nongovernmental) organizations, it generally refers to the chairman of a group within the association rather than to the president of the entire organization. For example, an association might have an executive board, house of delegates, council, or some similar high authority body, with a "speaker" as its presiding officer (see 401).

Standing Committee. The phrase "standing committee" is used in two overlapping senses. It may mean a committee which remains functioning (that is, "standing") through a change in administration, or it may describe a committee with a term coincident with that of the president. What is common to either kind of standing committee is that it has a predetermined area of jurisdiction and handles all matters that fall within that area. Unlike an *ad hoc* (or "select") committee, it is not specially created for each mission. Rather, it is established in advance, and "stands" there ready to receive any appropriate assignment.

Standing Vote. A standing vote is the members' answer to the chair's call: "All in favor, please stand." See "rising vote" in this glossary and 605 in the text.

Stating the Question. Before calling for a vote, the chair states, restates, or clarifies the motion. This is "stating the motion" or "stating the question." See 122.

Subsidiary Motion. A subsidiary motion is one which seeks to dispose of another motion without passing it or defeating it. The subsidiary motions are to amend, postpone, cut off debate on, table, or refer to a committee. Each exercises an effect on the main motion; none makes any definitive disposition of it. See "incidental motion" in this glossary and 202(c) in the text.

Surrogate. In parliamentary language a surrogate is a member who holds another member's proxy.

Suspension of the Rules. To permit compliance with the organization's immediate desire, it may be necessary to waive its regular procedure. This temporary modification of procedure is a "suspension of the rules." A fundamental change in policy, a deviation from the constitution, or a breach of the bylaws is *not* a suspension of the rules (see 306(b) and 307(e)).

Table, Lay on. The phrase "to table" or "to lay on the table" is to suspend, for the time being, any further consideration of a matter. When the organization, later, wants to consider it, it is voted to take it from the table. See "Lay on the table" in this glossary and also 801 to 810.

Table, To. This verb means "to lay on the table." See "Lay on the table," this glossary.

Take from Table. To take from the table is to put back on the floor a motion that had been previously laid on the table (see 806 to 810).

Teller. A teller is not one who tells but one who tallies. In the meeting room as in the bank, the teller does more counting than talking. He is a person (usually a member) named to count the votes (see 609).

Two-Thirds Vote. A two-thirds vote means that at least twice as many voted on the prevailing side as on the other side. Only legal and definitive votes are tallied. Blanks are ignored. If one hundred members are present, and eight vote yes while three vote no, then the motion has a two-thirds vote, even though only eight out of a hundred supported it. Only eleven voted, and eight is more than two thirds of eleven (see 614(c)).

Unfinished Business. If a matter is left pending because of adjournment, that matter is "unfinished business" at the next meeting and gets a priority there. "Unfinished business" does not survive a *sine die* adjournment (see 304 and 1210).

Viva Voce. The Latin phrase *viva voce* means literally, "by live voice." In operation, it means "by word of mouth." An inquiry, conducted orally (rather than by correspondence) is a *viva voce* examination. In parliamentary practice, *viva voce* most often refers to the method of voting described below as "voice vote."

Voice Vote. When the chair calls, "All in favor say 'aye,'" he is calling for a voice vote. It is measured by appraising the relative loudness of the "aye" and "no" responses as explained in 604.

Warrant. A warrant is a paper which authorizes a member or employee to do something for the organization or to represent the organization at an outside function. In the latter sense it is more often called a "credential." Also see "commission."

Yeas and Nays. A vote by roll call in which each member's answer is formally recorded is a "vote by yeas and nays." It is also called a "roll-call vote." See 607.

Yield. One motion is said to "yield" to another if the latter has higher rank. See "precedence" and "rank" in this glossary, and also 201 and 203 in text. The word "yield" also indicates a member's surrender of the floor (that is, of his right to speak) to another member (see 1512).

Index

References are to section numbers. The major definitive reference is indicated by an asterisk (*).

293

PRECEDENCE OF MOTIONS, POINTS, AND QUESTIONS

When any of these is pending, a matter listed *below* is out of order. A matter listed *above* is in order, provided either (a) the mover can get the floor, or (b) it is a matter that may interrupt the speaker.

See Number

Fix Time for Next Meeting	1212
Adjourn	1205-13
Recess	1211
Point of Privilege	701-3, 707
Point of Order	706
Orders of the Day (Call for)	307f
Parliamentary Inquiry	705
Division of the House	612
Lay on the Table	802-5
Reconsider	1101-9
Suspend the Rules	306b
Appeal from the Chair	408
Close Debate (Previous Question)	505b
Postpone to Specified Time	811
Refer to a Committee	1005-7
Amend a Motion or Resolution	902-4
Postpone Indefinitely	812
Take from the Table	807
Object to Consideration	116
Main or Primary Motion	202